D0857796

OXFORD
Historical and Literary
STUDIES

Issued under the direction of C. H. FIRTH
and WALTER RALEIGH Professors of
Modern History and English Literature in
the University of Oxford

THE HOUSE OF LORDS IN THE
REIGN OF WILLIAM III

By A. S. TURBERVILLE

GREENWOOD PRESS, PUBLISHERS
WESTPORT, CONNECTICUT

328,42
T931

Originally published in 1913
by the Clarendon Press, Oxford

Reprinted from an original copy in the collections
of the Brooklyn Public Library

First Greenwood Reprinting 1970

Library of Congress Catalogue Card Number 77-110877

SBN 8371-4558-9

Printed in the United States of America

PREFACE

THE following study deals with the House of Lords in one
of the most interesting periods in its history. The reign of
William III was ushered in by the movement which we term
the English Revolution, and it marks the beginning of a new
constitutional epoch. By such a crisis the House of Lords
could not fail to be deeply affected, so that its story during
the reign is well worth telling for its own sake. But while
making the influence of the Revolution upon the Second
Chamber the main pivot of the narrative, I have sought to
treat the subject in its broader aspects and to present a picture
of general aristocratic influence, whose interest belongs to the
province of social as well as that of constitutional history.
The House of Lords stood as the embodiment of a tradition
of government which entrenched upon numerous spheres.
Many of the incidents dealt with in this book are well known
to all students of the reign of William III; I can only hope
that there may be some to whom it will be useful to have the
familiar facts treated from a new point of view.

The most obvious authorities for the subject are the *Journals*
of the House and the Parliamentary Histories. The information to be gleaned from these sources is, however, very fragmentary, and it is fortunate that it can be largely supplemented
by details drawn from the prolific memoirs and correspondence
of the time, and by the dispatches of foreign residents in
England interested in parliamentary affairs. But much more
important than any of these are the *Manuscripts of the
House of Lords*, which have been recently printed for the

whole period under consideration. The publication of these invaluable documents has rendered possible a fuller and more detailed account of the Upper House than would have been possible hitherto.

Professor Firth suggested to me the undertaking of this work, and I have been indebted to his assistance throughout its progress. How much this has meant to me will be realized by all those who have had the rare privilege of drawing upon Professor Firth's unrivalled knowledge of the literature of the Stuart period. I wish also to express my thanks to my friend, Mr. F. J. Routledge, of Liverpool University and New College, Oxford, who gave much time and zealous care to the reading of my proofs, and to suggesting various improvements in matters of style and arrangement.

ARTHUR STANLEY TURBERVILLE.

CONTENTS

CHAPTER I

THE COMPOSITION OF THE HOUSE

THE history of the House of Lords divides itself into a number of well-defined periods. In the earliest days the assembly of the nation, the Magnum Concilium, is an assembly consisting of lords only. With the beginning of a parliamentary system there comes into existence a chamber of popular representatives. Burgesses and knights of the shire eventually elect to sit together; and so there arises the possibility of a strong House of Commons. A third epoch in the history is reached when the abbots and higher clergy, who had the right to sit in the Upper House together with the bishops, begin to meet in their own Convocation only. Thus the House of Lords becomes a chamber consisting of a preponderatingly temporal element instead of being as heretofore very largely a clerical body. The marriage alliances of Edward III may almost be said to have made the House into a congregation of relatives, all connected more or less nearly with the sovereign. The consummation of this remarkable system led to its speedy dissolution in the Wars of the Roses. The restoration of order out of chaos which came with the triumph of the strong Tudor monarchy did not, however, bring revival for the nobility. The Tudors had no mind to resuscitate a feudalism which had over and over again in the past rendered strong centralized administration difficult, if not impossible. Instead they encouraged the influence of a House of Commons destined to do battle with despotism, and in so doing to overthrow monarchy and peerage together. The House of Lords perished when the Commonwealth began. It is an interesting paradox that prior to the return of Charles Stuart in 1660 the monarchy had been restored in all but name. Certainly after the attempted 'rule of the saints' in the Little Parliament there is a distinct conservative process discernible, in which the Instrument of Government marks one stage, the Humble Petition and Advice another. The institution by the latter of a monarchy and a second chamber is the precursor to the re-establishment of the hereditary sovereignty and the historic House of Lords. The House returned apparently much the same as it had been before the days of its humiliation. In reality new processes were at work. It was no more possible for the hereditary chamber to remain unaffected by the Great Rebellion than it was for the hereditary monarchy to do so. The restored monarchy, tried in the balances, was in no long time found wanting, and was accordingly dispensed with. The Revolution of 1689, which saw the final downfall of the Stuart sovereignty, could not but prove a crisis in the history of the hereditary chamber which, together with that sovereignty, had been temporarily abolished and then restored.

Were gratitude for honours received a lasting tie, then never was bond stronger than that which bound the House of Lords to the Stuart dynasty. The extent to which the peerage in 1688 was of Stuart creation is very remarkable.[1] When William III ascended the English throne the House of Lords consisted of 153 members; eighty-four years previously it had consisted of only 59. During a single reign the number was almost doubled. When Charles I succeeded his father there were 104 temporal lords. James had made 62 creations, but 17 titles had become extinct during his reign. Charles I raised the number to 142, his creations totalling 59. His son was responsible for no fewer than 64 additions, but as 53

---

[1] See *Two lists showing the alteration in the composition of the House of Commons from the beginning of the reign of Henry VIII to the end of that of James I, and in that of the House of Peers from the accession of James I to the present time, with observations.* Published 1719 in connexion with the Stanhope Peerage Bill. Most of the particulars given as to peerage creations in the following pages are derived from these peerages: J. E. Doyle, *Complete Baronage of England,* 3 vols., London, 1886; Arthur Collins, *The Peerage of England,* ed. Sir E. Brydges, 9 vols., 1812; *The Complete Peerage of England and Ireland, &c.,* by G. E. C[okayne], 8 vols., 1887-98; *The Peerage of England, or An Historical and Genealogical Account of the Present Nobility,* in 2 vols. (printed by E. J. for Abel Roper and Arthur Collins), 1714.

peerages died out between 1649 and 1685 this only meant a net increase of 11. Despite the large number of extinctions the membership of the chamber had considerably more than doubled in the eighty years prior to the accession of James II. But this statement of the case does not quite accurately express the extent of the Stuarts' influence on the composition of the House, seeing that they had actually conferred as many as 185 peerages altogether.

A brief glance at the composition of the House of Lords in the reign ˘of James II—in the year 1687—will show in a striking manner in what degree it was of Stuart origin. In 1614 a chamber which consisted of but 65 lay members was composed of a single duke, a single marquis, 19 earls, 4 viscounts, and 40 barons. In 1687 there were 12 dukes, 2 marquises, 65 earls, 9 viscounts, and 66 barons. Five of the dukes were illegitimate children of Charles II, viz. Charles Lennox, Duke of Richmond ; Charles, Duke of Southampton ; Henry, Duke of Grafton ; George, Duke of Northumberland ; and Charles, Duke of St. Albans. Of the remaining seven one was a Villiers, the second Duke of Buckingham. He died in the April of this year 1687. Another was Christopher Monk, Duke of Albemarle, son of the famous general. Recently promoted to the highest rank of peerage was Henry Somerset, who had succeeded as third Marquis of Worcester in 1667, and was promoted to the dukedom of Beaufort in December 1682. James Butler, first Duke of Ormonde, had obtained his title only a few months earlier. Henry Cavendish was the second Duke of Newcastle, having in 1676 succeeded his father, the royalist general in the Civil War. There were only two of the dukes who could lay claim to antiquity in their titles—these being the Dukes of Norfolk and of Somerset. Henry Howard was the descendant of that John Howard who in 1470 became a baron and in 1483, as the reward of his attachment to Richard III, acquired the dukedom of the Mowbrays, and was at the same time made Earl Marshal of England. Charles Seymour was the sixth Duke of Somerset, and derived his title from the year 1547, though it has to be remembered that there was the long intermission between the execution of the famous Protector in 1552 and the restoration of the dukedom to the family in 1660.

The two marquises in 1687 were Charles Paulet, sixth Marquis of Winchester, whose title was also of sixteenth-century origin, and the celebrated George Savile, first Marquis of Halifax.

Among the earls were some names of historic interest. The ancient family of de Vere still held the earldom of Oxford; the holder of the honour in 1687 being the twentieth in the succession. Charles Talbot was the twelfth of his race to boast of the title of Earl of Shrewsbury. Anthony Grey, Earl of Kent, was the tenth in a line which stretched back to days before the dynastic war of York and Lancaster. Among peers of a more recent creation were men who had played so conspicuous a part in recent political events as Anthony Ashley Cooper, Earl of Shaftesbury; Thomas Osborne, Earl of Danby; Lawrence Hyde, Earl of Rochester. A large number of earls owed their dignity to Charles II. Such were Edward Montague, made Earl of Sandwich in 1660; Edward Hyde, made Earl of Clarendon in the following year, which also saw the elevations of the Earls of Cardigan, Anglesey, Bath, Carlisle, and Essex. The possession of the earldoms of Ailesbury and Burlington by the families of Bruce and Boyle respectively dated from 1664. In 1672 came Cooper's earldom; two years later there followed the creations of Powys and Danby. In 1676 Louis de Duras became Earl of Feversham.[1] The year 1679 saw the creation of the earldoms of Macclesfield, Radnor, Yarmouth, and Berkeley in the families respectively of Gerard, Roberts, Paston, and Berkeley. Six more earldoms owed their origin to the year 1682, viz. those of Nottingham, Rochester, Abingdon, Gainsborough, Holderness, and Plymouth. Of the total number of sixty-five earldoms existent in 1687 there were only ten that were not of Stuart origin.

Among the nine viscounties, there were three only of earlier date than the Stuart period, viz. those of Hereford, Montague, and Saye and Sele.

---

[1] He succeeded his father-in-law in the title by special remainder.

The first Viscount Fauconberg was Thomas Belasyse, created a baron in 1627 and a viscount in 1643. Francis Newport, son of the first Baron Newport, was raised to the higher dignity in 1675. The extraordinary Charles Mordaunt was the second Viscount Mordaunt of Avalon. Horatio Townshend had been created a baron in 1661 and had been given a viscounty in 1682. Thomas Thynne, Viscount Weymouth, was yet another who owed his rank to Charles II. Finally, Christopher Hatton, the son of the first Baron Hatton of Kirby, was promoted in 1683.

An examination of the list of baronies extant in 1687 reveals a situation very similar to that of the earls; but of the total number of sixty-five only fifteen dated beyond 1603, the oldest being those of Audley, de la Warr, and Abergavenny. Seventeen were created by Charles II, among them being one or two names of note. There was George Booth, Lord Delamere, destined to play a prominent part in the events of the Revolution; George Carteret, a member of the great Jersey family which had befriended Charles in his exile at their manor house of St. Ouen; George Legg, Lord Dartmouth, the admiral; Francis North, Lord Guilford; and greatest of all, Sidney Godolphin.

James II himself made but little change in the composition of the House of Lords. He made only eight new peers, and as the same number of titles became extinct during the reign, in actual numbers the House was the same in 1688 as it had been in 1685. Except for the Duke of Berwick the new lords were all barons. These were Henry Jermyn, the Catholic debauchee, created Lord Dover; John Churchill, already Baron Churchill of Eyemouth in Scotland, now made Baron Churchill of Sandridge; George Jeffreys, the judge of evil memory, made Lord Jeffreys of Wemm; Henry Waldegrave, Lord Waldegrave of Chewton; Lord Derwentwater; Lord Stafford; and Lord Griffin.

It is of interest to note the creations of peerages made by James after his abandonment of the English throne.[1] He was

---

[1] See *Jacobite Peerage, Baronetage, Knightage, &c.*, compiled by the Marquis of Ruvigny and Raineval (Edinburgh, 1904), pp. 150-1.

not prodigal of his rewards, and was more apt to be profuse in threats than in bribes.   But a few of his immediate followers were recompensed with peerages or promotion within the degrees of peerage.   In 1689 the Marquis of Powys, who subsequently became Lord Steward and Chamberlain of the Household at St. Germain's, was given a dukedom.   In the same year Lord Dover was given an earldom.[1]   Sir Edward Herbert, brother of the better-known Lord Torrington, was one of those adherents who accompanied James to France and Ireland.   For this conduct he was attainted in a bill, which, however, lapsed in parliament owing to prorogation, and his estates were handed over to his brother.   Compensation for the losses which his fidelity had brought upon him came from his royal master in the shape of the earldom of Portland.[2]   Another of the small band of the faithful was rewarded with a like honour in 1689.   This was Viscount Preston (in the peerage of Scotland), who was now created Earl of Esk.[3]   Sir Edward Hales was another recipient of an earldom in 1692.   He had accompanied the King in his first attempted flight out of England, had been fetched back ignominiously from Feversham, and lodged in the Tower.   In October 1689 he had been brought to the bar of the House of Commons on a charge of high treason, but less than eight months later he was so fortunate as to obtain his discharge, whereupon he speedily betook himself to St. Germain's, and in due course became Earl of Tenterden.[4]   The two most active of the Jacobites at the exiled court were the two secretaries, Melfort and Middleton.   The former was in 1689 created Baron of Cleworth, besides being given a Scottish dukedom.[5]   The honours to Middleton were somewhat belated.   He did not obtain an English title until 1701, when he became Earl of Monmouth.[6]   In 1696 the dukedom of Albemarle, which had become vacant on the death of Christopher Monk in 1685, was conferred upon Henry FitzJames, the youngest of James's illegitimate children by Arabella Churchill, and younger brother

---

[1] Ruvigny, pp. 42–3.
[2] Ibid., p. 150.
[3] Ibid., pp. 47–8.
[4] Ibid., pp. 171–3.
[5] Ibid., p. 37.
[6] Ibid., pp. 121–3.

of the Duke of Berwick.[1] This closes the list of the important Jacobite peerages created between 1688 and 1702. There were, however, three others. During his reign in England James had employed a certain John Caryll as his agent at Rome. The latter followed his master into exile. James would seem to have had a singular affection for him, as he asked that the estates of his agent should specially be exempted from confiscation. His request was granted, but unfortunately Caryll was suspected of complicity in the Assassination Plot of 1696, and he was attainted and his estates forfeited. Between 1694 and 1696 he acted with Middleton as joint secretary of state at St. Germain's; and a year or two later he was raised to the peerage as Lord Caryll of Durford.[2] As to the authenticity of the last two creations that remain to be mentioned there appears to be some doubt. A certain Walter Pye is said to have been made Lord Kilpee[3]; and one Humphrey Borlase is reported to have followed James to France, and to have been created Baron Borlase of Mitchell.[4] Nine men in all were honoured by James with the right to take their seats in the House of Lords during the period while the usurping William sat upon the throne of England.

During this period William made thirty elevations to the peerage. In comparison with the lavish grants of James I and Charles II this is not a large number, even taking into consideration the comparatively short duration of the reign. Twelve of the number belong to the first two years, 1689 and 1690. There was only one new peerage created after 1698. As twenty-one titles became extinct, William only increased the numbers of the House of Lords by nine in the aggregate. Six of the new peerages were conferred upon the eldest sons of peers, and their titles ultimately became merged into those of the fathers. This process had already taken place in five cases before the death of William. The barony of Willoughby de Eresby had become merged in the earldom of Lindsey; that of Berkeley in the earldom of Berkeley; that of Sidney in the earldom of Leicester; that of Granville in the earldom

---

[1] Ruvigny, p. 42.
[2] Ibid., pp. 20-21.
[3] Ibid., p. 73.
[4] Ibid., pp. 118-19.

of Bath, and that of Clifford in the earldom of Burlington. But as Thomas Osborne, successively Earl of Danby, Marquis of Caermarthen, and Duke of Leeds, lived on until 1722, the Osborne barony had a separate existence throughout the reign. Of William's new creations two were dukedoms, and both were made in 1689. The title of Duke of Cumberland was given to Prince George of Denmark in April of that year. At the same time William's Dutch follower, Schomberg, became a duke. None of the new lords were marquises. Nine of them were earls, viz. Cholmondeley, Portland, Romney, Torrington, Rochford, Albemarle, Jersey, Orford, Grantham. There was one viscount, Lonsdale. The new barons, in addition to the seven already mentioned, were Ashburnham, Capel, Lempster, Weston, Strafford, Herbert of Cherbury, Willoughby de Broke, Craven, Haversham, Somers, Barnard, and Halifax. It will be noticed how soon after the dying out of a title in one family it was revived in another, a fact which is apt to confuse the reader. Savile, Marquis of Halifax, died in April 1695. In December 1700 the title of Baron Halifax was conferred upon Charles Montague. The Portland title had been extinct but a short time when it was revived for the benefit of Bentinck. The most remarkable case is that of the title of Baron Herbert of Cherbury. One lord of that name died in April 1691. Exactly three years later another Henry Herbert, who, though his name was the same, came from a different family, took his place. In addition to Bentinck and Schomberg there were three other Dutchmen among the new peers: Zuilestein, Earl of Rochford; van Keppel, Earl of Albemarle; and d'Auverquerque, Earl of Grantham.

At the outset of the reign Savile urged upon William the desirability of raising existing peers who had been on his side to a higher degree. He argued that it would have two good effects. It would oblige the lords for their previous services; and secondly, it would engage their interests for the future.[1] As they would be indebted to William for their superior dignity, so they would be compromised and impelled by

[1] *Life and Letters of George Savile, Marquis of Halifax*, by Miss H. C. Foxcroft (1898, 2 vols.), vol. ii, p. 207 (in the Spencer House Journals).

motives of personal safety and aggrandisement to support the *de facto* sovereign. As Halifax notices, the new king was at first slow to embrace this proposal, as he was to adopt any new suggestion before he had had time to master his position. There certainly was plenty of pressure brought to bear upon William to make promotions. The attainment of a dukedom was the ambition of more than one of the most influential peers, and they did not hesitate to advertise their claims for advancement to the King. The Earl of Rutland had just succeeded in obtaining the promise of his dukedom from William before the latter's death.[1] He actually obtained the coveted distinction in March 1703. The Earl of Bedford had gained his dukedom as early as 1694. This encouraged another ambitious peer, Lord Montague, to proffer a request that the same honour should be done to him. The letter in which he addresses the King on the subject is so astonishing in its effrontery as to merit quotation *in extenso*[2]:

'I did not think it very good manners to trouble your Majesty in the middle of so great affairs as you had at your going away, else I should have made it my humble request that you would have been so gracious as to have done my family the same honour you have done to my Lord Clare, Bedford and others. This request had been made to you by the old Duke of Schomberg, who thought himself under some obligation to me for the encouragement I gave him to attend you in your expedition into England, but that I did not think it reasonable to ask the being put over the Duke of Shrewsbury's head, but now, Sir, that you have given him that rank, which the greatness of his family and personal merit has deserved, I may, by your Majesty's grace and favour, pretend to the same dignity as well as any of the families you have promoted, being myself the head of a family that many ages ago had great honours and dignities, when I am sure these had none ; and we having lost them by the Civil Wars

---

[1] *MSS. of the Duke of Rutland at Belvoir Castle*, vol. ii, p. 168. (Historical MSS. Comm. Rep. xii, Append., pt. 5). Rutland's son, Lord Roos, to his father, February 17, 1702.

[2] *Memoirs of Great Britain and Ireland from the last Parliament of Charles II to the Battle of La Hogue*, by Sir John Dalrymple (1720, 3 vols.), Appendix to Bk. VI, pp. 256–8. Lord Montague to William III, May 18, 1694. It is unfortunate that the pagination in Dalrymple is not by volume, but by Books.

between York and Lancaster, I am now below the two younger
branches, my Lord Manchester and Sandwich.   I have to add
to my pretensions the having married the Duke of Newcastle's
eldest daughter ; and it has been the practice of all your
predecessors, whenever they were so gracious to keep up the
honour of a family by the female line, to bestow it upon those
who married the eldest, without there are some personal
prejudice to the person who held that claim.   I may add,
Sir, another pretension, which is the same for which you have
given a dukedom to the Bedford family, the having been one
of the first ; and held out to the last, in that cause which, for
the happiness of England, brought you the crown.   I hope it
will not be thought a less merit to be alive and ready on all
occasions to venture all again for your service, than if I had
lost my head when Lord Russell did.   I could not then have
had the opportunity of doing the nation the service I did,
when there was such opposition made by the Jacobite party,
in bringing my Lord Huntingdon, the Bishop of Durham, and
my Lord Ashley, to vote against the regency, and for your
having the crown ; which was carried but by those three
voices and my own.   I should not put you in mind of this,
but hoping that so fortunate and so reasonable a service as
this may supply all my other wants of merit ; and which,
since you were pleased to promise me in your bed-chamber
at St. James', before you were King, never to forget, you will
not now that are so great and gracious a one.   The Duke of
Shrewsbury can further satisfy you what persecution I suffered,
and what losses I sustained in the last two reigns, which must
make the mortification greater if my humble suit be refused.'[1]

In his promotions William showed impartiality.   Both
Whigs and Tories obtained a share in them.   In the first
place the men who had been the prime movers in bringing
about the landing of the Prince of Orange were rewarded.
These, besides commoners who were now raised to the peerage,
were Lumley, who obtained a viscounty ; Danby, who became
Marquis of Caermarthen ; Churchill, given the earldom of
Marlborough ; Mordaunt, made Earl of Monmouth ; Delamere,
created Earl of Warrington.   Lumley was subsequently once
more promoted, taking the title of Earl of Scarborough.
The Earl of Shrewsbury obtained his dukedom in 1694.
Caermarthen was made Duke of Leeds in the same year ;

---

[1] It *was* refused.

when Devonshire and Bedford also obtained their dukedoms. Other promotions were those of the Marquis of Winchester to the dukedom of Bolton; of Viscount Sidney to the earldom of Romney; of the Earl of Clare to the dukedom of Newcastle; of Viscount Newport to the earldom of Bradford; of Lord Grey de Ruthyn to a viscounty;[1] of the Earl of Mulgrave to the marquisate of Normanby; of Lord Coventry to an earldom; of Viscount Villiers to the earldom of Jersey. It will be seen that the list contains a number of Tory names as well as Whig, although the latter preponderate.

The extent of the influence of William's creations upon the character, and particularly the party complexion, of the House is not an easy question. But it must be clear at the outset that there is a presumption against any very sweeping changes having been made by the addition of no more than thirty new peers. Put succinctly the case stands thus: of the sixteen dukes in the House in 1702 seven owed their present titles to William; of the sixty-seven earls, thirteen were of William's creation; of the nine viscounts, three; and of the sixty-three barons, nine only. The House of Lords in the reign of William III is often spoken of as a Whig House. So positive a statement as this is, to say the least, inaccurate. We are not justified in speaking of a House as being either Tory or Whig unless the preponderance of the one party over the other is really considerable. Otherwise some qualification is needed.

It is certain that in 1688 the House was preponderatingly Tory. It would be too much to say that a House principally of Stuart origin would necessarily be so. But it is reasonable to argue that this was the tendency. The Stuarts usually rewarded men who were of their own ways of thinking, and were not likely to approve the political principles of Whiggism. It is true that one of the tenets of the Whigs was toleration, and that both Charles II and James II issued declarations of indulgence. But the toleration which the Stuarts wanted was toleration of Roman Catholics, while the Whigs desired it only for Protestant dissenters. In any case

[1] He took the title of Viscount Longueville.

the question of toleration was a negligible quantity in comparison with the main issue—the different ways in which the two parties viewed the monarchy. When the House of Lords had to decide upon that subject in connexion with the Exclusion Bill they decided in favour of the established system by 63 votes to 30. Certainly the situation radically changed between that day and 1688, and peers who had been unwilling to exclude the Duke of York from the throne found his yoke, when he was on the throne, unbearable. At the same time the Exclusion Bill, notwithstanding the intervention of 'the trimmer', forms about as good an indication of the state of parties as the proceedings over the Revolution Settlement. The fate of the Regency motion—undoubtedly a Tory motion —does not provide a true criterion as to the state of parties in the House at the time. At that debate the supporters of William were able to defeat the proposal for a regency by only two votes, 51 to 49. The Whigs did their very utmost, and we may take it that the figure 51 represents their full strength. On the other hand, we know that the minority does not represent the full strength of their opponents. Some Tories voted in the majority, while the names of others, such as the Archbishop of Canterbury, the Duke of Newcastle, the Earl of Mulgrave, do not appear at all in the division lists. It should be remembered that Halifax, who voted with the Whigs at this juncture, not long after went over to the other party and ranked as a Tory till the end of his life. We have a better criterion in the majority by which the 'vacancy' motion was rejected in the Lords, viz. 55 to 41. The determined opposition made in the House to the words 'vacant' and 'abdicated' reveals the activity of the Tory majority. In addition to those present in the Convention, there were Tory peers who continued to support James till the last and did not come up to Westminster. The facts justify us in stating that in 1688 there was a considerable Tory majority in the Upper House.

But there is a prevalent idea that all this was changed during the reign of William, and that this epoch inaugurates the long period of Whig supremacy in the House of Lords which lasted through the eighteenth century until George III, principally by the aid of the younger Pitt, transformed the chamber into a stronghold of Toryism. That this idea is incorrect is proved by the simple fact that at the end of the reign of Anne there was a Tory and not a Whig majority in the House. It is with the utter downfall of the Tory party in 1714, and not with the accession of William III, that the period of Whig ascendancy in the chamber begins. As is notorious, it was by the creation of twelve peers to carry the Treaty of Utrecht that the Tories secured a majority in the Lords. The fact that such an expedient was required at all is scarcely more significant than that so small a number of new peers should have been required. If the ministry could be sure of being able to carry their peace proposals through the House by so small a creation, the inference is that the previous position was one of remarkable numerical equality between the two parties.[1] This becomes still clearer when we remember that the Whigs were at the time enjoying the support of such men as the Duke of Somerset and the arch-Tory Nottingham. It is true that the introduction of the sixteen Scottish representative peers in 1707 and a small number of creations made by Anne herself had done something to increase the strength of the Tories since 1702. On the other hand it has to be remembered that the two leaders of the Whigs in the reign of Anne—Godolphin and Marlborough—had both counted as Tories under William III.

Such transferences of political allegiance were not uncommon in those days. Indeed, the instability of principle revealed by not a few of the peers makes it very difficult to speak with accuracy about the party character of the House. The main motive with some would appear to have been personal ambition; their chief characteristic volatility. In any case, seeing that there were at one time during the reign of William as many as 190 peers, temporal and spiritual, it would be an

[1] As a matter of fact the government thought they could count upon a bare majority even before the creation of the twelve peers; though in this they were mistaken. See Swift, *Four Last Years of the Queen* (*Prose Works of Jonathan Swift*, ed. Temple-Scott, 12 vols., 1899-1908, vol. x, p. 36).

impossible task to say what was the political creed of each. Moreover, one had to distinguish then, as always, between the peers who led a political life and were effective members of the second chamber and those who took no part in public affairs and were scarcely ever present at Westminster. Even when the Lords were called upon to sign the Association after the Fenwick conspiracy as many as sixty-two peers never attended a sitting of the House. There were a number who during the war were generally absent serving in the army; there were one or two in the navy. In view of these circumstances it will be recognized that to draw up an accurate statement of the balance of parties from time to time would be impossible. One thing is clear, however. The change made by William III, whatever it may have been, was not so great but that it was possible for the Tories to obtain a certain majority in the Upper House in the following reign without any great difficulty. The change was not of a sweeping kind.

Of the thirty new peers created by William most were Whigs, but the number does include Tories, viz. Weston, Jersey, Lonsdale, and Cholmondeley. The elevation of the seven sons of existing peers, as we have seen, did not mean any permanent addition to the House, and as the Duke of Cumberland has to be omitted from our calculations, it will be seen that the permanent addition to the strength of the Whig party made by the new peerages was not very considerable; certainly quite insufficient in itself to transform the Tory majority of 1688 into a substantial Whig majority. We have to seek for contributory causes to explain the alteration in the position of parties which did undoubtedly occur while William III occupied the English throne. First and foremost we have to remember the really great change which came upon the episcopal bench. This aspect of the case will be considered more particularly in the next chapter. It is sufficient to note here that the bishops from being a predominantly Tory body became predominantly Whig. In the second place, there were Jacobite and non-juring temporal lords as there were Jacobite and non-juring clergy. They may not have been very numerous, but the Tories could not afford any abstentions. And it was not only voluntary exiles like Berwick and Dover, outlaws like Huntingdon and Salisbury, and non-jurors like Clarendon that the Tory party lost. There were besides Tories who were willing to submit to what they regarded as the inevitable, to take the oaths of allegiance to the new sovereign and live at peace under the new settlement; and yet were so completely estranged from the existing order that they abjured parliament and lived in retirement from the arena of politics. Such were Grafton and Beaufort.

In such ways as these is explained the change in the balance of parties in the House of Lords and the fact that the Tory majority, which was to be expected and which did actually exist in 1688, faded away and left the Whigs predominant, though the superiority of the latter was by no means overwhelming. The new creations to the peerage were not sufficiently numerous to bring about such a revolution. William himself was a trimmer, and had no purpose to aggrandize one party at the expense of the other. The essential fact about the situation is not that the Whigs became more numerous than their rivals; it is rather that during the reign the two parties maintained more or less an equipoise.

CHAPTER II

THE EPISCOPAL BENCH

IF the alteration made in the character of the temporal peerage by the creations of William III was small, it was far otherwise with the spiritual lords. During the reign there took place nothing short of a revolution in the composition of the episcopal bench. Changes were numerous and frequent. In only five dioceses was the see occupied by a single bishop throughout the short term of twelve years; in eight there were as many as three different bishops; in two of them there were as many as four.

At the very commencement of the reign a great difficulty was necessarily created by the non-juror schism. It may seem at first sight surprising that the very men who in their resistance to the assumed dispensing power of the King gave the signal of revolt from James II, and were consequently in no small measure responsible for the Revolution, should find the situation which they had helped to create too hard for them and refuse to take the oaths to the new sovereign, whose future triumph had been first heralded when a delighted populace acclaimed the acquittal of the Seven Bishops. Yet the position of the bishops is quite comprehensible when we take into consideration the peculiar position of the Anglican Church at this juncture. The Restoration had been both a restoration of the monarchy and of the national church. The events of the Civil War and the Commonwealth appeared to prove how indissolubly connected were the interests of Church and King. There was therefore a strong tendency after 1660 for the Church to cling more closely than ever to a sovereign ruling in virtue of divine right and to dread profoundly anything savouring of revolution. What, then, must have been the perplexity of the

Church's leaders when they found that revolution was threatened from the very quarter whence it was least to be expected, and that the same dynasty, whose restoration had brought with it the Clarendon Code and the Test Act, had set out upon a policy which would utterly wreck that intolerant system and which (worse still) was one of Popish propaganda? Surely passive resistance to such a policy was required by conscience? It was necessary to remind His Majesty that he was no longer the exponent of the divine purpose, of which the king is none the less the undoubted earthly guardian, and to pray earnestly that he might be brought to see the error of his ways and his prime duty to the established church of his country. It had been well for James II had he realized the peculiar nature of the conditions which the Restoration had involved, and that since so much of loyal enthusiasm was really devotion to the Anglican Church, the bishops were the last persons in the realm whom it was politic to offend.

For his failure to comprehend the facts James paid the penalty by being virtually deposed. And thus the Seven Bishops found that in resisting one revolution, which had threatened the whole fabric of their religious system, they had brought upon themselves another revolution, whose nature was altogether opposed to their scheme of political thought. For how could any believer in Laudian principles abandon his divinely appointed, although misguided, sovereign for an outsider whose presence upon the throne was unavoidably subversive of the whole High Anglican state theory? That is the reason why Sancroft, after a good deal of undignified shilly-shallying, failed to appear as the leader of the Tory party in the Convention, as he was expected to do, and eventually decided that he was unable to take the oaths to the new government. With him there also stood out Ken, Bishop of Bath and Wells, Lake, Bishop of Chichester, Turner of Ely, White of Peterborough, Frampton of Gloucester, William Lloyd of Norwich, and Thomas of Worcester. Of these the first four had been of the number of the Seven Bishops. Trelawney of Bristol and William Lloyd of St. Asaph, who must be distinguished from William Lloyd of Norwich,

one of the non-jurors, succeeded in reconciling their consciences
to the taking of the oaths.   Lake died early in 1689, asserting
on his death-bed his emphatic belief in the doctrine of passive
obedience and non-resistance : a declaration which aroused
some warm rejoinders.[1]   William was lenient to conscientious
objectors ; too much so in Burnet's estimation.[2]   He gave the
bishops plenty of time in which to reconsider their decision
and kept the sees open as long as was possible.   That the
Church lost men of high honour and distinguished character
in the non-juring bishops, there can be no question.   But it
was clearly impossible for the government, however willing
it might have been to retain them in their sees, to allow men
who incidentally held high positions in the state to continue
in the enjoyment of them without their owning allegiance to
the head of the state.

Within the first year of the new reign six bishoprics happened
to fall vacant, viz. those of Bristol, Chichester, Worcester,
Bangor, Chester and Salisbury.   The men whom William
appointed to these sees were of a different temper and intellectual character from High Church divines like Sancroft
and Ken.   They were, in a word, Latitudinarians.   Reason
and common sense began to be enshrined in the place of
sentiment and mysticism upon the episcopal bench.   There
was some outcry against the new appointments.   William
himself was known to have but little sympathy with the
Anglican Church.   He was indeed a Calvinist; he had abolished
Episcopacy in Scotland[3]; he favoured the dissenters in England.
It was bruited about that in future the great posts in the Church
would be engrossed by Socinians, as their enemies chose to
term the Latitudinarians.   These slanders against the new
bishops were ascribed by one of them, Burnet, to ' some angry
men at Oxford ', the Earl of Clarendon, and several of the non-
juring bishops.[4]   The six bishops appointed in 1689, who gave

---

[1] Bartholomew Pamphlets for 1689 in Bodleian : *Declaration of John,
Bishop of Chichester on his Death Bed.*
[2] Burnet, *History of My Own Time* (folio ed.), vol. ii, p. 9.
[3] The abolition was really the work of the Scottish Convention before
William was accepted as king ; William did but acquiesce.
[4] Burnet, vol. ii, p. 29.

such umbrage to the High Church party, were Nicholas Strat-
ford, who became Bishop of Chester upon the decease of
Cartwright; Humphrey Humphreys, who succeeded Lloyd at
Bangor; the great Stillingfleet, Dean of St. Paul's, who was
given the see of Worcester; Simon Patrick, who followed Lake
at Chichester; Gilbert Ironside, who took the place of the
popular Trelawney at Bristol, Trelawney having been transferred to Exeter to fill the bishopric rendered vacant by the
promotion of Lamphugh, now Archbishop of York; finally,
Gilbert Burnet, Bishop of Salisbury, best known of all the
new bishops.

No consideration of the House of Lords during the reign of
William III would be complete without some notice of this
remarkable man, who played so outstanding a part in the proceedings of the Chamber, and to whom also we are indebted
for so much of our information on the subject. Because he
was a chronicler as well as an actor, it follows that we know
more about the activities of Gilbert Burnet in the House than
we know about those of the rest of the episcopal bench together.
Burnet was in many respects typical of the new type of bishop:
he was certainly the best hated of them all. Denounced as a
Presbyterian, he was accused of every heresy. On one occasion,
when one of the not infrequent attacks was being made upon
him in parliament, this time upon his having been entrusted
with the education of the youthful Duke of Gloucester,
Christopher Musgrave inveighed against the Bishop's exposi-
tion of the Thirty-nine Articles. It was, he argued, obviously
written from the Presbyterian standpoint, by one who did
not understand Church of England dogma. Full of Arminian
opinions, it was mixed with a grain of Socinianism.[1] Both
parties in the Lower House were at this time rancprous against
the Bishop. The services he had rendered to the House of
Orange, his intimacy with William, his friendship with Mary,
all marked out Burnet for speedy advancement. Nevertheless,
William did not love him. Halifax notes in his diary of
conversations with the King that he never heard the latter say

[1] Dispatches of Friedrich Louis Bonet: British Museum Add. MSS.
30,000, vol. c, pp. 271, 274, December 12/22, 1699.

a good word of Burnet. The King once remarked to Savile
that he only wished he knew everybody as well as he knew
the Bishop of Salisbury.[1] And indeed the whole character of
the man stands out very clearly. Robust in intellect, good-
natured, exceedingly industrious, conscientious, he was, on the
other hand, conceited, a busybody and, it must be added, sometimes vulgar, as the well-known episode in Salisbury Cathedral
in the early days after the prince's landing proves.[2] He is his
own best biographer. Time after time he bears witness to
his own meddlesomeness and self-importance, as when with
infinite self-complacency he lectured Queen Anne upon the
dangers she incurred from the Jacobites and the Papists.[3] His
broad-mindedness was never proof against the fear, which
became almost an obsession with him, that fires would again
be raised in Smithfield. His faults are indeed on the surface,
and it is difficult to discern evidence for the view expressed
by William that the Bishop was a dangerous man with no
principles.[4] But it shows what a hostile feeling Burnet was
capable of arousing even in those to whom he was devotedly
attached ; and if so, what were the sentiments of those whose
principles, political or religious, the Bishop unfeignedly disliked ? But whatever may have been the weaknesses of the
Bishop of Salisbury, there can, on the other hand, be no
doubt of his many admirable qualities. Had more of his
brethren shown the same practical energy in their religious
work, the same zeal for reform, and the same seriousness of
purpose, had they, in a word, carried out the weighty and
eloquent injunctions which Burnet laid upon the clergy in his
splendid conclusion to his History, the accusation of lethargy
so justly levelled against the English Church in the eighteenth
century need never have been uttered. But, as we know, many

[1] Foxcroft's *Life of Halifax*, vol. ii, p. 216.
[2] Macaulay's *History of England* (1849-61 ed.), vol. ii, pp. 539-40 :
'As soon as the officiating minister began to read the collect for the king,
Burnet, among whose many good qualities self-command and a fine sense
of the becoming cannot be reckoned, rose from his knees, sate down in
his stall, and uttered some contemptuous noises which disturbed the
devotions of the congregation.'
[3] See Burnet, vol. ii, pp. 547-8 and 583.
[4] Foxcroft's *Life of Halifax*, vol. ii, p. 322.

in a puny spirit resented the desire for reform among the clergy coming from a man whom they labelled an interfering Scot, a Presbyterian.   And the episcopal bench was scarcely likely to look with favour upon one who made a point of speaking in the Upper House more than all the other bishops put together on any subject.[1]

The consecration of Burnet was accompanied by some little difficulty.   Sancroft—against whom it is plain that Burnet entertained a good deal of personal pique—had scruples.   In the end he compromised by granting a commission to all the bishops of the province of Canterbury or to any three of them to act together with the Bishop of London, and to exercise the authority of metropolitan between them.   In this way Burnet was consecrated Bishop of Salisbury in succession to Seth Ward. The inconvenience of having an archbishop who refused to perform his archiepiscopal functions was very obvious, and although, as has already been stated, William kept open the sees of the non-juring bishops as long as possible, the interregnum could not be allowed to continue indefinitely. Deprivation therefore became necessary, and in 1691 the vacant sees were filled up.   The most natural candidate for the position of metropolitan was undoubtedly the Bishop of London.   His was a very strong claim inasmuch as he had been one of the foremost promoters of the Revolution, had indeed been one of the signatories of the Association which invited the Prince of Orange to undertake his crusade.   He had, moreover, since the beginning of the reign actually performed the offices of Archbishop of Canterbury owing to Sancroft's failure to perform them.   Compton, however, to his great and not unwarranted chagrin, was passed over and the primacy was bestowed upon Tillotson, the Dean of St. Paul's. The choice was an admirable one.   Though not the ablest of the Latitudinarians—intellectually he was the inferior of both Burnet and Stillingfleet—Tillotson was in many respects excellently fitted for the great office which he was chosen to

---

[1] Extracts from the Reports of Friedrich Bonet to the Court of Brandenburg, printed in Ranke's *History of England* (trans. Oxford, 1875), vol. vi, p. 211, January 24/February 3, 1693.

occupy. The new archbishop had a gentle, mild and conciliatory spirit, but his broad-mindedness and his mildness of
disposition did not prevent his being at once vigorous and
resolute.

As successor to Ken in the see of Bath and Wells Richard
Kidder was appointed. Patrick, who had for a short time
been at Chichester, having succeeded Lake, was now promoted
to Ely, and Robert Grove followed him at Chichester. To fill
the vacant see at Gloucester the excellent choice was made of
Edward Fowler, a singularly able and open-minded man. The
other two bishoprics, made vacant by the deprivation of the
non-jurors, were those of Norwich and Peterborough. They
were now filled respectively by Moore and Cumberland. Upon
the death of Bishop Croft of Hereford, Gilbert Ironside was
transferred thither after his brief administration of the diocese of
Bristol, and John Hall succeeded him. Tenison, destined afterwards to become Archbishop of Canterbury, became Bishop of
Lincoln, and Sharp, like Tillotson, a noted preacher, but in
Burnet's opinion neither so experienced in the world nor so
steady in judgment, was made Archbishop of York on the
death of Lamphugh.[1] Burnet utters a panegyric on all these
men. He declares that all those whom the king had appointed
were ' generally looked on as the learnedest, the wisest, and
best men that were in the church '. He continues his eulogium
thus :

' It was visible, that in all these nominations, and the filling
the inferior dignities that became void by their promotion,
no ambition or court favour had appeared ; men were not
scrambling for preferment, nor using arts, or employing friends
to set them forward ; on the contrary, men were sought for,
and brought out of their retirement; and most of them very
much against their own inclinations; they were men both of
moderate principles and of calm tempers.'[2]

By the end of 1691 William had been responsible for as
many as eighteen episcopal appointments. Of these, fifteen
had been appointments of entirely new men. There had been
three translations. As there were only twenty-six sees in

[1] Burnet, vol. ii, p. 76.   [2] Ibid.

existence, it will be seen that already in three years a very remarkable change in the episcopate had been accomplished. But the process was by no means at an end. In 1692, on the death of Wood, Bishop of Lichfield, William Lloyd, the celebrated Bishop of St. Asaph, was promoted to fill the vacancy, his place at St. Asaph being taken by Edward Jones. In 1694, the same year in which Queen Mary died, there died also Archbishop Tillotson. Tenison succeeded to the archbishopric. He was in no sense the equal of his great predecessor. The man who was marked out by his gifts for the post was undoubtedly Stillingfleet, and the Queen was particularly anxious for his appointment. But the Bishop of Worcester was not a *persona grata* in some quarters. Although he was a Latitudinarian and a moderate man, the Whigs considered him too high a churchman, and apprehended that he might prove of too independent and uncompromising a temper. Although intellectually somewhat of a mediocrity, Tenison was well suited for this position by his conciliatory disposition and his conscientious industry.[1]

In 1696 the bishopric of Chichester again fell vacant, and Dr. Williams was appointed. On the death of Stillingfleet in 1697 Lloyd was transferred from Lichfield to Worcester, being followed in the midland see by Hough, Bishop of Oxford. The year 1701 saw two more appointments; Humphrey Humphreys being promoted to the see of Hereford, and his place at Bangor being taken by John Evans.

It will be noticed how frequent throughout the reign was the practice of promoting a bishop from one see to another. William Lloyd held as many as three different bishoprics successively in the period of twelve years. In 1701 an attack was made in the House of Commons upon this system of transference. It was stigmatized as 'a spiritual polygamy', the argument being that the effect of the practice was to make bishops too dependent upon the court.[2] It made possible a sort of bribery by means of sees; for the hope of being promoted from one see to another better and more lucrative successfully

---

[1] See Burnet's eulogy, vol. ii, pp. 135–6.
[2] F. L. Bonet, E. p. 75, March 11/22, 1701.

chained a man to the leading strings of his sovereign. Whatever little force this argument may be considered to have is diminished when we realize that it had a purely personal aim, as it was directed not really against a system but against the Bishop of Salisbury. It was thought that Burnet had hopes at the time of succeeding to the diocese of Winchester, and so exchanging a stipend of £2,000 for one of £8,000.

Although we need not suppose that William deliberately transferred bishops from one see to another in order to keep them in leading strings, it is certainly true that the new bishops were generally in the King's interest. The Latitudinarian in religion was as a rule a Whig in politics, just as the High Churchman was as a rule a Tory. A High Church Tory episcopate existed under James II. Stung into protesting against the policy of the Romanizer, it still maintained its political creed. Among the lords at the Guildhall who joined in declaring their intention of assisting with their utmost endeavour the Prince's efforts to call a parliament, 'wherein our laws, our liberties, and our properties may be secured, with a due liberty to Protestant dissenters, and in general, that the Protestant religion and interest over the whole world may be supported and encouraged', were the two Archbishops, with the Bishops of Winchester, St. Asaph, Ely, Rochester, and Peterborough.[1] Yet when the motion for a regency was discussed in the Upper House, all of these, with the exception of Sancroft and the Bishop of St. Asaph, were in favour of the motion, and the absent Sancroft was regarded as the proper leader of the Tories. Of the fourteen bishops present in the House on this occasion only two voted against a regency, viz. the Bishops of London and Bristol[2]; and of these Compton voted almost throughout the reign as a Tory. Near the end of the reign the position is reversed. There were again fourteen bishops present at the trial of Lord Somers. Eleven voted on the Whig side for his acquittal. The Bishops of London,

[1] James Ralph, *History of England during the Reigns of William III, Anne, and George I* (1744), vol. i, p. 1061.
[2] See the list given in the Diary of Henry Hyde, Earl of Clarendon, in vol. ii of his *Correspondence* (ed. S. W. Singer), London, 1828, p. 256.

Exeter, and Rochester were the only three who voted against him. The Whig complexion of the episcopacy is shown as early as January 1692/3, when all the bishops in the House, with the exception of the notorious Bishop of St. David's, Dr. Watson, were in favour of the Triennial Bill. On the other hand, the majority of the bishops voted against the other great reform measure obnoxious to William, viz. the Place Bill, and were well lectured by Mulgrave for so doing.[1] The bishops were once more on the side of the King on the question of the Irish Forfeited Estates, and a very serious crisis was only averted by the retirement of the bishops from the House at the eleventh hour. Tenison, the Archbishop, had been particularly vigorous in his opposition to a measure which might well seem to a just-minded man nothing short of iniquitous.

It is unfortunate that we do not possess speeches of the ecclesiastics in the House with the exception of the outlines of some of Burnet's. It is difficult therefore to estimate the extent and character of the influence exercised in the Chamber by the episcopal bench. We can say, broadly speaking, that it was for most of the reign Whiggish, and that it was moderate. Even the High Churchmen showed at the commencement of the reign that they quite realized that something must be done for the Protestant dissenters. The opposition to the Comprehension Bill, itself introduced into the Upper House under the patronage of the High Anglican party, failed not in the Lords but in the Commons. The general tolerance of the bishops was such that it is somewhat disappointing to find that no one of them offered any amendment to the scandalous bills against the Papists of 1699. With the first of these, which was introduced in the Commons, the Lords made no progress, and it was dropped. The second bill was even more intolerant. Among other clauses there was one banishing all popish priests from the realm, and condemning them to prison if they returned.[2] The Bishop of Salisbury himself defended the measure. Although laying claim to the principles of

---

[1] *Infra,* p. 183.
[2] See *Lords MSS. 1697-9,* No. 1419, pp. 389-91.

toleration, he could yet say that he had always considered 'that if a government found any sect in religion incompatible with its peace and safety, it might, and sometimes ought, to send away all of that sect, with as little hardship as possible '.[1] Moderation among Protestants of every denomination was far to seek where Roman Catholicism was concerned at the end of the seventeenth century. On the whole, however, it may be said that the voices of the bishops were raised in favour of moderate views in religious as in other affairs which came before the House of Lords.

The importance of the episcopal element in the Chamber was obviously far smaller in the seventeenth century than it had been in the past. At a time when the temporal peers numbered about 160 the episcopate consisted of only 26 members, an inconsiderable minority in the House. Nor does an examination of the *Journals* show that the bishops were at all regular in their attendance. In view of their diocesan duties it was not to be expected that they should be. It is rare to find more than a dozen of them present at a time, and only a few enthusiastic politicians were at all assiduous in their appearance at Westminster.

Again, in those cases in which the attendance of the temporal lords was especially required, i.e. judicial cases, the presence of the bishops was not wanted at all. It was a rule that in cases where the death penalty was involved they should absent themselves before sentence was actually given: it was quite in order that they should remain during the preliminary proceedings. Still, the very prominent position assumed by the Bishop of Salisbury during the Fenwick trial met with strong disapproval, and indeed his eagerness against the accused was altogether inexcusable. There is extant a speech of the Earl of Warrington, in which he brings out the main arguments of his day against the bishops being allowed to vote in cases of blood.[2] He is at pains to prove the inferiority of the spiritual peers in their claims as members of the House of

---

[1] Burnet, vol. ii, pp. 228-9.
[2] *Works of Henry, Lord Delamere and Earl of Warrington* (1694), p. 111 *et seq.*

Lords. Strictly speaking they are not peers at all, but only lords of parliament. An act of parliament is good even if the bishops be entirely absent from its consideration. It has been their custom when decisions in capital cases are in question to withdraw before sentence is given after making a formal protest. Lastly, they have not so absolute a right to sit and vote in the House of Lords as the temporal peers have because they are called to parliament so uncertainly. Warrington considers that no good case can be made out for the bishops sitting in judgment upon peers : which, as only a select number of peers were summoned to the Court of the Lord High Steward, they ceased to do.[1] They could, he insisted, find no precedent in peaceful times. When a peer had been tried out of parliament, had a bishop ever been nominated to sit upon the jury? It was in the interests of the temporal peerage to make common cause against the claim of the bishops to take any part in judicial proceedings. Surely it was expedient for the peers to keep their numbers as small as possible, and to take every opportunity to exclude those who had really no lot with the nobility?[2]

As a matter of fact, although the cleavage between the temporal and spiritual lords was no doubt a wide one in any case, and tended to become wider when the personnel of the episcopate was rendered unstable by constant changes, nevertheless the bishops could scarcely fail to imbibe some of the characteristic spirit of the nobility from sitting so much with them and sharing in so many of their distinctive privileges. Spiritual as well as temporal lords could insist upon their claims to immunity from the ordinary course of the law. Assuredly no member of the Upper House made more extensive or (it may be added) more discreditable use of his privileges than did Dr. Watson, the Tory Bishop of St. David's.

[1] After the passing of the Act, 7 Will. III, cap. 3, it became doubtful whether spiritual lords' were included in the word 'Peers', i.e. whether they could take place in trials of peers, 'but as they could not "vote at the trial", and have always withdrawn before judgment, it seems clear that they are excluded'.—L. O. Pike, *Constitutional History of the House oj Lords* (1894), p. 224 footnote. See *infra*, pp. 111-2.

[2] The bishops acknowledge themselves to be lords of parliament and not peers as early as the Reformation.—See Pike, p. 165.

Burnet cannot speak too badly of this bishop.[1] 'He was', he says, 'one of the worst men in all respects, that ever I knew in holy orders: passionate, covetous and false in the blackest instances, without any one virtue or good quality to balance his many bad ones.' An instance of the manner in which Dr. Watson utilized his parliamentary privileges is found in a petition presented by a man named Lucy against the Bishop in 1699.[2] The petitioner had been for thirty years registrar of the diocese of St. David's, by a patent granted to his father by the late bishop. He was entitled to the fees and perquisites of the office. Lucy's title had recently been confirmed by the Court of Exchequer in a suit which had been brought against him by a new patentee under the present bishop. Dr. Watson had for nine years been appropriating the fees due to the petitioner, and now detained them, insisting upon his privilege, despite the decision of the court. Moreover, he had failed to make an entry in the register of such matters dispatched by his lordship as was required by the canons, whereby the petitioner had been debarred from ascertaining what fees were due to him therefrom, and was in danger of losing them altogether. In the meantime the Bishop was suing Lucy for a small rent from tithes which he held from his lordship. Lucy very naturally wanted to have the same facility for recovering his considerable dues from the Bishop as the Bishop had for recovering his small debts from Lucy. The matter was referred to a committee of privileges, with the satisfactory result that it was decided in the report that the Bishop of St. David's was in this case merely a trustee and could not claim privilege.

Watson did not retain his bishopric for long after this. The evil practices of which he had been guilty were so patent and so scandalous that from the first it was not possible to doubt what would be the verdict of the Ecclesiastical Court, before which eventually he was summoned to appear.[3] The only point upon which there could be any question was the penalty.

[1] Burnet, vol. ii, pp. 226-7.
[2] *Lords MSS. 1697-9,* No. 1234, pp. 235-8, May 12, et seq.
[3] T. B. Howell, *Complete Collection of State Trials,* vol. xiv, pp. 447-71.

In the end he was deprived, though Burnet had been in favour of excommunication.[1] Watson was not the sort of man to submit quietly to his fate : when the court sat to give judgment, he chose to resume his privileges, and when deprived by the archbishop, he pleaded this and appealed to the House of Lords. The House of course did not go into the merits of the case which had come before the Ecclesiastical Court, but confined itself to the question of privilege, and decided that the bishop should not be allowed his privilege. Even after this Watson was not at once satisfied : he made another attempt to obtain relief from the Lords, but his petition was dismissed.

Fortunately the Bishop of St. David's stood by himself in marked contrast to the rest of an episcopate, whose united influence was decidedly for good. It was an influence which showed itself principally by its tone and dignity. The days when the whole bench acted together in the bonds of a common interest and united purpose, when the Church as such had to adopt a definite attitude towards the state, were gone. There were no overmastering claims upon the bishops which obliterated the distinctions between Whig and Tory, Court party and Opposition. Therefore the influence of the episcopate within the House of Lords was not likely to be at all considerable. It was not sufficiently distinctive, sufficiently vital.

Nevertheless, the history of the episcopal bench in the reign of William III is of very great importance. The fundamental change in its composition had far-reaching consequences. From this time we date a very remarkable divergence between the higher and lower clergy, which is revealed in the many acrimonious disputes between the two Houses of Convocation. The bishops were no doubt chosen from the most learned, from perhaps in all respects the most distinguished, party in the English Church at the time. But it soon became clear that however admirable they might be, however zealous, erudite and enlightened, they were almost wholly out of touch with the main body of the clergy, and so far as we can judge, with the majority of the Anglican laity too. The Sacheverell case proved

[1] Burnet, vol. ii, p. 250.

indisputably how strong and widespread in the succeeding reign was High Church feeling in the country. We know that the doctrines of passive obedience and divine right were never more zealously preached than in the beginning of the eighteenth century ; that the royal martyr was never more assiduously worshipped. Of such tendencies there was no trace at all among the bishops. With whichever side our sympathies may be, with High Church or Low, we must agree that it was an evil day for the Anglican Church when the nominal representatives of the Church in Parliament ceased to represent the Church as a whole.

CHAPTER III

THE SOCIAL POSITION OF THE PEERAGE

WHEN Gulliver visited Brobdingnag he gave His Majesty the King of that realm an account of the English constitution.[1] He explained that the Parliament was partly made up of an illustrious body called the House of Peers, ' persons of the noblest blood and of the most ancient and ample patrimonies '. He described ' the extraordinary care always taken of their education in arts and arms, to qualify them for being counsellors born to the king and kingdom, to have a share in the legislature : to be members of the Highest Court of Judicature, from whence there could be no·appeal ; and to be champions always ready for the defence of their prince and country, by their valour, conduct and fidelity. That these were the ornament and bulwark of the kingdom, worthy followers of their most renowned ancestors, whose honour had been the reward of their virtue, from whence their posterity was never once known to degenerate '. Gulliver also described the position of the bishops in the Upper Chamber of the Parliament. It was, he said, their business to take care of religion ; their function was indeed to be the spiritual fathers of both clergy and people. As was only right, therefore, the bishops were holy men, sought out from the whole nation and selected from the priesthood on account of the special sanctity of their lives and the depth of their erudition. The king was much interested in Gulliver's account, and proceeded to put a number of very pertinent questions. He was anxious to learn what were the methods of education used to cultivate the minds and bodies of the young nobility of England. In what kind of business were they engaged during their earlier years? In the second place, when vacancies occurred in the assembly owing to the extinction of

---

[1] Swift, *Prose Works*, vol. viii, pp. 130-3.

a noble house, what were the qualifications deemed necessary
when a new lord was created? Were the reasons for advancement ever such as the caprice of a prince, or a design of
strengthening a party opposite to the public interest? Or could
a peer's dignity ever be bought by a sum of money to a court
lady or a prime minister? Then as to the judicial qualifications
of the peers: what sort of knowledge of their country's laws
had they, and in what way did they come by such knowledge?
Were they always so free from avarice or bias as to be entirely
incorruptible? With regard to the spiritual lords, the king
inquired whether as a matter of fact it was always on account
of their personal holiness and their knowledge in matters of
religion that they were promoted, and never through time-
service to the spirit of the hour or meek compliance with the
opinions of a nobleman—opinions which 'they continued
servilely to follow after they were admitted into that assembly'.

Such questions as these are apposite at all periods. But
how wide in Swift's day was the severance between the ideal,
as sketched by Gulliver, and the reality, as suggested by His
Majesty of Brobdingnag? We may find an answer partly by
discussing the cases of particular peers. But it is clearly
impossible to examine one by one the numerous members of
the House, many of whom history scarcely remembers, even
if she deigns to notice them at all. It is necessary in order to
visualize the House of Lords to have some idea not only of
the distinguished minority, but also of the ordinary men in it.

We need a picture of the typical peer; of his pursuits and
interests, and of the daily life he led. Such a picture is much
more readily attainable in the pages of fiction than in those of
the history book. From the writer of fiction we may learn, at
any rate, what manner of man the peer was supposed to be,
and what measure of dignity attached to a title irrespective
of the personal merits of its holder. The literature of the
latter half of the seventeenth century provides us with a very
distinct and vivid impression of social conditions, and no figure
occurs more frequently in it than that of the man about town,
the man of quality; for these are the halcyon days of bucks
and beaux. We do not indeed often come across him in the

literary and critical *Spectator* or in the lady's paper, *The Tatler*. Defoe, the one novelist of the period, is chiefly interested in the lower classes in the social scale. But the dramatists, on the other hand, serve our purpose admirably. They are concerned almost entirely with the one class, writing for them, of them, and at them. The commonest figure in what we call Restoration Comedy is the man of fashion, and in not a few instances the man of fashion is a peer.

Most famous of all the noble characters in the fiction of the time is Lord Foppington, in *The Relapse*, by Vanbrugh, the play which Sheridan converted into 'A Trip to Scarborough'. When the play opens his lordship has just entered upon the pleasures of peerage.[1] Alone in his bedroom he soliloquizes upon his new-found delights. 'Well, 'tis an unspeakable pleasure to be a man of quality, strike me dumb—My Lord— Your Lordship—My Lord Foppington. Ah! C'est quelque chose de beau, que le diable n'importe.' Such is the creed of this very self-satisfied and entirely vacuous gentleman. It is admirably set forth in his remarks upon reading and the manner in which he spends his day. Sheridan has taken a slice of this eloquent address verbatim from Vanbrugh, but a good deal of it he has omitted. Lord Foppington confesses to a passionate fondness for reading, but adds that he never *thinks* of what he reads. For what must be the attitude towards literature of the man who aspires to be a leader in the fashionable world? The answer is given by my lord as follows:

'To mind the inside of a book is to entertain one's self with the forc'd product of another man's brain. Naw I think a man of quality and breeding may be much diverted with the natural sprauts of his own. But to say the truth, madam, let a man love reading never so well, when he comes to knaw the tawn, he finds so many better ways of passing away the four and twenty hours, that 'twere ten thousand pities he should consume his time in that. For example, Madam, my life; my life is a perpetual stream of pleasure, that glides thro' such a variety of entertainments, I believe the wisest of our ancestors never had the least conception of 'em.

---

[1] *The Relapse*, Act I, sc. 3.

'I rise, Madam, about ten o'clock. I don't rise sooner, because 'tis the worst thing in the world for the complexion;
nat that I pretend to be a beau; but a man must endeavour
to look wholesome lest he make so nauseous a figure in the
side-bax, the ladies should be compelled to turn their eyes
upon the play. So at ten o'clock, I say, I rise. Naw, if I find
it a good day, I resalve to take a turn in the Park, and see the
fine women, so huddle on my clothes and get dressed by one.
If it be nasty weather, I take a turn to the chocolate house;
where, as you walk, Madam, you have the prettiest prospect in
the world; you have looking-glasses all round you.'

'But I fear,' the narrator breaks off, 'I tire the company.'
Being assured that he does not, he then continues:

'Why then, ladies, from thence I go to dinner at Lacket's,
and there you are so nicely and delicately served, that, stap my
vitals, they can compose you a dish no bigger than a saucer,
shall come to fifty shillings; between eating my dinner and
washing my mouth, ladies, I spend my time, till I go to the
play; where till nine o'clock I entertain myself with looking
upon the company; and usually dispose of an hour more leading them out. So there's twelve of the four and twenty hours
pretty well over. The other twelve, Madam, are disposed of
in two articles. In the first four I toast myself drunk, and in
'tother eight I sleep myself sober again. Thus, ladies, you
see my life is spent in an eternal raund O of delight.'

'But,' objects Loveless, 'your lordship now is become a
pillar of the state; you must attend the weighty affairs of the
nation.' Foppington's reply is eminently characteristic. 'Sir,
as to weighty affairs—I leave them to weighty heads. I never
intend mine shall be a burden to my body.' Foppington,
having thus delivered himself, now proceeds to make love to
Amanda, Loveless's wife, declaring that he is in love with her
to desperation, strike him speechless; whereupon, Amanda,
with excellent justification, administers a sound box on the ear.
'Gad's curse, madam,' exclaims Lord Foppington, 'I'm a peer
of the realm.'

In another of his plays, *The Provoked Wife*, Vanbrugh
introduces to us the delectable company of another nobleman
of very similar character in the person of Lord Rake. With
his boon companion, Sir John Brute, his lordship sits toping.

When two such cronies are singing and drinking together, what matters affairs of state and acts of parliament?
The ditty runs thus:

> What a pother of late
> Have they kept in the state,
> About setting our consciences free!
> A bottle has more
> Dispensation in store
> Than a king or a state can decree.[1]

The singer is perfectly content. There are no penal laws that can curb him.

> Whate'er I devise
> Seems good in my eyes,
> And religion ne'er dares to disturb me.

He is not to be worried by 'saucy remorse' or 'impertinent notions of evil', and he is quite prepared 'in peace to jog on to the devil'. He will have another glass, and 'damn morality'.

Lord Plausible in *The Plain Dealer* of Wycherley is another of the same character as Foppington and Rake. Lord Froth in Congreve's *The Double Dealer* belongs less to the merely feeble and inane type, more to the defiantly vicious. He is notable as sharing Chesterfield's views on the subject of laughter. As he says, everybody can laugh, and to be pleased with what pleases the vulgar is not to be thought of.[2] Farquhar gives us in *The Twin Rivals* the unpleasing figure of Benjamin Would-be. The best scene in the play—a very lifelike one, which admirably represents the range of aristocratic influence—is the scene in which the supplanting brother is hailed as Lord Would-be at his levée.[3] To him enters first a poet, bringing with him 'an elegy upon the dead lord and a panegyric upon the living one—in utrumque paratus.' Enter also the suitors for places. There is the gentleman who craves the new peer's influence in order to obtain a post in the army 'that (as he puts it) the blood I have already lost may entitle me to spend the remainder

---

[1] *The Provoked Wife*, Act III.
[2] *The Double Dealer*, Act I, sc. 4.
[3] *The Twin Rivals*, Act III, sc. 1. *Works of George Farquhar* (ed. Alex. C. Ewald, 2 vols., 1892), vol. ii, pp. 49–51.

in my country's cause'. There is the alderman who wants
a commission for his scapegrace son, as the army is the natural
resort of the ne'er-do-weel.

The idea of the typical peer of the time which, notwithstanding such occasional exceptions as Lord Bellamy in
Shadwell's *Bury Fair*, we gain from the comic dramatists is
clearly most unflattering. There is an interesting passage
in Jeremy Collier's *Short View of the Immorality and Profaneness of the English Stage*, in which he discusses the treatment of the peerage by contemporary dramatists.[1] 'What
necessity is there', he asks, 'to kick the coronets about the
stage, and to make a man a lord, only in order to make him
a coxcomb? I hope the poets don't intend to revise the old
project of levelling, and vote down the House of Peers. In
earnest, the playhouse is an admirable school of behaviour!
This is their way of managing ceremony, distinguishing degree,
and entertaining the boxes.' The canons of criticism which
guided Collier are very different from those of our own day,
and it will be noted that he objected to the dramatists' treatment of the peerage not on the ground of any infidelity to
truth in it, but rather on the ground of impropriety. He
thought that it was highly indecorous to speak of a duke as
a rascal even in fiction.

Is it more to our own purpose to decide whether the
Restoration Comedy can be at all treated as a guide to social
facts. Is it really mere farce, where the humour is not of that
artistic kind, which, however broad it may be, is yet a criticism
of actual conditions? It will be remembered that Lamb's

---

[1] Jeremy Collier's *A Short View of the Immorality and Profaneness of
the English Stage* (1698), p. 175. Cf. p. 173: 'Let us now see what
quarter the *Stage* gives to *Quality*. And here we shall find them extremely
free and familiar. They dress up their *Lords* in Nick-Names, and expose
them in *Characters* of contempt. *Lord Froth* is explained a *Solemn Coxcomb*; and *Lord Rake* and *Lord Foplington* give you their talent in their
title. Lord Plausable in *The Plain Dealer* acts a ridiculous Part, but is
with all very civil. He tells *Manly he never attempted to abuse any
Person*. The other answers: *What you were afraid*? *Manly* goes on
and declares *He would call a Rascal by no other title, tho' his father had
left him a Duke's*. That is to say, he would call a Duke a rascal. This
I confess is very much *Plain Dealing*. Such freedom would appear but
oddly in life.'

excuse for the work of Congreve and Wycherley was based precisely on the ground that it was artificial, that it bore no relation to the world of reality; that the characters in it broke no laws, because they had got out of Christendom into a 'Utopia of gallantry, where pleasure is duty, and the manners perfect freedom.' Unfortunately, apart altogether from the question as to the validity of Lamb's main contention, the fact is that his premises are wrong. However artificial the Restoration Drama may appear to us, it is clear that it did not appear so to contemporaries. The vogue which it obtained was due to the fact that it did represent, though certainly from the comic point of view, the kind of life which the sort of people depicted actually lived. The picture of society vouchsafed us in the Memoirs of Grammont is remarkably similar to that given in the comedies. Both the memoirs of the man of fashion and the plays which are concerned with his counterparts are conceived in the same frankly cynical spirit. The Restoration Comedy existed because it was not artificial; because it was in harmony with the thoughts and interests of the class which patronized it. Dryden dedicates his *Marriage-à-la-Mode* to the amazingly dissolute Wilmot, Earl of Rochester, and makes the interesting confession that not only he but the best comic writers of the age will join in acknowledging 'that they have copied the gallantries of courts, the delicacy of expression, and the decencies of behaviour from your lordship, with more success than if they had taken their models from the Court of France[1]'. Wilmot the model for the comic dramatist!

We are too prone to think of the reign of Charles II as of a period standing apart, if viewed from the ethical standpoint; as though the laxity of morals which characterized his court died with the monarch. The term 'Restoration Comedy' is in itself misleading. A large proportion of the best-known works of the school were produced not in the reign of Charles at all, but in that of William III. The Restoration, however, did certainly mark the beginning of a new order of

---

[1] Dryden's *Works* (ed. Walter Scott), vol. iv, pp. 236–7.

things. It meant the resuscitation of court life. The court was restored, and that with a brilliance such as England had never known before. The renewal of the life of Whitehall meant for the peerage the reconquest of a position of social ascendancy which had inevitably been lost during the Commonwealth. Under the rule of the saints there had been no possibility of a Society, to use the word in its narrow sense. The peers had been the object of ridicule and contempt.[1] But now after a period of eclipse the central luminary of their constellation shone once more, and they could shine again in its reflected radiance. There can be little doubt that, whatever may have been the results of the Restoration upon the political influence of the peerage, their social influence was probably increased beyond what it had been prior to the outbreak of the Civil War. For the court after 1660 was more animated, played a more important part than it had done in the reign of Charles I. In the earlier period there could have been no doubt that the English court was less brilliant than the French. On the other hand, when Grammont landed in England he discovered ' so little difference in the manners and conversation of those with whom he chiefly associated, that he could scarcely believe he was out of his own country. Everything which could agreeably engage a man of his disposition, presented itself in its different humour, as if the pleasures of the court of France had quitted it to accompany him into exile.' [2] In fact, as the Count elsewhere observes, 'the court . . . was an entire scene of gallantry and amusements, with all the politeness and magnificence which the inclinations of a prince, naturally addicted to tenderness and pleasure, could suggest.' [3]

It is clear that in the eyes of Europe England in 1660 emerged from beneath a cloud; her court was admitted to be on an equality with those of the great continental capitals. This was largely due to the influx of French manners and ideas into London upon the accession of a prince largely French in taste

[1] Cf. C. H. Firth, *The House of Lords during the Civil War* (1910), pp. 238-9.
[2] *Memoirs oj the Count de Grammont*, by Anthony Hamilton (ed. Scott), London, 1876.
[3] Ibid., p. 186.

and upbringing. Pepys notices how soon after Charles' accession Lord Sandwich showed himself sensible of the new conditions. In his diary for October 20, 1660, he tells us he dined
with my lord and lady, and how the former was very merry,
and talked very high about having a French cook and a master
of his horse, and his wife and child to have black spots after
the French fashion. Lady Sandwich mentioned her hope of
getting a good merchant as her daughter's husband; but my
lord would have none of it, expressing himself warmly upon
the subject, and asserting that he would rather see his daughter
with a pedlar's pack on her back so long as she married a
gentleman, rather than that she should marry a citizen.[1]

It is not necessary to linger over the picture of Charles II's
court; it is sufficiently notorious. Royal favourites vied with
each other which should set the laws of decorum most utterly
at defiance. Sedley and Wilmot were only the most daring
members of a thoroughly depraved society. The question is:
how far were the conditions under William III the same as
they had been under Charles? At the threshold we are met
by one very obvious difference. The days of Whitehall had
passed away. Instead of a merry monarch entertaining his
laughter-loving guests in the centre of London, there was
a dour and taciturn Dutchman, who lived in retirement at
the suburb of Kensington. The central social luminary of the
realm was, to all intents and purposes, once more extinct.

The change in the situation is undoubtedly important; yet
its effects must not be exaggerated. Merely because there
was no longer any centre of gaiety at Whitehall, courtiers
who had learnt bad habits under Charles did not therefore
repent and amend their lives. To take an example: the
depravity which had marked Thomas, Lord Wharton, in his
early life he retained until his death, and he passed it on to
his son.[2] Even if we are to discount a good deal of the
denunciations which party opponents poured upon the head
of this notorious nobleman, he still remains exceptionally

---

[1] Pepys' *Diary* (ed. H. B. Wheatley, 1893), vol. i, p. 264.
[2] 'Wharton, the scorn and wonder of our days.'—*Moral Essays.* Pope's
Works (ed. Warton, London, 1822), vol. iii, p. 194.

iniquitous. Of the most abandoned, something good may be said. It is certain that Wharton possessed decided abilities, though they may have been of a debased order. The Whigs owed much to his great skill as a party manager and borough-monger. Again, Macky described him as ' one of the completest gentlemen of England, hath a very clear understanding, and manly expressions, with abundance of wit'.[1] He certainly had the gift of a ready, and, it must be added, of a very foul tongue, which was the terror of his opponents in the House. It has been said of him that ' his eloquence was coarse and popular ; his attacks merciless, and his wit ready and poignant, but often degenerating into ribaldry, which induced Boling-broke, in language equally coarse, to call him the scavenger of his party.'[2] It has been claimed that Wharton was not destitute of qualities of heart as well as brain. His son describes him as ' the best of fathers ' ; and the writer of an anonymous life, published in 1715, says of him that ' he was generous to all he employed and charitable to the poor, especially to old people and children ; never was a man of his quality more easy of access, and never one who was a kinder master '.[3] That the man who gave the populace ' Lillibullero ' to sing (by which he claimed he chanted a deluded prince out of three kingdoms) may have had the capacity to make himself pleasant to his dependants, if he chose to do so, we may well believe. Unfortunately there is another aspect of the character of ' honest Tom ', as the Whigs called him.[4] The evil side of the picture has been drawn with equal vigour and venom by Swift, who in two numbers of the *Examiner* attacked him under the guise of Clodius.[5] Again, as a second Verres he is denounced for his conduct as Lord-Lieutenant of Ireland. ' Didst thou think, O Verres, the government of Sicily was given thee with so

[1] John Macky, *Memoirs of the Secret Service* (1733, reprinted for Roxburghe Club, 1895), p. 33.

[2] *Memoirs of John, Duke of Marlborough*, by William Coxe (6 vols., 1820), vol. ii, p. 82.

[3] See *The Whartons of Wharton Hall*, by E. R. Wharton, p. 51 (Oxford, 1898).

[4] See *The Last Four Years of the Queen.* Swift's *Works*, vol. x, p. 28.

[5] *Works*, vol. ix, p. 169.

large a commission, only by the power of that to break all the bars of law, modesty, and duty, to suppose all men's fortunes thine, and leave no house free from thy rapine or lust, &c.'[1] Indeed, Swift accuses 'the most universal villain I ever knew' (as he calls him) of unmentionable crimes of indecency and sacrilege. Again, in the well-known *Short Character*, which opens with a disquisition on the private character of his excellency, and contains a catalogue of his crimes in Ireland, particular note is taken of his indulgence in lying. Though he was in fact an ill-dissembler, yet his talents for deceit he valued most highly. His lies might be detected within an hour, often in a day, and were always detected in a week. He would solemnly swear friendship for you one moment, and the next, when your back was turned, tell those about him that you were a dog and a rascal. He went constantly to prayers and yet would talk ribaldry and blasphemy at the chapel door.[2]

An even more notorious reprobate of his time than Wharton was Lord Mohun. He had the misfortune to come to his title when still young. He speedily became a most thorough rake, and an utter scandal to the peerage. Before he had come of age he had twice been on trial by his peers on the charge of murder. The first of these two cases arose from the passion of a worthless army captain, named Hill, for the beautiful Mrs. Bracegirdle, one of the queens of the contemporary stage. As she remained impervious to his advances, Hill came to the conclusion—probably unfounded—that he had been foiled by a successful rival in Captain Mountford. He determined to have vengeance on Mountford, and to carry off the object of his desires. The latter purpose he undertook with the assistance of Mohun, who was his bosom friend. The attempt was not successful. The screams of the actress roused the neighbourhood, and she was rescued. The disappointing result of this enterprise only served to whet the indignation of the two bravadoes against Mountford. They hung about the latter's house for a considerable time with drawn swords. The watch endeavoured to interfere, and requested

[1] Swift's *Works*, vol. ix, p. 178.   [2] Ibid., vol. v, p. 9.

the gentlemen to sheath their weapons. But Mohun haughtily informed them that he was a peer, and dared them to touch him. The guardians of the peace felt themselves powerless. The unfortunate man eventually made his appearance; messages sent to give him warning having failed to reach him. Mohun at once engaged him in a dispute. During the altercation Hill seized his opportunity, stabbed his enemy and fled. Mohun was indicted for murder, but as he had only been an accomplice, was acquitted. It might have been expected that, having passed through the ordeal of a murder trial, even the most irresponsible of men would have been scared into some sort of amendment; or at least that he would carefully have avoided the possibility of the recurrence of such an incident. Not so, however, Mohun. Five years later he was placed in precisely similar circumstances. This time in connexion with the death of that very Captain Hill with whom he had been associated in his former escapade. Hill perished in a tavern brawl, in which Mohun was engaged. The coroner's verdict was one of manslaughter, and so once more Mohun escaped scot-free. The House had grown tired of hearing of his lordship's delinquencies when only a short time later he once more appeared before them, together with Lord Warwick and Holland, in connexion with the murder of one Captain Coote. Mohun on this occasion was indeed found to be quite guiltless of any part in the crime; but it was felt to be singularly disgraceful that a peer should so often be involved in such ugly circumstances. There is some evidence for believing that subsequently Mohun made some efforts to live more reputably in accordance with the sense of contrition which he had expressed.[1] But he died as he had lived, perishing in a duel with the Duke of Hamilton, which Thackeray has made familiar to all novel readers.

A character for libertinism was shared by many of the most

---

[1] Macky, p. 72 : ' He hath been as good as his word ; for now he applies himself to the knowledge of the constitution of his country, and to serve it ; and having a great deal of fire and good sense, turned this way, makes him very considerable in the House ; he is brave in his person, bold in his expressions, and rectifies, as fast as he can, the slips of his youth by acts of honesty ; which he now glories in more than he was formerly extravagent.'

conspicuous nobles of the day together with the mere idle rakes. Henry Sidney, it is said, was for years drunk every day. Swift's summary of his character is very terse and decided. 'He was,' he says, 'an idle, drunken, ignorant rake, without sense, truth, or honour.'[1]   The two versions of Burnet's history give two very different accounts. The earlier is most eulogistic. Sidney's sweetness of temper, his truth and candour, are dwelt upon. All his inclinations were noble. He might be too apt to be led away from business into pleasure, 'but it is a great pleasure when all that is to be apprehended in a man of favour is an excess of gentleness and good nature.'[2]   The published version of the Bishop's memoirs gives a much shorter passage to Romney, and the illicit pleasures are more insisted upon.[3]   Evidently Burnet's further experience of the earl had been much less pleasing.

Another notorious ill-liver was Charles Mordaunt, Earl of Monmouth, and subsequently Earl of Peterborough, one of the most extraordinary men of his time. Marlborough had in his earlier day been famed even at a dissolute court for his gallantries. Even Somers had the reputation of being a libertine. The Tory Scarsdale, who loyally supported all the measures of his party in the Lords, was ever a man of pleasure rather than of business. A fat, red-faced man, very far from attractive in appearance one would suppose, and tongue-tied in the company of the fair, he was notwithstanding a great lover of their society and successful in his intrigues. A great sportsman, he possessed neither the taste nor the capacity for any pursuit more intellectual.[4]   It was noted of the Earl of Bradford, that, although a man of considerable parts and refinement, and a good judge of literature and art, he had been all his life a great libertine.[5]

---

[1] Swift's comment is made in his Notes on Burnet's *History*. These will be found in the foot-notes to the 1823 and 1833 editions. They are also collected together in Temple Scott's edition of Swift's *Works*, vol. x, pp. 327–68. The remark on Sidney is on p. 358.
[2] Burnet, vol. i, pp. 763–4.
[3] For the earlier version see H. C. Foxcroft's *Supplement to Burnet's History of His Own Time* (Oxford, 1902), p. 284.
[4] Macky, p. 66.   [5] Ibid., p. 56.

Other individuals might be mentioned, but it is. hardly necessary to do so. The low moral standard of the nobility can hardly be questioned. Few of them had any deep religious convictions ; while some, like Monmouth, were the open. enemies of all religion. Apart from the vicious gallantry which the court of Charles II had inculcated in so many, drunkenness and gambling were both widely prevalent. The love of play was with many all-absorbing. It was encouraged by the great growth of coffee-houses, to which the nobility, like everybody else, were wont to repair after dinner. To Tallard, it would appear, they seemed to have made a considerable change in the manner of life of the English peerage.[1] Swift's patron, the Earl of Oxford, we are told, never passed White's, the most notable of these places of resort, ' without bestowing on it a curse as " the bane of the English nobility " '[2]— so wild was the gambling which went on there every night. It was expected that Sundays would be exempt from the practice of gaming. The Duke of Norfolk was once fined £5 for ignoring the rule.[3] But for the man who had the fever in his blood it was impossible to refrain.[4] And in this way patrimonies, in some cases none too large, were squandered away. Devout believers in aristocratic government, who felt it to be a source of weakness to the nobility that, as it was, they did not possess sufficient property, were profoundly shocked by their inability to retain even what they had.

The author of the *Memorial to the Princess Sophia* attributed

[1] Tallard to Louis XIV, in *Letters of William III and Louis XIV*, edited by Paul Grimblot (1848), vol. ii, pp. 468–70 : ' Nothing is so different from the manners of former times as the present style of living among noblemen. They have no intercourse with one another after they quit the House ; most of them go to dine at some tavern ; and afterwards they repair to places called coffee-houses, where everybody goes without distinction. Of these there is an infinite number in London, and there they remain till they return home.'

[2] See Lecky's *History of England in the Eighteenth Century* (1904), vol. ii, p. 156.

[3] *MSS. of the Duke of Portland*, vol. iii, p. 472 (Hist. MSS. Comm. Rep. xiv, Append. pt. ii).

[4] The diversions of gambling, &c., were by no means confined to the male sex. Note the way in which Bridget Noel, Countess of Rutland, spends her time. *MSS. of the Duke of Rutland at Belvoir*, vol. ii, pp. 72, 97–98, 101, 104, 105, 108–110. (Hist. MSS. Comm. Rep. xii, Append. pt. v).

the decay which he believed he saw in the English nobility to their living in London and not in their country homes.[1] Here again we come across the malignant influence of the court at Whitehall. 'The debauched and loose way of living wholly in London, neglecting their estates and interests in the country, their monstrous gaming, and *that bottomless pit, their mistresses,* have confounded and brought the nobility very low.' The feeling that the peerage were losing their influence—and this largely on account of moral failings—was shared by many. The Jacobite, Ailesbury, raises a wail of lamentation, 'God knows,' he exclaims, 'the peerage in these my days are sadly degenerated, and I had rather trust a poor honest cobbler than a great part of my brethren. And the peerage also is become so cheap and despicable by such unwarrantable promotion and in such numbers that I insert what I have publicly asserted that if I had no succession, and that it was in my power to do it, I would resign up my title, and live as a single gentleman, and I would make up in lieu of greatness by a sincerity and moral deportment.[2]'

Another member of the Upper House, though a man of very different character and principles, delivered an eloquent attack upon the life of the lords of his time. Burnet never wrote anything else comparable in style and matter with the Conclusion to his History. In it we feel at once the touch of deep sincerity combined with real insight and wide experience. No doubt the Bishop's prophetic utterances have the too gloomy tone usually to be found in the harangues of seers and censors. But in the main we cannot doubt that the faults which he finds in the various classes of society were as he declares them to be. The faults of the nobility were, as he says, generally speaking, the faults of the gentry, and the latter were, in Burnet's opinion, 'the worst instructed and least knowing of their rank' he had ever met with.[3] Very

---

[1] *Memorial offered to the Princess Sophia,* 1712 (reprinted 1815), p. 31. This pamphlet has been attributed to Burnet, but the initials G. S. probably refer to a man named George Smyth, not to Gilbert Sarum.
[2] *Memoirs of Thomas Bruce, Marquis of Ailesbury* (Roxburghe Club, 1890), p. 304.
[3] Burnet, vol. ii, p. 658.

often they were both ill-taught and ill-bred, and so also both haughty and insolent.[1]   Burnet blamed the system of education as being radically at fault.   There was too much time spent on Latin, too little on the English and French languages, while a knowledge of law would be useful, especially for service in parliament.[2]   In after years the ordinary man learned nothing more than what was to be found in plays and romances, and the stage was the great corrupter of the town.   Religious principles were not sufficiently instilled into the young, and then the gentry 'grew soon to find it a modish thing, that looks like wit and spirit, to laugh at religion and virtue, and so become crude and unpolished infidels'.[3]   The universities are criticized, because those schooled in them came to have no love of country or public liberty, 'so that they are easily brought to like slavery, if they may be the tools for managing it.'   The remedy suggested is a course of Plutarch's Lives, together with English history.

The advice which the Bishop of Salisbury gave to the gentry generally he gave also to the nobility.   Only in their case the advice was more urgent, because just as they were higher in social rank than their neighbours, so they ought to excel in knowledge and virtue.   In particular, as members of the House of Lords, the supreme court of judicature, they ought to have some knowledge of the law.   Burnet maps out a special scheme of education for the sons of the nobility. Each should, he thinks, have two governors, the one to frame the mind, 'to give him true notions, to represent religion and virtue in a proper light to him,' and in particular to inculcate 'noble principles of justice, liberty and virtue, as the basis of government; and with an aversion to violence and arbitrary power, servile flattery, faction and luxury, from which the corruption and ruin of all governments have arisen'.   The other governor was to teach modern languages and to correct literary style and language.   It had often surprised him, continues the Bishop, to remark how often noble parents, who

---

[1] Cf. Pope, *Dunciad*, i. 220 : 'The polished hardness that reflects the Peer.'

[2] Burnet, vol. ii, p. 652.   [3] Ibid., p. 648.

were lavish in every other direction, would be frugal and narrow in the education of their children. A good education they owed to their children. But not only to them. They owed it as a debt to their country. Burnet looks upon education as 'the foundation of all that can be proposed for bettering the next age'. 'How,' he observes, 'do some of our peers shine, merely by their virtue and knowledge; and what a contemptible figure do others make, with all their high titles and great estates?'[1] The Bishop lays particular emphasis upon the proper employment of domestic chaplains by the peerage, and upon the well ordering of their households. He has in his mind's eye the vision of the ideal noble family, in which religion and virtue are enthroned, forming, as it were, a little provincial court, where all the members of the circle, servants as well as children, are brought up to be a pattern to the neighbourhood. The nobility should above all ever be affable and easy of access, and ought to achieve the best sort of popularity among their people by protecting the oppressed and 'entering into the true grievances of their country'.[2]

Such was Burnet's ideal for the English peerage.

'A continued pursuit of such methods,' he pursues in an eloquent passage, 'with an exemplary deportment, would soon restore the nobility to their ancient lustre, from which they seem very sensible how much they have fallen, though they do not take the proper methods to recover it. Have we not seen in our own time four or five lords, by their knowledge, good judgement and integrity, raise the House of Peers to a pitch of reputation and credit, that seemed beyond the expectation or belief of those who now see it? A progress in this method will give them such authority in the nation that they will be able, not only to support their own dignity, but even to support the Throne and the Church. If so small a number has raised the peerage to such a regard that the people, contrary to all former precedents, have considered them more than their own representatives, what might not be expected from a greater number pursuing the same method? These would become again that which their title imports, the peers of the crown, as well as of the kingdom, of which that noble right of putting on their coronet at the coronation is a clear

[1] Burnet, vol. ii, p. 655.   [2] Ibid., p. 656.

proof. Great titles, separated from the great estates, and the interest their ancestors had in their countries must sink if not supported with somewhat of more value, great merit, and a sublime virtue.'

It was, then, Burnet's ideal that the peerage should serve the purpose of a real aristocracy and be shining lights to the other classes of the social organism by their model behaviour. That they were very far from setting any such example is obvious. In the nature of the case, they were exposed to greater temptations to levity than other classes. On the other hand, however, we must be careful to remember that coarse manners were the rule in those days among people of every rank and station. They were days of brutal punishments, and days when brutal sports were popular. Thus a great deal which seems discreditable to our sense of refinement the nobility did but share with the rest of the community. In his lecture on Steele, Thackeray refers to Swift's *Polite Conversation*, and he retells the story of Lord Smart's dinner-party.

'Really,' says the lecturer with mock irony, 'fancy the moral condition of that society in which a lady of fashion joked with the footman, and carved a sirloin, and provided besides a great shoulder of veal, a goose, hare, rabbit, chickens, partridges, black puddings, and a ham for a dinner for eight Christians. What—what could have been the condition of that polite world in which people openly ate goose after almond pudding and took their soup in the middle of dinner? Fancy a Colonel in the Guards putting his hand into a dish of *briquets d'abricot* and helping his neighbour, a young lady *du monde*! Fancy a noble lord calling out to his servants, before the ladies of his table, " Hang expense, bring us a ha'porth of cheese!" Such were the ladies of Saint James's—such were the frequenters of " White's Chocolate House ", when Swift used to visit it, and Steele described it as the centre of pleasure, gallantry and entertainment, a hundred and forty years ago!' [1]

We do not need to take the *Polite Conversation* very seriously. The underlying truth which justifies the satire is the open coarseness which characterized society in certain of

[1] Thackeray's *Lectures on the English Humorists*. Works (Biographical Edition, 1902), vol. vii, pp. 316-17.

its moods. Swift has given us two pictures from fact in his
Journal to Stella. One is rather pretty.[1] Swift himself joins
Lady Kerry and two other ladies in one coach ; Lady Kerry's
son and three other gentlemen are in a second ; there is a third
containing Lord Shelburne's little children. Off the pleasure
party goes from Lord Shelburne's house in Piccadilly intent
upon seeing all the sights, which in those days included not
only the Tower and the lions, but Bedlam into the bargain.
They had dinner at the chop-house behind the Exchange, and
finished the evening at the puppet-show. Then there is the
picture of a dinner at Lady Betty Germain's.[2] It is a very hot
day, and the narrator is feeling the heat excessively, and is
therefore peevish. After dinner, Swift was not allowed to put
ice in his wine, being warned of its ill-consequences. This does
not increase his good humour. Then in the drawing-room the
cross and perspiring cleric is made a butt by the company.
Lady Berkeley, who was there with her lord, possesses herself
of Swift's hat and claps it on another lady's head, who in her
turn roguishly puts it on the rails. Swift was very sullen ; he
minded them not, he says. But two minutes later he is called
to the window, and Lady Carteret shows him his hat up at her
window several doors off. So he is forced to walk away, and
pay Lady Carteret and old Lady Weymouth a visit in order
to obtain his stolen property.

Diaries and memoirs such as the *Journal to Stella* are of
great utility in creating a definite impression of social life. By
scores of little touches, too minute, and often in themselves
without reference to others too uninteresting for quotation,
Swift helps us to realize in the pages of his journal the manner
of life of the great ones in society. Such works as these
enable us to check the statements of the professed humorist
or satirist, and to sift from general criticisms those which apply
in particular to a definite period. For example, when Pope
talks about the 'right hereditary to be fools',[3] he is uttering

---

[1] Swift's *Works*, vol. ii, p. 72.
[2] Ibid., p. 189.
[3] *Letter to a Noble Lord* who had written *An Epistle to a Doctor of
Divinity from a Nobleman at Hampton Court.* Pope's *Works*, vol. iii,

a gibe which has been brought against the hereditary principle
at all times.   There is no reason to believe that there was
a larger proportion of noble asses in his day than at any other,
though it is on the other hand probable that there was a larger
number of rakes.   It is a very common error to suppose that
the ne'er-do-weel is necessarily mentally deficient.   There were
noble youths of the Plausible and Foppington description
perhaps in plenty.   But more typical of the time than they
are men of Bolingbroke's kind.   After a long night of carousal
in which he has vindicated his ability, notwithstanding his
more serious duties, to be a man of the world and to share
in the dissipations of the idle, the statesman will rise from his
troubled bed, wrap a wet towel round his aching head, and sit
down doggedly to tackle piles of diplomatic correspondence or
official documents.   It is impossible to withhold a tribute of
admiration from the extraordinary versatility and buoyancy of
temper which characterized so many of the illustrious politicians
of the latter part of the seventeenth and the opening of the
eighteenth century.

After all, the nobility—and here was their saving grace—
aspired to be more than the leaders of society, had other
interests than those of mere dissipation.   Even the dissolute
Wilmot and others like him prided themselves upon their
literary attainments ; and, what is more, some of them had
real literary gifts.   In our period we stand at an interesting
parting of the ways in literary history.   The day was shortly
approaching when Johnson should strike his famous blow at
patronage.   The growth in the influence of Grub Street, the
development of the professionally literary class, portended
a new era.   But the new state of things was only in its
infancy.   There was as yet little of what we can call popular
literature.   The audience to which satire is addressed, except
this be of the very broadest description, must inevitably be of
the educated classes.   The pungency of satire depends in part
upon its being esoteric.   In a word, literature is not popular,
but aristocratic.   In the reign of Charles II we may almost

p. 328.   Cf. *The Dunciad*, vol. v, p. 280 : ' The sire is made a Peer, the
son a Fool.'

say the court was an academy.   In such circumstances patronage was a necessity.   As in the nature of things the circulation
of any book could not be very extensive, so the author was in
large measure dependent upon his patron.   There is extant
some interesting correspondence between Dryden and Philip,
Earl of Chesterfield—the latter a man of subtilty and cunning,
who is described in *Grammont's Memoirs* as being not deficient
in wit and agreeable in appearance, but of 'indifferent shape
and worse air'.[1]   The Earl had already sought retirement at
the accession of William III.   The poet writes offering him
the dedication of his translation of the *Georgics*.   The dedication would be suitable, as the Earl in his retreat spends his
time in the study of philosophy.   Dryden declares that ever
since he had the pleasure of making his lordship's acquaintance,
he has always preferred him to all other noblemen of the
kingdom, and that in all respects.   Finally, he declares that
he is desirous of making the dedication, not from any thoughts
of personal profit, but simply from the consideration that he
honours himself in doing so.[2]   Although Dryden gave priority
to the noble earl among all the nobility of England, a glance
through his published works will show that he was yet able to
say things of the most laudatory description and in very flowery
phraseology to many of the Earl's compeers.

The dedications of contemporary authors are indeed quite
instructive reading, as evidence of the system of patronage
which was so prevalent.   Congreve, in tendering *Love for Love*
to the Earl of Dorset and Middlesex, speaks in this strain :

'Whoever is king is also the father of his country ; and as
nobody can dispute your Lordship's monarchy in poetry, so
all that are concerned ought to acknowledge your universal
patronage.   And it is only presuming on the privilege of
a loyal subject, that I have ventured to make this, my address
of thanks, to your Lordship, which at the same time includes
a prayer for your protection.'

Shadwell, again, dedicates his comedy, *The Miser*, also to
Dorset, and asserts that 'the favour which your Lordship was

---

[1] *Grammont's Memoirs*, p. 168.
[2] *Letters of Philip Stanhope, second Earl of Chesterfield* (1829), p. 376.

pleased to shew this play I value more than all the loud
applauses of the theatre '.[1]   Several of his works he dedicates
to the Duke of Newcastle, whom he regards as still maintaining the magnificence and grandeur of the ancient nobility.
Welbeck is indeed the seat of the Muses.[2]   *The Sullen Lovers*
is addressed to this Maecenas.[3]

' Had I no particular obligation to urge me ', writes Shadwell,
' yet my own inclinations would prompt me not only to dedicate
this to you, but myself to your Grace's service, since you have
so much obliged your country by your courage and your wit,
that all men who pretend either to sword or pen ought to
shelter themselves under your Grace's protection; those ex-
cellences, as well as the great obligations I have had the
honour to receive from your Grace, are the occasions of this
dedication.   And I doubt not but that generosity, wherewith
your Grace has always succoured the afflicted, will make you
willing (by suffering me to the honour of your name) to rescue
this from the bloody hands of the critics, who will not dare to
use it roughly when they see your Grace's name in the beginning, that being a stamp sufficient to render it true coin, though
it be adulterate.'

Such are a few examples of the kind of language habitually
addressed to the peerage, in their capacity as leaders in the
literary world, though some of them, so addressed, had no
pretensions to literary capacity whatever.   With some it was
otherwise.   Dorset was certainly a poet.   Admirers even held
that he was ' the author of some of the finest poems in the
English language '.[4]   Dryden, archflatterer, being asked to

---

[1] *Works of Thomas Shadwell* (4 vols., 1720), vol. ii, p. 5.
[2] Ibid., vol. iv, p. 184, Dedication of *Epsom Wells*.
[3] Ibid., vol. i, p. 3.
[4] Macky, p. 55.   Cf. :
　　　Dorset, the Grace of Courts, the Muses' Pride,
　　　Patron of Arts, and Judge of Nature, died.
　　　The Scourge of Pride, tho' sanctify'd or great,
　　　Of Fops in Learning, and of Knaves in State ;
　　　Yet soft in Nature, tho' serene his Lay,
　　　His Anger moral, and his Wisdom gay.
　　　Blest Satirist ! who touch'd the Mean is true,
　　　As shar'd, Vice had its hate and pity too.
　　　Blest Courtier ! who could King and Country please,
　　　Yet sacred keep his Friendships, and his Ease.

name authors of his own country superior to the authors of
antiquity, instanced his lordship in satire and Shakespeare in
tragedy.   'Would it be imagined', asks Johnson, 'that, of this
rival to antiquity, all the satires were little personal invectives,
and that his longest composition was a song of eleven stanzas?'[1]
But, as Johnson adds, the blame of exaggerated praise falls
upon the encomiast, not upon the belauded author, and Dorset
was certainly responsible for a number of pieces which show
real poetic fancy.   Another peer who wooed the Muse was
John Sheffield, Earl of Mulgrave, subsequently Marquis of
Normanby and then Duke of Buckinghamshire.   He has
left behind him two volumes of works, including an account
of the Revolution and a quantity of verse.   His *Essay on
Satire* is so good that it was at one time thought that Dryden
must have had some hand in its authorship, if indeed he were
not really the sole author.   Charles Montague, Earl of Halifax,
has the honour of a place in Johnson's *Lives*, but no one has
been admitted to that company on slighter pretext.   But
though his original work was small in quantity and of no great
merit, Montague was remarkable as performing the same sort
of function as literary protector for the Whigs that Oxford performed for the Tories.   A man of far greater literary eminence
was George Savile, Marquis of Halifax, who revealed his great
intellectual powers in political writings of real genius.

It is probably easier for most people to think of the noble
of the period, not in his capacity as literary dictator, but as
a territorial magnate.   We picture him rolling along in his
equipage over the none too even high roads, being received by
village innkeepers with an excess of deference ; or red-faced
and jolly as he rides to hounds, goes a-hawking, or patronizes
the local sports of the country-side.   On his country estate
the lord was an influence altogether paramount, and he ruled

> Blest Peer ! his great Forefather's ev'ry Grace
> Reflecting, and reflected in his Race ;
> Where other Buckhursts, other Dorsets shine,
> And Patriots still, or Poets, deck the time.'
>   Pope's *Works*, vol. ii, p. 365.

[1] Johnson's *Lives of the Poets* (ed. Cunningham, 1834), vol. ii,
p. 11.

his dependants in the good old feudal manner with certain modern improvements and modifications.

We are fortunate in possessing the records of their journeys by certain travellers, who visited England on its emergence into the sphere of polite intercourse after the Restoration. Among these was Cosmo, Grand Duke of Tuscany, the narrative of whose visit, with its interesting illustrations in sepia, is especially instructive. Cosmo made what was almost a triumphal progress through the country ; the consummation of which was his entertainment in London. Both on his journey and in the capital he was the guest of different members of the nobility. Hence we have a picture of their country seats and of the pomp and splendour of their establishments. Everywhere he was magnificently fêted. He stayed at the palace of the Earl of Northumberland ; with Sunderland at Althorpe. He visited Audley End, the superb mansion of the Earl of Suffolk. Its wide courtyard, its minarets, spacious rooms and galleries surpassed anything which the royal residences could show. Indeed, Charles II looked upon Audley End with envious eye, and bought it, though he never paid the whole price.[1] Later on, and shortly before the termination of his stay in England, the Grand Duke paid a visit to the Duke of Albemarle (Monk) at his spacious and magnificent abode, Newhall. Several of the seats of the great nobles who entertained Cosmo are illustrated in the book ; and altogether we obtain quite a valuable impression in these pages of the social prosperity of the peerage.[2]

We have, too, an actual criticism of the English nobility.[3] The writer expends some pages on a description of the ordinary people, especially of the London populace. He describes their pastimes and amusements. Among their

---

[1] Audley End had originally cost £200,000. James, Earl of Suffolk, agreed to sell it to Charles for £50,000, of which only £30,000 was actually paid. See the petition of Henry Howard, the brother of the Earl of Suffolk, in *Lords MSS. 1689-90*, No. 63, p. 93.

[2] For an interesting list of the members of the establishment at Belvoir in the reign of Charles II see *Rutland MSS.*, vol. ii, p. 54.

[3] *The Travels of Cosmo III, Grand Duke of Tuscany, through England*, translated from the Italian of Lorenzo Magalotti (London, 1821), pp. 397 407-8.

characteristics he particularly notices their pride. The nobility, he goes on to say, are also proud, but they have not usually the defects of the lower orders. They display politeness and courtesy in their reception of strangers. As might be expected, those gentlemen are most well-bred and ceremonious who have travelled abroad and have been able to take lessons in politeness from the manners of other peoples:

' Almost all of them speak French and Italian, and readily apply themselves to learn the latter language, from the goodwill which they entertain towards our nation ; and although by their civil entertainment of foreign gentlemen, whom they endeavour to imitate, they moderate a little that stiffness or uncouthness which is peculiar to them, yet they fail in acquiring such good manners as to put them on a level with the easy gentility of the Italians, not being able to get the better of a certain natural melancholy, which has the appearance of eternally clouding their minds with unpleasant thoughts.'

The idea of melancholy in connexion with the English nobility at the date of Cosmo's journey may seem somewhat incongruous. It has to be remembered that it is an Italian that is writing ; and English jollity has never been of the same flavour as that which comes from the warm South. The haughtiness of the English nobility is commented upon by another foreign visitor, Sorbière, who declares that such is the pride of the English peer that he seems to regard himself as quite a different sort of being from his fellow mortals.[1] It may perhaps seem a little difficult to reconcile such an account with the descriptions by Swift, which give an impression of open-heartedness and familiarity. The Dean, however, had been permitted to enter the sacred gates, which were barred and padlocked against the ordinary person. The great pride of caste which characterized the English peerage during our period is emphasized again and again. Foppington's ' Gad's curse, madam, I'm a peer of the realm' is a delicious revelation of an actual state of things. Lord Longueville happened to be once insulted in the theatre. This affront was made the subject of

[1] *Relation d'un Voyage en Angleterre*, by Samuel de Sorbière (1664), p. 193. Another foreigner who experienced the hospitality of the English nobility was the Swiss, Muralt. See *Lettres sur les Anglois et les François et sur les Voiages*, by Béat de Louis Muralt (Cologne, 1725), pp. 88, 99.

a long debate in the Upper House.   Indeed, the temper of the
hereditary councillors was so much ruffled that the Earl of
Stamford rose to move that playhouses should be totally
abolished, as they were illegal and tended to the increase of
debauchery.   The Earl of Manchester and several others were
very earnest in the matter and contrived to have an order
promulgated to suppress all acting; which order was, however,
soon after taken off.   Still, it is interesting to notice that such
drastic steps should have been taken as the result merely of
an insult done to a single peer's high-mightiness.[1]   Another
remarkable incident occurred as the result merely of a laugh.
The Earl of Lincoln was noted for his excessive corpulence.
He had, in fact, to be excused from kneeling when occasion
required it, on account of his unwieldiness.[2]   The appearance
of his lordship's paunch once provoked the curiosity, if not the
laughter, of a youth named Webb.   Bitterly did the boy rue
his presumption in gazing at this sensitive peer.   Two of his
lordship's servants assaulted the boy, threw him down, and
beat him so severely that, when he died shortly afterwards, it
was the verdict of the coroner's jury that he had succumbed
as the result of the wounds he had received on this occasion,
though it was subsequently decided that Webb would have
died in any case from consumption, so that the murder charge
failed.[3]   Such tales as these make us feel that we are dealing
with a strange world.   A man, who was examined before a
committee of the Upper House in connexion with an inquiry
into the circumstances surrounding the death of Lord William

---

[1] *MSS. of the Duke of Portland* (Hist. MSS. Comm., 14th Rep., App.
pt. ii); *Harley Corr.* vol. iii, p. 485.   See also *Lords MSS. 1690-1*, No.
493, pp. 464-5.   Lord Longueville and his servants were assaulted by
the guard at the playhouse.

[2] *Lords MSS. 1692-3*, No. 524, p. 24.

[3] See Luttrell's *Diary*, February 27, 1691-2.   It is Luttrell who
informs us that the assault upon Webb was due to his gazing upon the
Earl in the street.   The jury at the trial declared the prisoners not
guilty, on the ground that Webb on February 24, 1691-2, and long before-
hand, had been sick of ' "a consumption", and died of this disease, by
the visitation of God '.   After the assault, however, both the Earl himself
and one of his men had fled and hidden themselves, which shows clearly
that they realized that the damage inflicted had been serious.—Narcissus
Luttrell's *Historical Relation of State Affairs, 1678-1714* (6 vols., Oxford,
1817), vol. ii, pp. 369-71.

Russell, declared that he had told the Earl of Lincoln that 'he would be torn in pieces before he would discover anything against any nobleman'.[1] We cannot wonder that common people went about in fear of the vengeance of a noble potentate, should he happen to be offended.

Squire Western's objection to the proximity of a peer in his part of the country is well known. There were, no doubt, many who shared in this objection before his day. It was indeed claimed by enemies of the peerage that, when an estate was to be sold, it was a great addition to the purchase that there should not be a lord within a radius of ten miles.[2] To country folk there may not have appeared to be any great difference between landlord squire and landlord earl. As landowners their interests were very much the same. They were probably too nearly the same to please the squirearchy. The typical country gentleman of the Western type, living comfortably on his own estate from year to year, travelling but rarely and lacking in the refinements of urban polish, might well feel himself put in the shade by a more powerful neighbour, who united the experience of court or official life with the pride of peerage.

Fortunately this pride of peerage did not alone reveal itself in an excessive determination to insist upon its dignity and to resent all encroachments thereupon. There may have been something ludicrous in the pose of the Duke of Somerset— 'The proud Duke', as he was called—particularly as he would appear to have been a man of no great intellectual capacity.[3] He made a magnificent ornamental figure at coronations, royal funerals, and on all great state occasions. But people realized that there was something in this portentous Duke besides mere

---

[1] *Lords MSS. 1689-90*, No. 154, p. 289.
[2] See a pamphlet on *The Limitation of the Peerage* (1720), p. 10.
[3] Macky's account of the Duke is : 'Is of a middle stature, well-shaped, a very black complexion, a lover of music and poetry ; of good judgment.' (p. 39). Swift's comment : 'Not a grain ; hardly common sense.'— *Works*, vol. x, p. 274. There is a well-known anecdote related of his Grace. His second wife one day had the temerity to tap him roguishly with her fan. The Duke solemnly reprimanded her for taking so great a liberty with his person. 'My first wife was a Percy, and she never did such a thing,' he told her.—*Dictionary of National Biography* (1st ed.), vol. li, pp. 294-9.

outward show, when he categorically refused to conduct the papal legate in procession at James II's bidding, and consented to be dismissed his regiment rather than do what he considered would derogate from the high dignity of the peerage of His Majesty's realm.   Again, there were not wanting among the peerage men who united seriousness of life with considerable powers, and in some cases even genius.   A good example of the earnest-minded lord, possessed of ordinary abilities, was Thomas, Earl of Pembroke.   His political views were moderate, and he was esteemed by both parties.   A plain, quiet-spoken man, his life is said to have been like that of the primitive Christians.   Fate placed him at the Admiralty Board, even against his own wishes.   As to his success there, there would seem to be some doubt.   Admirers actually maintained that had he had any experience of the sea, he would have been as good an admiral as any we had.   As he had none, the compliment does not appear to mean very much.

The Earl of Nottingham was of such serious manner and appearance as to earn the name 'Don Dismallo'.   He is best remembered as an enthusiastic Anglican.   Very early in life he had donned the mantle of religious gravity.   When he was at Christ Church, and before he had reached his sixteenth year, his father wrote to him exhorting him to preserve the reputation he had got of 'a very serious man'.[1]

---

[1] *The History of Burley-on-the-Hill, Rutland*, by Pearl Finch (2 vols., 1901), vol. i, p. 168.   P. 166, his uncle writes in a similar strain : ' I charge ye to frequent ye publique prayers and study to Reverence and defend as well as to obeye the Church of England, you will give me but a sad account of your time at the University if you return either factious or indifferent in ye point of Religion.   Nothing can betray you to errors in Religion sooner than the having too good an opinion of those who are not sound themselves.   Bee sure you never trust your own judgment in things of this nature, nor submit to Arguments only because you have not wit enough to answer them.'   It must be admitted that the advice was earnestly taken to heart, and that Nottingham became so much of an orthodox Anglican that he could hardly continue to remain in common charity with Dissenters.   The bargain which he made with the Whigs in 1711 is famous, by which he agreed to lead their cause in the Lords on condition that they should consent to the passing of the Bill against Occasional Conformity.   For William's opinion of Nottingham see Foxcroft's *Life of Halifax*, vol. ii, p. 206.   For Mary's see *Memorial of Mary, Princess of Orange, Queen Consort to William III*, by Gilbert Burnet Bishop of Sarum (Edinburgh, 1842), Appendix, p. xxii.

The Earl's openness and apparent singleness of purpose won him William's regard, though it was not always easy to square the King's policy with Nottingham's high principles. He also impressed Mary favourably. Though he took no pains to ingratiate himself, indeed spoke but rarely of himself at all, she confessed that she was inclined to have a good opinion of him and to believe in his sincerity, though she confessed that she might possibly be deceived by his formal grave look. The heavy formal look, of which the Queen speaks, was really the index of a very large measure of conscientiousness and industry in his official capacity. Ailesbury tells us that ' in comparison to Secretaries before and after him, he played the clerk as well as the chief, and he often told me he never ate until he had finished in the office in parliament time, and that he was obliged to go to Kensington . . . for to have the king to sign, and although fasting, he stayed often one or two hours before the king came out, who was in Council with his Dutch favourites'.[1]

Godolphin, dark and stern in mien, retiring and hard of access, was a man of somewhat similar type to Nottingham, although of infinitely greater power and ability. Again like Nottingham, he gave William the impression of being ' a very honest man '. He believed Lord Godolphin, the King once said, because he had given him his word.[2] Apart from his love of dice and horse-racing—he was an invariable visitor to Newmarket at the Easter and Autumn meetings—his habits were singularly austere. ' He is ', writes Spanheim who visited England in 1704, ' an enemy to all splendour and outward parade in his household, in his equipage and indeed in general, and perhaps to excess, as he has contented himself up to now with the lowest degree of peerage, which is that of baron, and only agreed with difficulty to be made Knight of the Garter, as he became only a few weeks ago.' [3]

[1] *Ailesbury*, p. 247.
[2] Foxcroft's *Life of Halifax*, vol. ii, pp. 219, 223, 242. Swift, making much of Godolphin's supposed Jacobitism, draws a rather unfavourable portrait in *The Last Four Years of the Queen*. *Works*, vol. x, pp. 26-7.
[3] Ézéchiel Spanheim, *Relation de la Cour de France en 1690, suivie de la Relation de la Cour d'Angleterre en 1704* (ed. Émile Bourgeois, 1900), p. 640.

Even in this period of dissolute living and volatility of purpose, there were noblemen who were not afraid of hard work. Nor does this statement refer only to men like Godolphin, Somers, and Montague, Earl of Halifax, who had been born commoners. One has always to bear in mind that the social priority of the peerage was not the cause of their other dignities and importance, but the result. Their social eminence was a factor derivative from their parliamentary privileges; and these privileges they owed to the fact that the nobility of England had originally been the servants of the sovereign. Historically considered, the peers were great because they had served. They enjoyed privileges because they had borne burdens. And now when many of these burdens had gone altogether and others had come to be regarded in a very different light, ambition egged on the noble subject to be the servant of the state. The aristocracy must be leaders in the sphere of literature. So must they also be in the various departments of government, in the navy and in the army. In the House of Lords there were soldiers like Marlborough, Ormonde, Monmouth, Feversham, and many others; sailors like Orford, Torrington, and the elder Dartmouth, Kiveton and Berkeley of Stratton; diplomatists like Jersey, Manchester, and Shrewsbury. Even the young Mulgrave must needs go to sea—he was in command of a ship when only twenty-two. It may have been a mistaken system which sent irresponsible young sparks to take posts in the forces. However that may be, it is certain that it was good for noblemen themselves to take part in serious occupations and in the defence of their country; and it must be allowed that the English lords were good fighters as a rule; some of them remarkably good officers. They had whole centuries of a military tradition behind them.

Finally, for all the nobility the wide field of politics lay open, and the door to office in the state might be entered by those who had ability and application. To some, politics might appear principally as an excitement; to others they formed a duty. There were those who deliberately turned their backs on White's and Wills's, and the amusements of court and theatre, and sought the more solemn pleasures of St. Stephen's and the Cockpit.   There were a good many more who found it possible to combine both the pleasures of labour and of dissipation.   There can be little doubt that the purely social attractions which a brilliant court in London had originated, or those bestowed by a position of semi-feudal authority in provincial seats, were often a snare for the young noble who found himself born to a place of great dignity and of at any rate comparative affluence.   Rank necessarily brings its temptations in every age.   In the later years of the seventeenth century they were no doubt particularly severe.   It were a futile task for any one to take upon himself the rôle of apologist for the escapades of Mohuns, who made the special privileges of their rank a nuisance to society, or for the tergiversation of politicians like Marlborough and Godolphin, upon whose allegiance either to principle or party it was impossible to rely.   But this at least we may say—that even in those days there did not lack among the peerage those who aspired to other ends than that of mere social predominance, examples of the motto *Noblesse oblige.*

CHAPTER IV

PARLIAMENTARY PRIVILEGES OF THE HOUSE

AN exhaustive list of the privileges of the English peerage would be lengthy, and it would have to include a number which really belong to the province of the laws of etiquette and are of but slight historical importance. Such small matters, however, deeply interested those concerned. An illustration of the minute interest taken by the Lords in matters relating to their dignity, however insignificant, is found in proceedings arising from a complaint brought forward by the Earl of Macclesfield,[1] that commoners were wont to be covered equally with peers when the sovereign went to the play. Evidence was adduced to prove that in the time of Charles I only peers used to sit covered. It was so also when the king was in the Mall or playing tennis. When Charles I put on his hat in the King's chapel, he used to give a sign to the peers to put on theirs. A committee of privileges reported in accordance with the evidence; but there were no further proceedings, possibly because the subject was regarded as being too trivial to warrant any very serious attention. One curious privilege—highly valued, no doubt—was to the effect that an earl might have eight tuns of wine free of impost every year, and the rest of the peerage amounts proportionate to their rank. But such exemptions are unusual in connexion with our English peerage.[2] There has always been much less

---

[1] *Lords MSS. 1689-90*, No. 61. See foot-note on p. 86.

[2] Muralt, p. 5, records the melancholy jest of an English peer at the futility of his privileges. 'On ne peut pas, dit-il, nous arrêter pour dettes, mais aussi ne trouverons nous point de crédit; pour tout serment, nous ne sommes obligez de jurer que sur notre Honneur, mais peu de gens nous en croient; il y a une Loi, qui défend de mal parler de nous, mais il nous arrive, comme à d'autres, d'être bâtus dans les rues!' 'Il pouvait ajouter', adds Muralt, 'que leur naissance leur donne entrée au Parlement, mais que ce n'est pas tout-à-fait leur Chambre qui gouverne.'

tendency in England than on the continent for the nobility to degenerate into a mere caste, partly on account of their official origin, partly by reason of the system of primogeniture. Thus all the important privileges of the English peerage are parliamentary. Peers possess them because they are lords of parliament, not because they are members of an aristocratic class. Their social dignity is—historically considered—a derivative factor. Several of their parliamentary privileges the Lords share with the Commons, such as that of freedom of speech.[1] On this it is not necessary to dwell; and of the privilege of trial by one's peers in cases of treason or felony it will be more convenient to speak in another place, when discussing the judicial powers of the House of Lords.

Freedom from arrest during the sitting of Parliament the Lords shared with the Commons; nor could they be impleaded in a civil action during time of privilege. As a matter of fact, in both cases the period of exemption extended beyond the nominal period, for it included anything from twenty to forty days both before and after the session.[2] In no civil case could a peer be impanelled upon any jury; not even if the dispute lay between peers. In no case could he be compelled to swear not to break the peace. He need only promise upon his honour, which was accounted sacred and inviolable. In any suit in which a peer was concerned no day of grace was allowed to the plaintiff. It is clear that it was no easy matter for the ordinary subject to obtain right from a peer, so thoroughly hedged round was the latter by exemptions from the ordinary processes of justice, and so long did the period of such exemptions extend. Often, indeed, one parliament might come to an end and another meet without the plaintiff's having

---

[1] On the subject of Privilege of Peerage see Chamberlayne's *Angliae Notitia* or *The Present State of England*, the *Whittaker* of its day. It contained a good deal of permanent matter together with details which varied from year to year. The pagination of the publication for different years naturally varies somewhat. It is immaterial to what year in the reign reference is made. In the 1692 issue, for example, the section on Privilege is on p. 220 *et seq.*

[2] A period of forty days was claimed in 1664. No decision as to whether the period should be one of twenty or forty days was arrived at, but in practice the longer period was no doubt adhered to.

any opportunity of bringing his action. In any case, the time available for legal proceedings was very short, and the wheels of the judicial machine, whenever a lord was concerned, were apt to move with exceeding slowness.

Occasionally it did happen that a peer became enmeshed in the network of the law courts. In such cases there was very likely to be an outcry. Several cases of importance came up at the beginning of William's reign. The momentous question respecting the covering of peers in the presence of the King was discussed at a time when there was a particular reason for eagerness on the part of the peers to assert their right. When the committee of privileges first met after the beginning of the reign, the redoubtable Earl of Macclesfield brought forward some more serious grievances than the trivial matter already referred to.[1] He made the general complaint that whenever a peer was unfortunately brought into a court of law, he met with unjust treatment there. The peerage, as he said, was invaded in their trials, which were not as fairly conducted as those of commoners. He went on to urge that lords should never be tried but in Parliament, and cited ancient usage. A statute of Edward III was read, in which it was enacted that no peers were to be tried except in Parliament. The particular circumstances which gave rise to this discussion were the trials in the Court of King's Bench of Lord Lovelace in 1685, of the Duke of Grafton in 1687, that of the Earl of Devonshire in the same year, and also the Seven Bishops' trial. The further proceedings of the House were confined to the case of Devonshire. This had arisen from a quarrel between the Earl and a certain Colonel Culpepper, which had aroused widespread attention at the time. It is clear that the former had received considerable provocation ; which did not, however, excuse his use of personal violence against Culpepper. Still, quite apart from the question of privilege involved, the punishment was exceedingly severe and altogether out of proportion to the offence. Summoned before the Court of

---

[1] *Lords' MSS. 1689–90*, No. 62, pp. 86–93, Macclesfield's complaint, p. 87.

King's Bench, the Earl had pleaded privilege of parliament against an accusation of misdemeanour. This did not hold good, and the plea was quite rightly overruled by the court. Eventually Devonshire was fined £30,000, was committed to the King's Bench prison until the sum should be paid, and was bidden to find security for his keeping the peace for one year.

The case is made the occasion of an eloquent dissertation by the Earl of Warrington.[1]

'The overruling of the Earl's plea of privilege', he contends, 'is a thing of that vast consequence, that it requires a great deal of time to comprehend it aright, and is of so great extent that more may be said of it than any man can say. . . . Because it is in case of Privilege, which is the most tender part of our Court, for if the Rights and Privileges of any Court are made light of, the Court itself will soon come to nothing, because they are as it were the most essential part of it, if not the very essence of the Court, for what signifies a Court, if its Orders cannot be executed ? It is better that a Court were not, than that its Privileges should not be observed, for without that it becomes a snare and mischief to the People, rather than an Advantage.'

The noble author goes on to attack the actions of the King's Bench judges in setting the feet above the head. Such is his lordship's phrase. These judges have arrogated to themselves superiority over the House of Lords, which is the supreme judicial body in the kingdom. This must lead to a complete inversion of the whole course of nature.[2] In fine, the Earl sees in the case a most manifest attempt upon the status of the peerage. In common with so many others of his day he bemoans the destructive policy of the Tudors towards the nobility, who had been undermined by lavish creations, and rendered contemptible by the honours given to men of mean extraction. Only one thing more was needed to complete the ignominy of the peerage. That finishing touch has been added by the Earl of Devonshire's case.

---

[1] *Works of Warrington*, p. 563, on the case of William, Earl of Devonshire, and Colonel Culpepper.
[2] Ibid., p. 566.

' Nothing can make it [the peerage] more despicable, than
that its Privileges should depend upon the beck of the King's
Bench, and therefore considering how groundless and without
president [*sic*] it is, what they have done in the case of the said
Earl, it is no more than probable [? *no less*] that they thereby
aimed at pulling down the peerage. For what seems so likely
as it does? It carries its evidence in its Face, for it manifestly
takes away the privilege of the Peers, and till it does appear
for what other end it was done, all Men of Sense, and that are
unprejudiced, must believe it was to pull down the Peerage ;
for all that can be pretended is, either to secure the Peace, or
to punish the offence.'

It is clear that it is for the noble caste that Warrington
is arguing here, and that his case deserved better arguments
than he has supplied. The Earl had done better to confine
himself to the grievance which was really relevant. The
assertion by the King's Bench judges of their competence
to try Devonshire's case was no infringement upon the dignity
of the peerage.[1] It was the infliction of a fine of the most
exorbitant figure, out of all keeping with the gravity of the
offence, that constituted the gravamen of the charge against
the judges. The Lords summoned the offenders before them.
It should be noticed that they did this, not as a court of appeal,
but in virtue of their original jurisdiction. In pursuance of
an act of Edward III, Macclesfield and several others were
appointed as a committee to inquire into delays and failures
of justice. The committee were anxious that not only Devonshire's case, but also those of Lovelace, Grafton, and the Seven
Bishops should be investigated. None, however, of these lords
attended, and although it was agreed to move the House for an
order to compel them, no more is heard of the matter. The
further proceedings had reference only to Lord Devonshire.
Sir Robert Wright, one of the judges concerned, cited the
precedents for peers not enjoying privilege in breach of the
peace. The other, Sir Richard Holloway, was more apologetic.
He admitted that the fine had been excessive. Personally, he
said, he had been in favour of the lowest fine, but he had been

---

[1] It is an ancient maxim of the law that the King's judges are the equal
of any man, be he peer or commoner.

overridden by the court. He did not attempt to justify anything, but submitted himself to their lordships. The advice of the Lord Chief Justice and others of the judicial bench was invited by the committee on the question as to how the law stood as to the commitment of a peer upon a fine to the King, for the trial had been at the King's suit. The Lord Chief Justice, although finding it difficult to answer on the spur of the moment, was of opinion that a peer could be committed upon a fine, at the suit of the King. Another of the justices put the case very clearly. Here was a lord brought before the King's Bench, and they had taken cognizance of it. As this was so, their censure could not but fall upon the peer as it would have done upon any other individual. Another legal adviser added that once a fine had been imposed, the court was justified in taking means to secure the payment of the fine. Notwithstanding this evidence, the judgment of the House was that a peer's privilege did protect his body. Accordingly, on May 15th, the resolution of the House was entered in the *Journals*, in which emphatic protest was made both against the commitment of a peer to prison for non-payment of a fine and also against the excessive nature of the fine in this case.[1]

Memories of the Devonshire incident were revived in October 1690 in connexion with the imprisonment of Torrington after Beachy Head.[2] The details of his trial are principally of interest to the naval historian ; but one or two points of parliamentary importance arose from it. Torrington was in the first instance committed to the Tower by the Privy Council, and this during time of privilege. The Earl petitioned for his release and for trial by his peers. The question before the House was whether, having accepted a commission, Torrington had any right on account of privilege of peerage to be exempt from trial by the Articles of War. The opinion of the judges was that he was triable by the Admiralty. The House drew up a resolution in accordance with the judicial advice.[3] The claim of privilege having been disallowed, Torrington was now by warrant of

---

[1] *Lords' MSS. 1689-90*, No. 62, p. 90.
[2] For proceedings in this case see *Lords' MSS. 1690-1*, No. 285, pp. 93-6.
[3] October 13, *Lords' Journals*, vol. xiv, pp. 521-2.

the commissioners of the Admiralty committed to the Marshalsea. The question then arose whether this was a legal
warrant. Two issues were involved in this question. In the first
place, did such power of commitment belong to the Admiralty?
In the second, could the power be exercised as well by Admiralty
commissioners as by the Lord High Admiral? Both issues
were determined in the affirmative by the judges. There was
a martial law in the kingdom. By it Torrington might be tried,
and if he could be tried he could also be committed. A third
question the judges also answered in the affirmative, when they
decided that for the offence specified in the articles of commitment issued by the Lords Commissioners of the Admiralty, the
Earl might also have been committed by the Privy Council.

The judicial decision on the subject of the Council's power
to commit was not accepted by the Lords.[1] They were satisfied
that the Admiralty commissioners had legal power to try
Torrington, and that his privilege did not exempt him from
such jurisdiction ; but they would not agree to the argument
that necessity of state justified the Earl's being sent to the
Tower by the Privy Council. For treason he might be, but not
for high crimes and misdemeanours. The report of the select
committee appointed to examine the question was accepted by
thirty-two voices to seventeen, several amendments having been
rejected. They thought fit to enter their opinion in their books,
that the case ' may not be drawn into an example for the future '.[2]
The epilogue to the Torrington affair is interesting. In view of
the forthcoming trial there was a feeling in the House that the
judicial powers of the Admiralty commissioners should be
made clear beyond dispute. Accordingly a bill was introduced
with this object in view. Macaulay is very eloquent in his
denunciation of the opposition made to the passing of this
bill.[3] He refuses to believe that the argument used against it,

---

[1] See Report by F. Bonet (Ranke, vol. vi, p. 152), October 28/Novem-
ber 4, 1690. ' Il y eut un long débat dans la Chambre, et plusieurs, non
contens que cet emprisonnement fut déclaré une brèche à leurs priviléges,
insistèrent à ce que les 9 conseillers fussent citez et censurez par la
Chambre, et les principaux de ce parti estoient le Marq. d'Halifax et le
Comte de Rochester, tous deux peu amis du Président du Conseil.'

[2] *L.J.*, vol. xiv, p. 525, October 20, and p. 527, October 21.

[3] Macaulay's treatment of this episode of Lord Torrington is typical of

that it was a retrospective penal law, could have been used in good faith. He concludes that the opposition proceeded merely from a strong feeling of caste. 'If their noble brother had offended, articles of impeachment ought to be exhibited against him : Westminster Hall ought to be filled up : his peers ought to meet in their long robes, and to give in their verdict in his favour : a Lord High Steward ought to pronounce the sentence and to break the staff. There was an end to privilege if an Earl was to be doomed to death by tarpaulins seated round a table in the cabin of a ship.'[1] At any rate Macaulay is led into exaggerating the strength of the opposition by following Ralph, who states that the majority for the passing of the bill was only two, whereas the third reading was in reality carried by twenty-five votes to seventeen.[2] In the second case there was a very good argument against the bill—that it was un-necessary ; the almost unanimous opinion of the different judges consulted being that the new act did but affirm what already existed. In reality there was not even a change of procedure, as Macaulay states. No one will maintain for a moment that jealousy for their distinctive immunities did not have influence in the House of Lords in connexion with the whole Torrington episode. Notwithstanding this, however, the facts are that the House agreed that the Admiralty com-missioners had been justified in their action, and went the length of passing an uncalled-for act upon the subject.

A third important case of privilege, which arose in November 1692, has given rise to considerable difficulty. The facts are indeed somewhat complicated. There can be no doubt that feeling was very much excited over the matter. There were 'very warm debates'. As Burnet says, when commenting upon

---

his less admirable methods. In the first place he quotes no authority for the account he gives, except Ralph on a point of numbers. He is con-tent to suppose that Ralph had 'some authority which I have been unable to find', as he confesses. As a matter of fact he was misled by Ralph. But for the much more important matter, viz. the arguments adduced against the bill, he gives no reference whatever, and for evidence sub-stitutes rhetoric of his own on the subject of tarpaulins.

[1] Macaulay, vol. iii, pp. 715–16.
[2] *Lords' MSS. 1690–1*, No. 307, p. 147.

the situation, 'where the privilege or the dignity of peerage is in question, it is not easy to keep the house within bounds.'[1] The Lords' sensitiveness on all such matters may be taken for granted. But the view that their attitude on this particular occasion was purely selfish seems to be founded upon a misunderstanding. The facts in the case are these.[2] The Earls of Marlborough, Scarsdale, and Huntingdon had been committed to the Tower on the grounds of alleged complicity in a Jacobite plot. On November 7th they formally informed the House that they had been committed and that they were now on bail within the time of privilege of parliament. It was moved that they should be discharged from their bail. Nothing came of this, however; and, in accordance with a previous motion, it was ordered that the Lord Chief Justice and the King's Bench judges should attend. They did so, and all agreed that the recognizances could not be removed to the House save upon a writ of error; secondly, that they (the judges) could not discharge until the last day of the law term. It was now moved that the King's Bench be ordered by the House to discharge the bail of these lords. This motion was not passed. As the result of the debate which followed, the matter was referred to the committee of privileges, who, however, eventually confessed that the question was too hard for them. Law and privilege often seemed to clash in a most perplexing way.

It is important to notice that after this the matter shifts to different ground. The House now took into consideration the reasons for the commitment. It so happened that in the cases of the Earl of Huntingdon, the Earl of Middleton, Lord Dunmore, and a commoner, Sir Andrew Forester, their release had been successfully resisted by means of the affidavit of one Aaron Smith, Treasury solicitor. Smith was sent for by the House, and as the result of a searching cross-examination

[1] Burnet, vol. ii, p. 102.
[2] See *Lords' MSS. 1692-3*, No. 581, pp. 86–91. See also *Journals*, vol. xv, pp. 105-15 passim. A great deal more is to be gleaned from the MSS. than from the latter, where the notices are meagre. It is notable that in one place a marginal note in the Minutes is inserted, 'Nothing to be entered.'

he failed to make good his affidavit. The point was, had there been the two requisite witnesses against Huntingdon? Being pressed, Smith acknowledged that he could not say there were two witnesses *upon oath*. There was one witness upon oath, and other evidence besides. It had now to be decided whether by the Habeas Corpus Amendment Act such testimony was sufficient to justify a remand. The judges' declaration upon this subject was to the following effect : first, that if there was but one witness it was the judge's duty to grant bail ; secondly, that other circumstantial evidence, if it was not upon oath, was no evidence.[1]

On November 12th the judges, being again examined, drew an important distinction between the evidence required for conviction and that required for a remand. They were clear that the act did not necessitate that for the latter purpose there should be two witnesses upon oath. The word 'witness' was to be taken as meaning 'any person'—it had to be a person ; no other sort of evidence would serve—'capable of giving testimony'. The judges' justification of their action was that Aaron Smith's affidavit might as a matter of fact have been faulty ; formally, however, it answered to the stipulations of the act. It was not their duty to inquire into the King's evidence at that stage in the proceedings. Therefore, it was contended they had done right in remanding the lords.

Having gone into the legal aspects of the matter, the Lords now acted in a manner precisely similar to their action in the Torrington case. They proceeded to make it quite plain what the law was, and framed a resolution with this purpose

---

[1] Ralph on this subject is guilty of a most extraordinary confusion : ' The judges managed their defence in such a manner as gave Mr. John Hampden occasion to say "that the very same opinions were now delivered for law, which King Charles' and King James' judges were infamous for. It is but a few days ago ", continues he (*Short Considerations*, p. 18), "that some of the judges declared in the Lords' House that one witness to a principal treason and another to a circumstance was sufficient to convict a man that is indicted for treason ; which was the worst of all the opinions delivered upon the Bench by the late Chief Justice Jeffreys." ' Ralph, vol. ii, p. 389. As a matter of fact the judges had said nothing of the kind. They said exactly the reverse.—*History of England during the reigns of William III, Anne and George I*, James Ralph (1744).

to the effect that for a remand two witnesses were necessary. But there was no insistence upon their being witnesses upon oath. This resolution was agreed to by thirty-five votes to twenty-eight. It must be carefully noticed in the first place, that the Lords were simply stating the judges' own doctrine, and therefore were not 'implying'—as Macaulay would have it they did—'a censure on the Judges of the King's Bench, men certainly not inferior in probity, and very far superior in legal learning, to any peer of the realm [1]'; secondly, that the resolution was no assertion of a distinctive privilege on their own behalf. Not a word was said about peers in particular.[2] It was the right of every freeman, in accordance with the Habeas Corpus Act, that the Lords asserted. In their resolution they asked nothing for themselves which they did not ask for all; but in the particular case of the three earls they were not satisfied. The subject was still discussed at length and with heat; and it was moved that an address should be made to His Majesty for taking the bail off the said lords. This was rendered unnecessary by William's voluntarily consenting to cancel the recognizances, and thus setting the souls of his nobility at rest.

The three cases just referred to stand out as being of particular importance; but privilege cases of varying consequence were constantly coming before the House. None were more frequent than those relating to litigation in connexion with estates. It often happened that a peer would at one time agree to waive his privilege and then suddenly resume it. For example, in the case of Cecil v. the Earl of Salisbury, which was proceeding in 1690, the younger brothers of the Earl brought a bill against him in Chancery, wishing to gain their portion under the will of their father.[3] Salisbury consented to waive his privilege when he found it to his advantage to do so, but subsequently insisted upon it when the case seemed likely to go against him. In these circum-

---

[1] Macaulay, vol. iv, p. 300.
[2] Luttrell is responsible for a misunderstanding on this point (vol. ii, p. 617).
[3] *Lords' MSS. 1690–1*, No. 336, pp. 185–6.

stances the Cecils brought up a petition before the House of Lords, with the result that Salisbury was ordered not to insist upon his privilege. In 1685 it had been decided that privilege should not be allowed as a bar to legal proceedings in the case of peers who were acting solely as trustees. Nevertheless, the settlement of estates continued to create difficulties if peers were involved. In March 1696/7 the Earl of Derby was concerned in several such cases.[1] Charlotte Catherine Savage, only child of the late Viscount Colchester, became entitled to £10,000 by the will of the late Earl Rivers, but she could not obtain her legacy owing to the obstruction of the Earl of Derby. In pursuance of the petition to the House on the subject, Derby was ordered to attend, and then signified his willingness not to insist upon his privilege, either as trustee, or legatee, or executor in trust. Again, the Earl's mother petitions that her son should be made to waive his privilege, because the payment of a dowry is in arrear, and she is largely dependent upon it, and yet can get no satisfaction from the Earl, who is responsible.[2] In the third place the two executors for the late Lord Widdrington pray that the Earl may so far waive his privilege that they may be able to prove the wills both of Widdrington and also of Lord Stanley.[3] An affair of very similar character came before the notice of the House in April 1699.[4] Upon the death of the first Duke of Bolton, the Earl of Bridgwater and the other executors tried to prove the will in the Prerogative Court, but were prevented from doing so by the new duke, who had entered a caveat. His Grace's agent and proctor being summoned to show cause, pleaded privilege, and the claim was admitted by the court, to the great detriment of the executors, who had to pay debts and legacies, to discharge servants, &c., none of which could be done until the will had been proved. The House, upon hearing Bridgwater's petition, very properly drew up a new Standing Order, '.That no peer of this House

---

[1] *Lords' MSS. 1695-7*, No. 1141, p. 532.
[2] Ibid., p. 537, No. 1148, p. 537.
[3] Ibid., p. 536, No. 1144, p. 536.
[4] Ibid., *1697-9*, No. 1446, p. 420.

hath privilege, whereby any stop or hindrance may or can be given to the proving the will of any person whatsoever.'[1]

The judicious inconsistency of peers in connexion with their privileges is well illustrated by a dispute which arose out of the sale of Lord Berkeley of Stratton's house in Piccadilly.[2] One morning Berkeley agreed to sell the house to the Duke of Devonshire. The same afternoon he arranged that the Marquis of Normanby should have it. The latter, hearing of the earlier transaction, brought in a bill in Chancery against both Berkeley and Devonshire. Berkeley at once waived his privilege, as after some little delay did Devonshire. A short time later, however, he changed his mind and resumed his privilege. Normanby appealed to the House. The three lords were heard, and an attempt was made to bring them to an agreement by seven of the foremost peers in the land— the Lord President, Nottingham, Rochester, Marlborough, Monmouth, Cornwallis, and Godolphin. But the Duke gave considerable trouble. It was proposed that he should be permitted to retain his privilege until the termination of the present parliament, but that after then none of the persons concerned should be permitted to insist. Devonshire found it hard to make up his mind whether he would waive his privilege immediately or not, but eventually decided to do so.

The celebrated and excessively complicated suit of the Earl of Montague v. the Earl of Bath came before the notice of the Lords on several occasions, as for example during the months of January and February, 1693/4.[3] An appeal was brought by the Earl of Montague and Elizabeth, Duchess of Albemarle, his wife, against the Earl of Bath. The question at issue was between two wills of the late Duke of Albemarle, the one in favour of the Earl of Bath, the other in favour of the Duchess. Both parties at different stages in the proceedings claimed privilege of Parliament, and so interfered

---

[1] *L.J.*, vol. xvi, p. 437, April 29, 1699.
[2] *Lords' MSS. 1695–7*, No. 1067, pp. 259–60.
[3] *Lords' MSS. 1693–5*, No. 776, p. 331. See also Chandler's *History and Proceedings of the House of Lords from 1660 to 1743* (8 vols. 1742–3), vol. i, p. 424.

with the progress of the case. A third claim in connexion with the Duke's estate was brought forward by one Pride, who complained that he was prevented from maintaining his cause by the use of their privilege made by the two earls. The latter were bidden to waive their privilege 'as to all persons who pretend to any title to the estates'. An afterburden of this notorious case is heard of in 1699/1700,[1] when we find the unfortunate Earl of Bath complaining that he had for several years been living in quiet possession of Finchley Park in the county of Southampton, part of the late Duke of Albemarle's estate settled upon himself, when suddenly in October last he had a declaration of ejectment served upon him by one Middleton, agent of William Sherwin. The Earl insisted upon his privilege against a cause carried on for scandal and vexation only (so he declared) in the face of two verdicts at King's Bench, and he prayed the House to take into consideration the breach of privilege: which it did.

One other case of a similar nature may finally be mentioned.[2] It was the result of the quarrel between the Earl of Peterborough and the Duchess of Norfolk, which had been engendered by the circumstances attending the Fenwick trial. The former laid claim to the Duchess's Northamptonshire estates, of which, despite his efforts, the Duchess and her trustees succeeded in retaining possession. The Earl had, however, succeeded in obtaining an injunction for stopping waste. Notwithstanding that her Grace had pleaded her title as heiress and purchaser, this injunction had been continued from time to time at Peterborough's suggestion, and upon his agreeing to proceed to some decision in law and equity next Easter term. In November 1699 the Duchess's servants were employed by the yeomen of the toils in removing some deer from one park to another. In doing so they had occasion to cut down some underwood, not more than £1 in value, according to her Grace, in a part of Drayton Park, of which Peterborough never had possession. The Earl had moved the Court of Chancery to take the Duchess's servants into custody for

---

[1] *Lords' MSS. 1699–1702*, No. 1485, p. 68.
[2] Ibid., No. 1464, pp. 6-7.

breach of the injunction. He had failed in this, and so now appealed to the House of Lords, making the case one of breach of privilege. The appeal being made, the House ordered Hoyte, the Duchess's servant responsible for clearing away the wood, to be attached. The Duchess therefore petitioned in his behalf, and Peterborough failing to prove his case, Hoyte was dismissed. This case brought about the addition of two new items to the Standing Orders of the House.[1] They were as follows :—

(1) 'That in case of complaint by any lord of this House, of a breach of privilege, whereupon any person shall be taken into custody for the future; if the House, upon examination of the matter complained of, shall judge the same to be no breach of privilege, the lord who made the complaint shall pay the fees and expenses of the person so taken into custody.'

(2) 'That no person shall be taken into custody upon complaint of a breach of privilege, but upon oath made at the bar of the House.'

Cases such as those already outlined might be multiplied almost indefinitely. They are frequently quite devoid of intrinsic interest; but taken together they are deserving of considerable notice. For one thing, their great number shows how a good deal of the House's time was occupied. It shows, too, how constant a resource the privileges of the House were whenever a member of it became involved in any difficulties. It was remarkably easy—so to speak—to assume the magic mantle of peerage and become invisible to the ordinary eye. Certainly it was not always that the claim could be made good or that the House would befriend its member. But there was always the chance that it might, and, at the worst, time was gained. The Chamber could be used as a sort of refuge or asylum, as when Lord Saye and Sele appealed to it with piteous cry to prevent his stepmother from ousting him from his estates during his absence abroad.[2]

[1] *L.J.*, vol. xvi, pp. 488–90.
[2] *Lords' MSS. 1697–9*, No. 1363, pp. 391–2.

It has to be admitted that for no purpose was parliamentary privilege more valued than for escaping from the payment of lawful debts. Sorbière sketches the English peer, who has a great rent roll and four houses.[1] He is courteous and civil, obliging and even liberal, something of a philosopher and man of letters. He spends a good deal upon the collection of curios or objects of interest. In fact he is an admirable person altogether; only he forgets his debts and his creditors. A number of measures were during the reign introduced in the House of Commons for the assistance of creditors. Two of these, viz., the Creditors' Relief (Privileged Places) Bill and the Creditors' Relief (Composition) Bill passed into law in 1696/7. But it is noticeable how little anxiety the Lords appear to have shown for them. Time after time, when similar measures, some of general, some of local import, were brought up from the Lower Chamber, they were laid aside, and there were no further proceedings.[2] It looks as though the sympathies of the Peers were all on the side of the debtor. They certainly made at times most discreditable use of their immunity in order to escape from the payment of their debts. Occasionally an arrest might be made, as was the case, for instance, with the Countess of Newport, who was seized on account of her son's debts, he having succumbed to wounds received in His Majesty's service.[3] The Countess had legitimate grounds for grievance. The arrest was certainly in defiance of her privilege ; and she appears to have been barbarously used into the bargain. On the other hand, there are instances in which no excuse is possible. For example, in December 1696 we find several persons petitioning the House because the Earl of Nottingham, a bad offender, has been indebted to them severally for the last six years, but has continually refused or delayed payment, and the sessions of

[1] Sorbière, p. 161.
[2] Some of these measures were of local importance only. See, for example, *Lords' MSS. 1689–90*, No. 195, pp. 388–92. Norwich Court of Conscience Bill. One principal aim was to put an end to the abuses of Whitefriars. See *Lords' MSS. 1689–90*, No. 244, pp. 17–25. The Creditors' Relief (Privileged Places) Bill at last accomplished this.
[3] *Lords' MSS. 1699–1702*, No. 1527, pp. 121–2.

parliament have been so frequent that there has been no interval sufficiently long in which to take action against him.[1] The petitioners pray for leave to prosecute actions of law against the Earl, or else to sue out originals and summons him thereon and procure a return thereof. The answer to their petition is the Standing Order of December 14, 1696, to the effect that the filing of an original against any lord of this House shall not be taken to be a breach of privilege of parliament. Again, in March 1699/1700 we find a builder named Jackson praying the House that the Duke of Devonshire may not be permitted to resume his privilege in order to stop a suit which had been brought against him for payment of work due in the building of Chatsworth.[2] In a previous suit the Duke had agreed that in the event of further differences he could waive his privilege. Now, however, he chose to disregard his promise. The case was referred to two committees of privileges, but we hear nothing more of the matter.

It was, one would have thought, sufficient that peers themselves should enjoy such choice exemptions as freed them so largely from the clutches of the ordinary tribunal. But the privilege went further than this. The servant was allowed to share in his master's virtue. In other words, the peer communicated his immunity to his dependants. No privilege of the Upper House is more interesting, none was more frequently discussed, none more liable to misuse than this. It has in fairness to be stated that the House was fully alive to the objectionable character of the abuse, and made efforts to regulate the enjoyment of the privilege. In March 1690 it ordered lists of protections to be produced by the sheriffs of London and Middlesex, the bailiff of Southwark, the marshal of the Marshalsea, and the steward of Westminster.[3] These lists were considered, and as a result an order was made 'that all protections are to be vacated and

---

[1] *Lords' MSS. 1695-7*, No. 1092, p. 375.

[2] Ibid. *1699-1702*, No. 1531, p. 125. Macky notices of the Duke of Devonshire that he is 'of nice honour in every thing, but the paying his tradesmen '.—Macky, p. 40.

[3] *Lords' MSS. 1690-1*, No. 241, pp. 11-15.

none allowed but what are entered in the office of the Clerk of the Parliaments'.[1] The full lists of protections, which was compiled as a result of the investigations made upon this occasion, is of peculiar interest. The total number of those proved by the sheriff of Middlesex is 126, distributed among thirty-four peers and one peeress. The majority of these had granted but one or two apiece, but the Duke of Northumberland was responsible for nine, and Lord Morley and Mounteagle for as many as fifty-four. Of the latter, all but nine had to be withdrawn.

As an example of the scandals which were apt to arise from the granting of protections we may take a case in which the Earl of Lincoln was concerned.[2] Some one, named Dixon, presented a petition to the House, complaining that he had without any legal warrant or process been seized by the Earl and imprisoned for certain misdemeanours of a trivial character, and kept in confinement by a certain James Taylor. The chief contriver of his misfortunes was a woman, named Anne Lamb. Yet Dixon was unable to proceed against either her or Taylor because they were 'protected' by the Earl. The affair was so outrageous that a serious, though unsuccessful, effort was made at the time to deal with the abuse which rendered such episodes possible. On December 12, 1690 the whole House was put into committee to consider the general question. It was proposed that all lords who gave irregular protections should either be reprimanded or sent to the Tower. The proposal came to nothing. Indeed, it was not until the 27th that anything further of moment was done in the matter. On that date the House was moved 'that all Protections be vacated, that the Lords declare they will never give any more but to their menial servants'.[3] But this motion met with no better success than the other, and even the record of it was cancelled. And although Dixon's case was heard, still on the question whether written protections should be granted in future, it was resolved in the affirmative by forty-three to

[1] L.J., vol. xiv, p. 441, March 18, 1690.
[2] Lords' MSS. 1690-1, No. 372, pp. 231-4.
[3] L.J., vol. xiv, p. 607, December 27.

twenty-five. In these circumstances it was useless to expect that the misuse of a valued privilege should be discontinued. George Wilson complained to the House that in the counties of Lancaster, York, and Westmoreland there were sixty persons who produced protections from Lord Morley, though none of them had been entered by the Clerk of the House.[1] In fact, the petitioner went on to state, ' in the town of Hornby, where his lordship lives, no sheriff's officer dare attempt to arrest any inhabitant without his lordship's license first had, several bailiffs who have attempted to do so, having been whipped and put in the stocks by his lordship's order.' Another witness said that Hornby had the name of the Whitefriars, as the result of Lord Morley's wholesale distribution of protections. This makes rather a striking picture of aristocratic influence in distant counties ! As a result of the case Lord Morley was bidden to ask pardon of the House, and was committed to the Tower, where, however, he stayed only a week or two. It was only to be expected that as their protectors made use of their privilege to escape the payment of their debts, those protected would follow their example. James Howard, a relative of the Duke of Norfolk, though a man of substance, for years made use of illegal means to defraud his creditors, and when at last a warrant for arrest had been obtained produced a protection from his noble relative and was discharged.[2] There was indeed a potential Whitefriars on every nobleman's domain.

A secondary abuse which arose out of the system was the counterfeiting of protections. A case early in the reign drew attention to a gross scandal.[3] A counterfeit protection came to the notice of the Lords, which purported to emanate from Lord Kingston, and was said to have been given by him to a surgeon called Kirby. The evidence showed that as a matter of fact the latter had, in order to escape his creditors, bought the forgery from two men, one of whom confessed to having disposed of a similar counterfeit for £2.

A petition presented to the House in 1699 may be cited,

---

[1] *Lords' MSS. 1692-3*, No. 514, pp. 7–8.
[2] *Lords' MSS. 1695-7*, No. 1098, p. 380.
[3] Ibid. *1690-1*, No. 251, pp. 27–9.

because the circumstances are of a different kind from any of those which have yet been mentioned.[1] It reveals a really intolerable state of things. Susannah, wife of John Harrington, has taken out a process against her husband in the Consistory Court of the Bishop of London, to answer a cause of separation or divorce by reason of cruelty and adultery, and for alimony, but John refuses to appear, exhibiting a protection from the Earl of Warrington, upon which the Court has declined to proceed. Petitioner prays that the protection may be set aside, as she is thus forced to live with an adulterous husband or to live away from him unalimented and perish through want, although she had brought him nearly £2,500. The House read the petition and rejected it, 'it appearing that the said John Harrington was a servant to the Earl of Warrington and had been so for some years'.[2]

It is true that the Lords were fully alive to the abuses to which their privileges were apt to lead. But even if they did not *personally* benefit by it, a privilege was a privilege, and as such it was hard to give up. Nevertheless, the House was frequently engaged in discussing means by which abuses might be prevented and in putting a stop to all irregularities. Efforts were made to restrict the use of protections to menial servants only of peers. An order was entered in the *Journals* in November 1691, by which it was decreed that no attorney or solicitor should be entitled to privilege.[3] Notwithstanding this, there seems to have still lingered some doubt on the subject, for in December 1692 the Earl of Oxford desires the opinion of the House whether he may protect his solicitor, who is a person that he can trust in his business;[4] and in 1696 the question was broached once more, when the Earl of Derby complained that his steward had been committed to the Fleet prison.[5] The point at issue was whether his lordship's agent was to be regarded as an attorney. This was the view ultimately taken by the House, though even

---

[1] *Lords' MSS. 1697-9*, No. 1152, pp. 541-2.
[2] *L.J.*, vol. xvi, p. 138.
[3] See *Lords' MSS. 1690-1*, No. 423, p. 283.
[4] Ibid., *1692-3*, No. 618, pp. 248-9.
[5] Ibid. *1695-7*, No. 1065, pp. 251-3.

then it was probably by no means easy to satisfy Lord Derby's counsel, who could not see why an attorney, in serving a nobleman, was unfit to have privilège.

More important than any such restriction as the exclusion of lawyers from the benefit of protection, was a general rule laid down in April 1694 as the result of a case involving the Duke of Southampton's privilege.[1] Richard Shelmer petitioned on his own behalf and on behalf of his attorney and of the bailiff of the sheriff of Middlesex. The petitioner had been owed a debt amounting to £200 by George Elwes, who had absconded. Having heard that Elwes claimed a protection, he had searched the Parliament Book, and not finding any such protection there, he had had Elwes arrested. Thereupon the latter produced an obsolete protection signed by the Duke. When the case was brought before them, the Lords resolved that the arrest was a breach of privilege, but they followed this up by framing an important order to the effect that any protection was void unless it had been entered ten days before the end of the session.[2] Another important order made to regulate protections required 'that no lord shall enter any written protections in the book of protections, until after he shall have personally attended this House in the same session of parliament'. The Duke of Norfolk thought it incumbent upon him to append his solitary signature to a protest against the order. He considered that 'to take away any part of the undoubted privileges of the peerage by a vote in a pretty thin House, particularly when it had actually been moved by a member on behalf of absentees that a day might be appointed for the discussion of a matter so nearly concerning them, seemed in the manner of it to make too light of what their House ought to esteem so sacred as the privileges of the Peerage of England.'[3]

[1] *Lords' MSS. 1693-5*, No. 856, pp. 891-2.
[2] *L. J.*, vol. xv, p. 422.
[3] J. E. Thorold Rogers, *Complete Collection of the Protests of the Lords* (Oxford, 1875), vol. i, p. 115. It will also be found printed in vol. iii, p. 483, of *A Collection of the Parliamentary Debates in England from the year 1668 to the Present Time* (Dublin; reprinted London, John Torbeck, 14 vols., 1741).

These being the Duke's sentiments, it would have been interesting to know what he thought of the attempt which the House made in the late months of 1696 to deal with the difficulties with which creditors met in consequence of peers' privileges enjoyed either by themselves or by their servants. At this date the case of Nottingham and one or two others, in which protections had been utilized by commoners in order to evade their debts, had brought the problem prominently forward. One in particular had come under the notice of the Commons, who on November 30 decided *nem. con.* that no member of their own body should have any privilege save for his own person only.[1] They communicated this decision to the Lords, at the same time asking for a conference, which was granted. As a result the Upper House on December 20 appointed a select committee to consider heads for a bill upon the subject.[2] Next day the Lord Chief Justice of the King's Bench and Mr. Justice Powell were directed to draw up a bill upon the following heads: (1) That all privileges, except personal privileges, shall be taken away during the sitting of Parliament. (2) That there be the same process at Common Law against a commoner, sitting in Parliament, as against a peer out of Parliament. (3) That if the trial must necessarily be in the country, then privilege shall prohibit the same as it does now; but if at the bar, then no privilege to be allowed, because it is near the place where the Parliament sits. This bill was truly of an epoch-making character. But it never became law. The first clause was rejected by 40 voices to 22. Subsequently it was ordered that the bill should not be engrossed, and thus unsuccessfully ended the first attempt to deal with the problem of how to recover debts from privileged persons.

In May 1701 a new bill for the greater ease of the subjects in recovering their just debts was introduced in the Upper House; but it was laid aside in favour of a bill of the same purpose, originating in the Commons.[3] The stipulations of

---

[1] *C.J.*, vol. vi, p. 642.
[2] *Lords' MSS. 1695-7*, No. 1089, pp. 371-2.
[3] Ibid. *1699-1702*, No. 1643, pp. 363-4.

the Commons' proposal did not differ materially from those included in the Lords' recent measure, but they were somewhat fuller.   It is to be observed that neither of these two later bills were as stringent as that of 1696, for in the measures of 1701 it was still forbidden to commence an action against any member of either House or any privileged person during session of Parliament or during adjournment lasting less than a fortnight.[1] The last provision was an addition made by the Lords, whose amendments were accepted by the Commons ; the bill thus passing both Houses and becoming law on June 12.   That the new act was a boon, notwithstanding 'the restrictions contained in it, cannot be doubted. The advantages which accrued from it were further reinforced in 1711 when the House of Lords entered a Standing Order in their *Journals*, abolishing protections altogether.

A privilege which the Peers share with the Lower House is that of control over the composition of their own Chamber ; although in this connexion it has to be remembered that it is a prerogative of the Crown to decide claims to peerages, which are, however, as an almost invariable rule referred to the House for decision.   Two claims to peerages during the reign of William III received a great deal of attention in the writings of contemporaries, viz. those of Charles Knowles to the earldom of Banbury and of Sir Richard Verney to the barony of Broke.   Knowles was arrested for killing his brother-in-law in a duel, and was thrown into Newgate.[2] Two bills of murder were preferred against him, the one as against a commoner, the other as against an earl ; and the trial was postponed until the question as to whether the prisoner was peer or commoner had been decided.   Knowles petitioned the House of Lords that he might be tried by them as a peer. Into the question of the validity of the claim to the earldom of Banbury it is not necessary to go.   It may, however, be remarked that the King expressed surprise—so the Attorney-

---

[1] See *Statutes at Large*, vol. iv, p. 59, Anno 12 W. III, cap. iii.   'An Act for preventing any Inconvenience that may happen by Privilege of Parliament.'

[2] *Lords' MSS. 1692-3*, No. 631, pp. 267-71.   See foot-note on p. 267.

General informed the House—that any one should come to ask to be tried as a peer before he had asked the King for a writ of summons. The House decided against the claim.[1] The case of Sir Richard Verney was a good deal more complicated.[2] The pedigree was not disputed. The question turned upon the descent of the barony, created by writ in 1492, to co-heiresses thirty years later. What became of the honour in this case? On the one hand, it was contended that an honour could not be lost save by attainder; on the other, the Attorney-General argued that the barony by writ could not go by inheritance. It reverts to the Crown. If the King chooses to renew it in the family he may do so; but descendants have no *right* in the matter. The case was decided against Sir Richard Verney. But this query was put by certain lords interested in the case: What happens when a person summoned to Parliament by writ, and sitting there, dies leaving two or more daughters, who also die, the issue of one of them surviving? In January 1695/6 Verney propounded a new claim, basing it upon his right as descendant of the sole issue of one of the co-heiresses. The title which he now claimed was that of Lord Willoughby de Broke. The King's counsel argued that the former decision of the House was a bar against the new demand. The claimant was either Lord Broke or Sir Richard Verney. The original claimant had been referred to in the *Journals* as ' Dominus Broke '. But the petitioner in his second venture had two points in his favour; first, the disarming of the opposition of the existing Lord Broke by the change of title, and secondly, an array of precedents laid before the House by his counsel, Sir Thomas Powys: and this time he succeeded in making good his claim.[3]

A problem of some perplexity taxed the minds of lords at the time when the first Verney claim was being discussed. The question, as put to the committee of privileges, was whether

---

[1] *L. J.*, vol. xv, p. 187, January 17, 1692–3.
[2] *Lords' MSS. 1693–5*, No. 859, pp. 403–10.
[3] *L. J.*, vol. xv, p. 668. Lord Willoughby de Broke took his seat, February 27, 1695/6. Ibid. p. 684.

the son of a peer's son, called by writ into his father's barony, becomes a peer on his father's death.[1] It is so ambiguously expressed that the general is best explained in terms of the particular. The son of the Earl of Burlington had been summoned to the House of Lords as Lord Clifford of Lanesborough. He died in his father's lifetime. Did his son, grandson of Burlington, become a peer on his father's death? The committee was unable to discover any precedent in the *Journals*; but the House after debate agreed that Charles Lord Clifford, son and heir of the late Lord Clifford of Lanesborough, had a right to a writ of summons to parliament. Accordingly he took his seat next day.[2] A few months after this the minds of noble lords recurred to the subtle question which had been propounded to them, and some person or persons thought it well that Lord Clifford's claim should be formally explained. The House adjourned the consideration of the matter, arranged that the judges should attend and that the Attorney-General should be heard. Apparently, however, they fought shy of their self-appointed task, for there appear to have been no further proceedings on the subject.

A distinctive privilege of the Lords, one not shared by the Commons, was the right of voting by proxy. Like most other privileges it was liable to abuse and apt to create difficulties. For instance, a proxy might be used contrary to the wishes of the principal. The Earl of Chesterfield in 1689 gave his proxy into the hands of the Earl of Mulgrave, only to find that, a hundred miles distant as he was from Westminster, he was made to differ from those friends to whose judgment, had he been on the spot, he would probably have submitted his own.[3] He had been much deceived—so he said—in the character of Mulgrave. There were certain restrictions on the use of proxies, some of which were recognized, others of which were questioned. A curious situation

---

[1] *Lords' MSS. 1693–5*, No. 843, p. 393.

[2] *L.J.*, vol. xv, p. 488, November 21, 1694. See on the Verney case and the question of peerages falling into abeyance, Pike, p. 135. The doctrine of abeyance was first recognized in the case of Lord Windsor in the reign of Charles II. Pike, p. 133.

[3] *Letters of Chesterfield*, p. 352.

arose in connexion with the use of proxies in the proceedings in the Norfolk Divorce case in February 1691/2.[1]   In its earlier stages one or two divisions were determined by proxies.   For example, on February 12, the motion for adjournment was lost, although those present in favour numbered thirty-two and those against were only thirty.   The contents could, however, muster ten proxies only; the non-contents had fourteen.   Despite the fact that proxies had been used and had actually, as in this case, turned the scale in divisions, it was on February 16 moved to consider whether they should be allowed at all in connexion with this bill. After debate the question was formally put, to be met by the counter-motion of the previous question, whether this question should now be put.   It was decided in the affirmative by three votes only, the contents including nine proxies, the non-contents seventeen.   The main question was then put and carried by thirteen votes against the use of proxies.[2]   Obviously this situation involved an anomaly.   For, as the lords who protested very aptly objected, it was absurd for those to use proxies who were voting against the use of proxies.   Two other reasons were propounded in the protest.   First, voting by proxy was an inherent right of peerage, and therefore could not be taken away by a chance vote in the House; secondly, those who were interested in the matter had not been heard. It was unfair that those who wished to retain a right, which they considered inherent in their rank, should be deprived of it by those who did not value it.   After the decision of the House on this occasion, it is curious to find that when the second Norfolk Divorce Bill was thrown out, seven proxies were used in the division, four on one side, three on the other.[3]

It was a question whether proxies, which might be used in the preliminary business, could be made use of in the final decision on bills of a judicial nature, or indeed, whether in such cases they ought to be used at all.   Standing Order CIX

[1] *Lords' MSS. 1692–3*, No. 524, pp. 23–4.   See also Chandler's *Lords' Debates*, vol. i, p. 409.

[2] The main question itself was voted on without the use of proxies. *L.J.*, vol. xv, p. 78.   February 16.

[3] *Lords' MSS. 1692–3*, No. 642, p. 279.

forbade their use altogether during judicial proceedings. The matter came up in connexion with the trial of Duncombe, when the bill for his punishment was rejected by a single voice.[1] There being a number of peers absent, it was proposed that their opinions should be taken by proxy. It was, however, resolved that not only in this case, but in the future generally, no proxies should be taken at all in judicial proceedings. Another regulation regarding the use of the privilege was made in March 1696/7, when an order was made 'that no proxy entered in the Books after Prayers shall be made use of the same day',[2] and this was added to the Standing Orders of the House in January, 1702/3.

The right of entering formal protests against decisions of the House was constantly exercised throughout the reign. There were few interesting debates in connexion with which no protests are to be found. As to the value of being able to set on record one's disapproval of one's comrades' opinions there may be some doubt. Once or twice, after a protest had been entered in the *Journals*, it was subsequently deleted by order of the House. This only occurred when the 'reasons' given by the dissentients were particularly obnoxious to the majority. Still, it is true that the right of protest—the right of a minority —was always dependent upon the good will of the majority. There was no fundamental law sustaining the privilege of 'entering dissents'; so that if a majority in the House chose to order that the records of a protest should be expunged, it could always do so. This fact deducts somewhat from the value, however great it may be held to be, of the privilege of protesting.

The list of Peers' privileges may be concluded with the brief mention of three others. First, when search was made for conventicles or prohibited books, the house of a peer could not be entered by the officers of justice save with a warrant signed by the King's own hand and the hands of six of his

---

[1] See Dispatches of L'Hermitage in State Correspondence between England and the Netherlands, MS. transcripts in the British Museum. Add. MSS. 16,677, vol. N.N., p. 191, March 15-25, 1697-8.

[2] *L.J.*, vol. xvi, p. 130, March 20, 1696-7.

privy councillors, of whom four must be peers. Secondly, the peers enjoy the right of personal access to the Sovereign. Thirdly—to quote Chamberlayne—'The Laws of England are so tender of the honour, credit, reputation and persons of noblemen, that there is a statute on purpose to hinder all offences by false reports, whereby any scandals to their persons may arise, of debate and discord between them and the commons; and because it is to defend not only lay lords, but bishops and all great officers of this realm, it is called *scandalum magnatum*.[1] Libel was particularly heinous when it attacked the sacred dignity of the peerage. The lords themselves took care in Parliament to make clear the superiority of the lord over the mere commoner, of the Upper over the Lower House. The rules which they themselves framed upon the subject of conferences between the two Chambers run as follows:—'The place of our meeting with the Lower House upon conference is usually the Painted Chamber, where they are commonly, before we come, and expect our leisure. We are to come hither in a whole body, and not some lords scattering before the rest, which both takes from the gravity of the Lords, and besides may hinder the Lords from taking their proper places. We are to sit there, and be covered ; but they are at no committee or conference either to be covered, or sit down in our presence, unless it be some infirm person, and that by contrivance in a corner out of sight, but not covered.'[2]

Always rights should imply duties. We have seen that the English peerage owe their rights to their being members of a political, not a social body, to their position in days gone by as counsellors of the Crown, servants of the realm, bearers of the nation's burdens. Secondly, the House in its corporate capacity has always assumed control over its members. One of the essential ideas of the trial of peers by their peers is that they are peculiarly responsible for their actions to their fellows.

---

[1] Chamberlayne's *Angliae Notitia* (for 1692), p. 22.
[2] See T. Erskine May's *Parliamentary Practice* (10th ed. 1893), p. 419. Also Edward Porritt's *The Unreformed House of Commons* (Cambridge, 1903), vol. ii, p. 588.

When the House had official notification of a quarrel between Lord Granville and Lord Kiveton, it ordered the arrest of both parties.[1] It might have been well had the superintendence of the House over some of its younger and more turbulent members been stricter than it was. Particular mention should be made of one way in which the House endeavoured to exert disciplinary powers over members, viz., in endeavouring to enforce attendance. Even in the later years of the seventeenth century there were excuses for non-attendance. Locomotion was difficult at a time when roads were exceedingly bad and the effect of unfavourable weather upon them very severe. Lengthy sessions were greatly disliked by both Houses. London in the heat of summer was often very unpleasant, and the list of casualties was apt to be heavy when the session was prolonged in the summer months.[2] The call of the country with its freshness and purity was in such circumstances exceedingly alluring.

It must be confessed that the House was often very peremptory indeed in its messages desiring the attendance of absent members, and difficult to satisfy. No doubt there was sometimes good reason to suspect the genuineness of the excuses made. At times they were of the most piteous description. Chesterfield was an offender more than once. Summoned to appear in the House in November 1689, he thus writes to Halifax:

I confess I do think this very hard; for since a man who is not well does not sometimes know himself whether he is able to undertake such a journey, how can he honestly send two persons to swear that they believe he is not in a condition to come up? Besides this is but a late custom; and when I moved the House last session to have it renewed, it was upon a change of government, to oblige all the peers to come and take a new oath to a new master. But now that the kingdom

---

[1] *Lords' MSS. 1690–1*, No. 309, pp. 150–1.
[2] See *MSS. of Earl Cowper at Melbourne House* (Hist. MSS. Comm. Rep. xii, App. pt. i), vol. ii, p. 40. Charles Davenant to Thomas Coke, '. . . though it be now sixteen years ago I still bear in memory the evil smells descending from the small apartments adjoining the Speaker's chamber, which came into the House with irresistible force when the weather was hot.'

is so well settled, I cannot conceive why your Lordships should endanger us poor country lords and our servants, by tempting them to forswear themselves'.[1]

Chesterfield was once more in difficulties in November 1696, when the House took special means to ensure the presence of all its members so far as possible, to discuss the Fenwick case. It was ordered first, 'that such lords as do not attend the service of the House, by a day to be appointed, shall be sent for in custody;' and secondly, 'that no lord absent himself from the service of the House [by being out of town] without the leave of the House, upon pain of being sent for in custody, and that no such leave be asked for, but between the hours of 12 and 2 of the clock.'[2] Chesterfield was at this time very seriously indisposed, and the demand made him indignant. ' I must say ', he exclaims, ' they [the House] seem to usurp a power, by bidding a sick man to take up his bed and walk, which I never heard belonged to any body but Jesus Christ.'[3]

Upon this occasion there were a number of other peers in the same predicament with Chesterfield. The aged and infirm Earl of Berkshire was excused, as were one or two others, on the grounds of advanced years or dangerous illness. But the House was not easily propitiated. The Earl of Rutland, although he declared that a journey to Westminster would hazard his life, was not excused. The Duke of Bolton was in very ill health, plagued with dyspepsia, could ' not digest the least bit of meat'; he was afraid he could not arrive at the proper time, but would endeavour to reach the House on the 25th. The answer of the Lords was that unless he succeeded in carrying out his intentions and arrived not later than the 26th, he should be taken into custody. Particularly unfortunate was the Duke of Beaufort, who seems to have experienced considerable difficulty in persuading the House of the reality of his ailments. When summoned, he sent a letter of excuse, with which he enclosed a certificate from his physician. But this did not satisfy. He was sent for

---

[1] *Letters of Chesterfield*, p. 352.
[2] *Lords' MSS. 1695-7*, No. 1071, p. 263.
[3] *Letters of Chesterfield*, p. 374.

in custody.   This elicited a dolorous protest from the Duke,
who felt himself much aggrieved.   He was surprised that the
House should be so ready to take away the liberty of one
of its members.   It was punishment enough not to be able to
sit with his brothers ; but to be punished for this punishment
was hard indeed.   He owed it to himself and his family not
to endanger his life or at least court pain by abandoning
Bristol waters and setting forth on so long a journey.[1]   Such
instances as these serve to indicate the strictness which the
House could show upon occasion.   The Fenwick case does
not stand alone.   Similar severity had been shown in connexion with the first Mohun trial.   Early in the proceedings
it was moved that all the lords then present should attend on
the morrow, and that if any were absent he should be sent
to the Tower.   The motion was lost by a substantial margin,
but the next day the subject of attendance was revived, and
a stringent order was brought in.[2]   The four lords who had
left the House on Tuesday during the trial and had gone out
of the court before the summing up of the evidence and before
the adjournment were to be fined £100 each.[3]   Eventually the
fine was exacted from Ailesbury only.[4]   Still the action of the
House was undoubtedly severe.   In days before the advent
of the party whip, when the privilege of voting by proxy was in
itself a temptation to absenteeism, frequent calls of the House
and occasional measures of severity were justified.[5]

[1] Cf. *Lords' MSS. 1689–90*, Nos. 9 and 21, pp. 13–14 and 37–9.   The
excuses of Sancroft and the Bishop of St. David's for non-attendance
were not considered satisfactory.   A cancelled entry (p. 39) in MS.
Minutes for March 22 states, ' Ordered that this House shall be called
ten days hence, and that all peers that do not attend shall be fined £500.'
[2] *L.J.*, vol. xv, p. 211.
[3] Luttrell, vol. iii, p. 27.   January 31, 1692–3.
[4] Ibid., p. 30.   February 4.
[5] *Lords' MSS. 1692–3*, No. 603, p. 122.   A letter from Lord Ferrers.
' My Lord, I reseved yᵉ six and twentieth of this monnth your Lordˢᵖ. of
yᵉ one and twentieth, by which you acquant me that unles I attend yᵉ
house ye fifth of December I shall incur yᵉ farther displeasure of ye
House (if sicknes do not prevent me) which I thanke God I can not
aledg, but I can this in excuse of my past absence, that having a Proxe
allowed of and in such good hands as my vote wold not be beter given by
my presence, did not thinke my selve as altogether absent, which made
me on yᵉ account of sum exterordinary famaly bisnes defer my attendance
and yᵉ same still remaining I hope there Lordˢᵖˢ. will grant me sum longer

A very interesting proposal was made in October 1690, whose object was to enforce the attendance of lords, the House being in committee with that purpose.[1] Precedents for fining absent peers were read. It was then proposed 'That any lords that shall omit their attendance here one session of Parliament shall lose the privilege of parliament. A fine to be on all the lords alike.' A sum of £100 was proposed and agreed to, and it was resolved that no privilege should be allowed against the execution of such a sentence. The Earl of Bridgwater reported the results of the committee's consultations, but there were no further proceedings. Still, the incident would be significant even if it stood alone ; but, as we have seen, it does not. The proposal of 1690 can be paralleled by the order actually made in 1694 with regard to protections, to which reference has already been made. Let it be admitted that individual peers often abused their privileges and set too great store by them. On the other hand, the House as a corporate body was a court of appeal against its own members, if they offended ; it possessed and exercised disciplinary powers which kept the abuse of privileges in check.

time, which request I desier your Lord⁸ᵖˢ. will make for me in ye most prevaling terms you can.' To Sir R. Atkyns, Speaker of the House of Lords.

[1] *Lords' MSS. 1690-1*, No. 314, p. 153.

CHAPTER V

THE JUDICIAL PROCEEDINGS OF THE HOUSE

ONCE when two toleration bills lay before the House of Commons, one their own, the other from the Second Chamber, Mr. Hampden, junior, who opened the debate, reminded his hearers that as a rule in such circumstances they selected the bill from the Upper House. 'You always', he said, 'respect a bill from the Lords, the judges and bishops being there present.'[1] The frequent, indeed the almost constant, presence of members of the judicial bench in the House of Lords is a very interesting feature. Negligence in attendance on the part of the judges once led to a very severe reprimand from the Lord Keeper, and it was ordered that two of the judges at least should be present in the Lords every day during term time.[2] It may seem rather an exorbitant demand that the judges should attend the pleasure of the Peers as well as perform their ordinary functions in the courts. It has, on the other hand, to be remembered that the Upper House was no great distance from Westminster Hall. The judges were virtually on the spot. The Lords also expected to receive the advice of the Attorney-General.[3] The Peers could always obtain the very best possible advice on the legal aspect of all matters which came before their notice. They

---

[1] *Debates of the House of Commons*, Auchitell Grey (London, 1703), vol. ix, p. 252.

[2] *L. J.*, vol. xv, p. 364. February 9, 1693–4, 'I am commanded by the House, to tell you, you have the honour to be the assistants here ; and the House takes notice of your great negligence in your attendance. You have had sometimes warning given you, though not with so much solemnity as I am directed now to do it. If this fault be not amended for the future, the House will proceed with great severity against you.'

[3] When in connexion with the Banbury peerage case the Solicitor-General appeared in place of the Attorney, objection was raised to the substitution and measures were proposed for securing that in future the Attorney-General should always be an assistant to the House. See *Lords' MSS. 1692–3*, No. 631, p. 268.

availed themselves of the expert knowledge at their disposal in the drafting of bills, the most important being as a rule drawn up by the judges. Hence the significance of Mr. Hampden's argument that bills originating in the Upper House had a special authority as coming from the judicial chamber. So far as the mere legal framework went, there was a presumption that such measures would be superior to those of the Commons.

The House of Lords would have had a certain judicial appearance in any case simply because of the presence in it of judicial functionaries; but the judicial atmosphere was derivative chiefly from the Lords' possession of judicial powers. The original identity of the Parliamentum with the Magnum Concilium had meant that, when the Council became differentiated from the Parliament and separate law courts were established, such judicial powers as remained to Parliament were possessed by the Lords and not by the Commons. The ever-increasing activity and influence of the courts of justice, the use by Tudor sovereigns of new and extraordinary courts, the rise to political power of new official classes were all factors leading to the gradual loss of judicial authority by the Peers. But under the Stuarts, particularly in the reigns of Charles I and Charles II, the Lords made a number of spasmodic efforts to revive their jurisdiction.[1] In the latter reign one or two cases of exceptional importance gave rise to exceedingly bitter quarrels between the two Houses. These concerned both the original jurisdiction of the Lords, as in the celebrated case of Skinner *v.* the East India Company and in the Fitzharris case, and also the appellate jurisdiction of the House, as in the case of Shirley *v.* Fagg. It may be said that the authority of the Upper House as a court of first instance terminates with the case of Skinner. Indecisive as the results of this case were, it was clear that the Peers would always have very great difficulty in maintaining their claim. Moreover, the opportunities for doing so could in the nature of things be only very infrequent. Quite different was the result of the case of Shirley, in

---

[1] L. O. Pike, p. 231.

connexion with which the Commons had denied that there lay any appeal from the Court of Chancery to the House of Lords. The proceedings in the cases of Skinner and Shirley *v.* Fagg were somewhat similar. In each the Lords remained obdurate in the defence of what they considered their undoubted right. In each the Commons refused to withdraw their objections. But in the latter case it was the Peers that won. The petition of Dr. Shirley was not pursued to the bitter end. The particular case dropped, but others of a like nature followed, and the Lords exercised without protest their appellate jurisdiction in cases of equity. Still, the question was evidently regarded as one which was not quite satisfactorily settled. A good act of parliament which should define the position of the Court of Chancery quite clearly was in some quarters thought to be needed. Atkyns dedicates his treatise on the subject to the House of Peers, as being the last resort in cases of equity as in those of common law.[1, 2]

Appeals upon writs of error are of fairly frequent occurrence, as the most cursory examination of the *Journals* of the Second Chamber will show. They are usually of no great intrinsic interest or consequence ; and it is only the fact of their frequency that is to be noticed. The House was constantly occupied with purely judicial questions—especially appeals. These cases almost invariably called for the presence of the judges, who had to deliver their decisions upon points of law. Occasionally they took up a considerable time, as for example did one in which Isabella, Duchess of Grafton, was concerned in 1693. It lasted six days, at the end of which the

---

[1] See *An Inquiry into the Jurisdiction of the Chancery in Causes of Equity*, by Chief-Baron Atkyns (1695).

[2] Pike, p. 297 : 'It has often been questioned by lawyers of eminence whether the jurisdiction really belonged to the House of Lords, without any special commission of the sovereign, such as there was in the case of a writ of error to rectify judgment in a court of common law. The point is one which has reference to form rather than to substance. The Parliament, in the sense of the King, Lords, Judges, and high officers of State, was the original fountain of justice from which flowed remedies not to be obtained elsewhere. It might have been technically incorrect to address a petition in the nature of an appeal to the Lords alone, but hardly more incorrect than to address a petition in the first instance to the Chancellor alone.'

Duchess, being sensible of the trouble she had given their lordships, withdrew her petition.[1] The roll of the House was called over on more than one occasion, and it was ordered on the 20th of December that all those peers who had been present when the case was first brought before the House should attend on the morrow. The ordinary peer, layman as he was in legal matters, might at any time be summoned to act as judge of the judges.

Of greater interest than these numerous miscellaneous cases is the appeal made by the Society of Ulster in 1697. The circumstances were somewhat complex, involving a dispute between the society which had built Londonderry and Coleraine in earlier days and the Bishop of Derry.[2] The latter had made an appeal against certain orders of the Lord Chancellor of Ireland to the Irish House of Lords which had reversed the decision of the Court of Chancery. Thereupon the Ulster Society sent up a petition to the English House of Lords against this reversal, arguing that there was no appeal from the Irish Court of Chancery to the Irish House of Lords, but direct to the English House of Lords only. The cause was discussed at great length and the proceedings were protracted, lasting off and on from January 1697/8 until December 1699. A large number of precedents were cited, and eventually the House showed but little hesitation in resolving that an appeal from the Chancery in Ireland to the Irish House of Lords was *coram non iudice*. The proceedings of the Irish Chamber were consideied void. This decision was subsequently re-affirmed in connexion with the reversal by the Irish Peers of an order made by the Chancellor of the County Palatine of Tipperary.[3] Any furtive attempts on the part of the Irish Legislature to act with independence were doomed to failure, if they came in conflict with the adamantine determination of

[1] *Lords' MSS. 1693–5*, No. 775, pp. 31–45.
[2] Ibid. *1697–9*, No. 1194, pp. 16–24. On this case see *Revolutionary Ireland and its Settlement*, by Rev. Robert H. Murray (London, 1911), pp. 318–28. The case of the Ulster Appeal was the occasion of the appearance of Molyneux's work, *The Case of Ireland's being bound by Acts of Parliament in England stated*, to which Dr. Murray attaches considerable importance (p. 322).
[3] *Lords' MSS. 1697–9*, No. 1369, pp. 297–9.

the English Peers to maintain their supremacy in judicial matters.

One or two interesting points relating to impeachments arose in the reign of William III. The case of Sir Adam Blair is a curious appendage to that of Fitzharris in the reign of Charles II. Then the House of Lords had refused to listen to the impeachment of a commoner. The case was impending in a court of common law, and the Peers refused to interfere in it. The Commons, conceiving that their right of impeachment was in jeopardy, drew up a resolution, declaring 'that it is the undoubted right of the Commons in Parliament assembled to impeach before the Lords in Parliament any peer or commoner for treason or any other crime or misdemeanour, and that the refusal of the Lords to proceed in Parliament upon such impeachments is a denial of justice and a violation of the constitution of Parliaments'.[1] The case of Fitzharris was a complicated one. The man was already in prison. He was about to be charged in an ordinary court. The Lords, therefore, in refusing to proceed with his impeachment, were not necessarily asserting that in no case would they allow the impeachment of a commoner.[2] The situation was made clear when in 1689 the Commons impeached Sir Adam Blair and certain other commoners. The Lords examined precedents, and discussed the question whether the term 'great men' might include commoners. Eventually they decided by the narrow margin of 44 to 43 to proceed with the impeachment.[3]

Another important decision with regard to impeachments followed in October 1690. The Earl of Peterborough complained that he had been detained in the Tower for upwards of two years notwithstanding a dissolution and several prorogations of parliament. The Earl of Salisbury had suffered a similar fate. The question raised was whether impeachments remained *in statu quo* from parliament to parliament. A great number of precedents were exhumed, and it was finally decided that impeachments were discharged by either a

---

[1] *C. J.*, vol. ix, p. 711.
[2] *L. J.*, vol. xiv, pp. 260 and 362-4.
[3] *Lords' MSS. 1689-90*, No. 118, pp. 203-4.

dissolution or a prorogation. The two earls were accordingly discharged.

The most celebrated impeachments of the period, viz. those of the Whig Junto, as also the most celebrated attainder, that of Fenwick, belong to the realm of political rather than of constitutional history, and do not call for general treatment in this place. But the attitude of the House of Lords to the bill of attainder against Fenwick ought briefly to be noted here.[1] Process against a man by means of attainder instead of by impeachment meant that although in effect the results would be the same in either case, the Upper House was converted from a judicial into a legislative assembly. In the case of an impeachment the Lords are acting as judges, therefore as the superiors of the Commons; in the case of a bill of attainder they enjoy only their usually co-ordinate authority. The second method of procedure would be preferred whenever evidence was not sufficiently good for the exactness of the law or whenever instantaneous action was necessary in the interests of national security. But precisely because there was greater latitude allowed for the passing of a bill of attainder than would be permitted in judicial proceedings, it was essential in the interests of individual liberty that the special causes supposed to necessitate recourse to legislative methods should be closely scrutinized. Accordingly when the bill reached the Peers, who as revisers had to act a part exactly analogous to that which they would have performed in connexion with an impeachment, they had to determine whether the guilt, and incidentally the importance, of Fenwick merited so extreme a method of procedure as an attainder.[2] They had also to

---

[1] Pike, pp. 228–9: 'There had always been some confusion between the judicial and legislative powers of the Lords, and thus the proceeding by Bill of Attainder appears, for a very long time, to have superseded the proceeding by impeachment, where, at any rate, the offence was High Treason. This may have tended to obscure the right of the Commons to impeach a commoner of treason, and the jurisdiction of the Lords to try him. The subject was still further complicated by the usual practice of introducing a Bill of Attainder first in the House of Lords.'

[2] For the proceedings in the Lords in connexion with the Fenwick case see the following authorities: Burnet, pp. 182–90; Torbeck's *Parliamentary Debates*, vol. iii, p. 88 *et seq.*; *Lords' MSS. 1695–7*, Nos. 1071, 1081; L'Hermitage, Q.Q., p. 632, and R.R., pp. 140–77 (*passim*),

consider whether in the absence of one of the two witnesses, Goodman, there was sufficient evidence against the accused. Three Tory lords, viz. Nottingham, Rochester, and Godolphin, wished for a preliminary inquiry upon these heads : but they were overruled.[1] On the question of the use of Goodman's deposition there was considerable difference of opinion. Leeds, Ormonde, St. Albans, Normanby, Rochester, and Nottingham urged that the law required two witnesses; and if the law were disregarded in such an instance as the present, how was any subject of the realm to feel secure? Any arbitrary act would be possible.[2] If it were argued that the written deposition of Goodman was sufficient, it could be answered that written evidence was from the point of view of the accused no evidence at all, as he could not enjoy the privilege of cross-examining.[3] Their opinion on the more general question of the desirability of bills of attainder is summarized in the protest entered by the fifty protesting peers when the bill against Fenwick was eventually passed.[4] 'Bills of attainder', they assert, 'against persons in prison, and who are therefore liable to be tried by common law, are of dangerous consequence to the lives of the subjects, and as we conceive, may tend to the subversion of the laws of this kingdom.'

The two most ardent champions of the bill were Monmouth and the Bishop of Salisbury. The former, endeavouring to answer the contention that the Treason Act necessitated the production of two witnesses, made the brilliant explanation that that act had been passed for the liberty, and not for the license of the subject : which argument merely comes to mean that the privileges of the subject, as guaranteed by law, can be interfered with by the executive whenever it thinks fit. His

December 8/18, 1696, to January 12/22, 1696/7 ; Howell's *State Trials*, vol. xiii, pp. 538–758; Ailesbury's *Memoirs*, pp. 413–14; *Letters from 1696 to 1708 to the Duke of Shrewsbury by James Vernon* (ed. G. P. R. James, 1841), vol. i, pp. 81–140 (*passim*); Cobbett's *Parliamentary History*, pp. 998–1156; for proceedings in the Upper House, pp. 1149–1156.

[1] L'Hermitage, Q. Q., p. 632, December 8/18, 1696.
[2] Ibid., R R., p. 140, December 18/28.
[3] Burnet, vol. ii, p. 185 ; see Dartmouth's note on this passage.
[4] Thorold Rogers, vol. i, pp. 128–9.

own arguments are given by Burnet with considerable fullness. They were stuffed with a great deal of matter which was nothing to the purpose, in Dartmouth's opinion, and probably the modern reader will agree with Dartmouth. The chief argument was that necessities of state may override all securities of law, the latter being for convenience' sake termed 'forms'. A number of curious historical examples, culminating in the cases of Strafford and the Duke of Monmouth, were cited. So also was the procedure of ancient Rome. Burnet's harangue apparently had greater weight than might now be imagined, for it was largely owing to the Bishop's eloquence that, despite the strenuous opposition of Godolphin, the bill passed the third reading. Marlborough influenced Prince George to give his vote among the contents. Monmouth's partisanship was also valuable. Yet the third reading was carried by a majority of no more than seven in a crowded house, several lords—Devonshire, Pembroke, Ormonde, and Dorset—who had previously voted for the bill now voting against it, and explaining that their support hitherto had been given simply with a view to bringing pressure to bear upon Fenwick in order to make him speak, and that they were against the attainder in itself, as they dreaded its consequences and the use that might in future be made of such a precedent.[1] There was, then, quite a considerable force of opinion in the Upper House against the Fenwick Bill of Attainder, both upon the ground that such procedure might be dangerous to the liberty of the subject and because such an extra-judicial method of accomplishing a judicial act was in itself dangerous, and would make an ugly precedent. It will be generally admitted that while Fenwick merited his fate, the opposition in the Lords were justified in the exception they took to the means employed in order to get rid of him.

We again find objection being raised in the Upper House to the method of proceeding by bill in a judicial matter in the case of Duncombe.[2] Charles Duncombe was a prominent

---

[1] L'Hermitage, R. R., p. 157, December 26/January 4.
[2] For the Duncombe case see the following authorities: *Lords' MSS. 1697-9*, Nos. 1232, 1238, 1248, 1257, 1258; L'Hermitage for 1698,

banker who had, when cashier of the Excise, led an attack upon the government, and had in particular singled out Montague as the object of his diatribes, accusing him of peculation. This charge the great minister had little difficulty in refuting; and he was able to turn the tables by proving that his assailant had been responsible for serious irregularities in the issue of exchequer bills. The Commons, accordingly, introduced a bill of pains and penalties, the penalty being exceptionally heavy. The bill was passed in the Lower House and in due time reached the Lords on March 1, 1697/8. The situation created considerable excitement. Duncombe and those who had been accused with him, Knight and Barton, took heart of hope from the lambent jealousy between the two Houses subsisting at this time. The bill might be regarded as an attack by the Commons upon the peculiar judicial privileges of the other Chamber. At the first reading of the bill it became clear that Duncombe had powerful support in Bolton, Leeds, Nottingham, Peterborough, Rochester, and Halifax. They argued that the Commons possessed no judicial powers, were no court of justice, and had no power to impose an oath or to hear testimony. The bill of attainder against Fenwick afforded no precedent. Fenwick had conspired against the state. It could not so much as be proved that Duncombe had directly broken the law. The sound arguments which can always be adduced against unusual methods of judicial procedure were forcibly maintained in this case. If such a comparatively venial offence as the putting false endorsements to exchequer bills was to be punished by act of parliament, the liberties of the people were very seriously menaced ; men could no longer rely upon their being tried by ordinary law and in ordinary courts of law. The answer to these statements was that to bring in the question of the rights of the two Chambers was to confuse the issue. The only point to be decided was whether the accused in point of fact deserved

vol. S. S., pp. 183–202 (*passim*), March 8/18 to March 25/April 4 ; F. L. Bonet, B., pp. 61–89 (*passim*), March 8/18 to April 8/18, 1698 ; Howell's *State Trials*, vol. xiii, pp. 1062–1106 ; *Vernon Corr.*, vol. ii, pp. 19–26.

the punishment which the Commons sought to impose. It was asserted that he did. Use was made of the rather far-fetched argument that he had really been guilty of a grave offence against the state, because he had endangered its credit. When the question was put whether the bill be read a second time, it was resolved in the affirmative by 48 votes to 36.

At this juncture Duncombe, who had recovered from the immediate and somewhat paralysing effects of the indictments, denied that he had made a confession, as had been supposed. The Commons must prove their case. They were very indignant, as they showed when the Lords asked for a conference to discuss the reasons for which Duncombe had been condemned. Let the Lords look to the bill itself for the reasons, rejoined the Commons. However, the conference was agreed to. The Lords were resolved to treat the case judicially. Counsel were heard on both sides, and a telling speech for the defence was made by Sir Bartholomew Shower. Had Duncombe merited that a bill of pains and penalties should be brought against him? Surely not? The bill in effect punished a crime which had only just been recognized as such. Putting false endorsements to cheques is a very different thing from high treason. The payments which Duncombe had made, whether irregular or not, had been good and lawful payments and could not possibly be refused. It was not denied that the accused had merited censure; but to deal with such a case as his the ordinary courts of law were quite adequate. After the hearing of counsel a heated debate took place, and continued for three hours. It was moved to commit the bill, and the motion was lost by a single vote. The question was raised whether proxies might be called for; but it was decided 'that no proxies shall be made use of in any judicial cause in this House, although the proceeding be by way of bill'. The Commons' case having thus been rejected, Rochester moved that Duncombe, whom the Lower House had placed in the Tower, should be removed thence; and an order to that effect was granted. This further action on the part of the Peers incensed the Commons. What right, they demanded, had the Lords to set at liberty a man who was not their prisoner? Duncombe was a member of the

Lower House, and its participation should have been obtained before the accused could be released from the Tower. The Lords replied with a quibble. The Commons had sent up the case to them; in doing so they had sent up Duncombe too. He had been handed over altogether into the hands of the Lords, who, as they had been able to summon him from the Tower without the Commons' objecting, were also able to set him free if they found him to be guiltless.

It will be generally agreed by most candid critics that the Lords were not justified in their action in setting Duncombe free. And in the end the Commons gained the day on this point, for they restored Duncombe to the Tower, where he remained until the close of the session. But in their decision with regard to the bill of pains and penalties there can be no doubt that the Lords were right. The points at issue have been clearly put by Macaulay.[1] He contends that ' the bill for punishing Duncombe was open to all the objections which can be urged against the bill for punishing Fenwick, and to other objections of even greater weight. In both cases the judicial functions were usurped by a body unfit to exercise such functions. But the bill against Duncombe really was, what the bill against Fenwick was not, objectionable as a retrospective bill. It altered the substantive criminal law. It visited an offence with a penalty of which the offender, at the time when he offended, had no notice.' Macaulay goes on to maintain the apparent paradox that the Duncombe bill was the worse of the two inasmuch as it touched not life, as the bill against Fenwick did, but property. Duncombe was to have been mulcted of two-thirds of his great wealth. But whereas men are always chary about taking the life of a fellow creature, they have not always such qualms about taking a man's possessions, particularly when, as in this case, the victim would still be very well off when the fine had been paid. There was a positive inducement to severity in the fact that the application of the amount of the fine—£300,000—would in those days have meant a quite appreciable reduction in taxation. Thus such a bill of pains and penalties as the

_____
[1] Macaulay, vol. v, pp. 44-5.

Commons brought against Duncombe might come to have an irresistible attraction for the House which voted the revenue, and which would find confiscation a singularly simple expedient for raising it. The Duncombe case is indeed a remarkable instance of the utility of a revising chamber in defending the interests of property ; as also of a judicial chamber in preventing the use of irregular weapons of justice to the detriment of individual freedom.

It would be giving a false impression to let it be supposed that the House of Lords stood firm upon a bedrock of principle in their resistance to legislative methods of judicial procedure. The opposition to the Fenwick Attainder Bill was defeated ; the opposition to the bill against Duncombe won the day by one vote only. That they were quite ready to make use of a bill of attainder when it suited them to do so, the Lords showed in the attainders against the Pretender and Mary of Modena brought forward towards the end of William's reign. The bill against James was introduced in the Lower House and came before the Peers in January 1701/2. It was proposed as an amendment that a clause should be added attainting the Pretender's mother as well as himself. The Commons disagreed for the excellent reason that an attainder was far too serious a thing to be introduced simply as an amendment. It could not in that form receive sufficient attention. So the Lower House lectured the Upper upon its lack of due gravity. At first the Lords insisted on their position and busied themselves in the discovery of precedents and discussion of the heinousness of Mary of Modena's offences. Then they gave way and introduced a bill specially to accomplish their purpose, only to be seized later on in the proceedings with qualms as to whether a foreigner could be attainted at all. A number of peers protested against the third reading ' because there was no proof of the allegations in the bill so much as offered before the passing of it, which is a precedent that may be of dangerous consequence.[1] It will be seen that the Lords could at times be somewhat precipitate even with regard to attainders, although it must be admitted that the attainting

[1] Thorold Rogers, vol. i, pp. 160–1.

a deposed royal family is not analogous to a bill which may
be of imminent danger to the subjects of the realm. In the
cases of Fenwick and Duncombe much was undoubtedly due
to party divisions and to the animus existing between the two
Houses, apart altogether from any question of principle.

It was this latent jealousy between the two Houses that lay
at the root of the difficulties which were found in settling
the question of treason trials. There was no privilege upon
which the Lords set greater store than that of trial by their
peers. They had been much exercised in mind by the case of
Lord Delamere, subsequently Earl of Warrington, who in the
previous reign had successfully emerged from the ordeal of
trial by a grossly partial tribunal, presided over by Jeffreys as
Lord High Steward. The Peers certainly had a legitimate
grievance in the composition of the Court of the Lord Steward
during recess of parliament.[1] While Parliament was sitting the
whole House were the judges, but in recess the Lord Steward,
always nominated by the king, summoned only a select number
of triers, the number being indefinite, and at the discretion of
the Lord Steward. The system obviously afforded opportunities for packing, by which means the sovereign might contrive
to get rid of any obnoxious magnate.

To remedy this patent abuse the Lords introduced in
February 1688/9 a bill for the better regulation of trials of
peers. The measure underwent considerable changes during
its progress through the House.[2] In the original draft it was

[1] See *His Grace the Steward and Trial of Peers*, by L. W. Vernon
Harcourt (1907). Mr. Harcourt traces the history of Trial of Peers, and
in particular of the Steward Court up to the important case of Buckingham
in 1521, by which date the Court may be said to have become standardized.
Mr. Harcourt concludes that the Court 'has an origin, which is neither
ancient, nor obscure, nor creditable', p. 433. Discussing the question of
the influence of the Court on the status of the spiritual lords, as lords of
parliament and not peers, he shows that so far was it from being an
engine for the degradation of the spiritual lords and to the aggrandizement
of the temporal lords at their expense, that 'this court was a fraudulent
device for the degradation of the nobility generally; it was intended to
supersede and altogether deprive them of trial in parliament' (p. 442).
Mr. Harcourt's book does not deal at all with the post-Tudor history of
the Steward's Court.

[2] For the text of this bill, together with the amendments, see *Lords'
MSS. 1689-90*, No. 18, pp. 31-4. See also Chandler's *Lords' Proceedings*,
vol. i, p. 348.

stipulated that at all treason trials fifty-one peers should be summoned, of whom thirty-five at least must attend. In select committee it was proposed that instead it should be enacted that whether during session of Parliament or not a peer should be tried by the whole House. Eventually the number was altered to sixty-one, of whom at least forty must attend. The prisoner was to be allowed to challenge twenty of these. So far the bill was, as indeed it only purported to be, purely selfish. But there followed several clauses, which applied to the ordinary subject as well as the peer, though this fact has sometimes been overlooked. One clause was to the effect that 'in all cases of treason, other than concerning the king's coin, there shall be two witnesses of express overt acts of treason'. Another clause regulated the property qualifications of persons called to serve upon juries in various cases. For instance, no one should serve upon the grand jury in a criminal case or upon the petty jury in case of high treason who was not possessed of 'lands and tenements of some estate of freehold of the clear yearly value of twenty pounds at the least'. In the third place, it was proposed 'that every peer and peeress *and other person* that shall hereafter be indicted of any capital offence for which he or she shall be tried by his or her peers or in the court of King's Bench, shall have a copy of his indictment translated into English, whereupon he or she is to be arraigned by the space of a week before such arraignment and also of the panel by the space of two days before the trial'. Again, the defendant shall be allowed to have counsel to advise him and evidence shall be given upon oath on his behalf. The bill passed the Lords, though an important protest was entered against it. It is interesting to notice the grounds of dissent set forth by the seventeen peers who signed the protest. They objected to the bill precisely because it was not selfish, because, while purporting to secure the privilege of the nobility, it benefited the commonalty as well. It reflected greatly upon the honour of the Peers, they maintained, because it placed Lords and Commons upon an equal footing, whereas the distinctive privileges of the former were based upon the very special regard which the law of England had for the honour and integrity of Peers above that of the Commóns —a regard exemplified by the statute *de scandalis magnatum*.[1] Although such objections could be raised to the Lords' proposals by members of the Upper House themselves, the Commons did not regard the bill with any favour. The majority agreed with Sir Thomas Lee that it would not be for the peace of the government if the bill were passed. Its result would be that the Peers might do as they pleased with impunity. They, the Commons, had no use for the bill.[2] It must be confessed that there was strong justification for their conduct in refusing to accept the measure. The truth is that it was, even as things were, extraordinarily difficult to convict a peer who had been engaged in treasonable practices, so hedged in was he by the privileges of his class. Even Delamere, despite the great efforts made to secure his conviction, had been acquitted.[3] On the other hand, the Lords had their very reasonable grievance; and it was natural that they should fight strenuously for their privilege, and endeavour to avoid measures which tended to bring them more within the reach of the common law.

Two bills whose object was the regulation of treason trials were before Parliament in November 1691.[4] The first originated in the Lords, and was an attempt to revive the bill of 1689. It was stated to be 'for the more equal trial

---

[1] *L. J.*, vol. xiv, p. 140, March 6, 1688/9.

[2] Grey's *Debates*, vol. ix, p. 173. It has to be remembered that trial by one's peers means one thing among the mass of Englishmen, and quite another among a small and privileged class. Ordinary commoners are not united by any sense of comradeship simply because they are not noblemen. But the peerage possesses a distinct solidarity. The judges are always the same men; not simply twelve jurymen selected from an ever-changing multitude. The men whom you are trying to-day may be trying you yourself to-morrow. In such circumstances the rule 'Do as you would be done by' becomes the soundest maxim of expediency and most eminently practical.

[3] The garrulous Ailesbury tells us the following story in connexion with the Delamere trial. 'There happened a thing extraordinary enough in its nature. Henry, Earl of Peterborough, Groom of the Stole, a man of a hot and fiery temper, rising up, said the same as did the rest of the lords, but then whispered his next neighbour in the ear, "Guilty, by God." And indeed the whole number of the lords was of the same sentiment, but, as I said, men of honour and conscience could proceed no otherwise by the strict rule of the law.' Ailesbury, p. 135.

[4] For the Lords' measure see *Lords' MSS. 1690-1*, No. 417, pp. 278–9.

of every peer, peeress, and every commoner of the realm '.[1]
It went no further than the committee stage, as the attention of the House was then arrested by another bill of the
same nature emanating from the Commons. In this, as was
only to be expected, there was no special reference to the
Peers' grievance.[2] The latter were, however, determined to
make use of the bill for their own purposes. The Commons'
proposals included several which had been included in the
abortive Lords' measure of 1689, i.e. those which related to
the use of counsel and witnesses for the defendant. The Lords
made a number of amendments, the principal being the addition
of the following clauses :

' And be it further enacted, That upon the trial of any peer
or peeress for any such treason or misprision of treason as
aforesaid, all the peers who have a right to sit and vote in
Parliament, shall be duly summoned, twenty days at least
before any such trial, to appear at every such trial, and that
every peer so summoned and appearing on such trial shall vote
in the trial of such peer or peeress so to be tried, he and they
first taking the oaths mentioned in one Act of Parliament
made in the first year of King William and Queen Mary....'[3]

The Commons received the amendment with no favour at
all. It was urged, in particular by Somers, that the nobility
are not merely each other's peers, they are often each other's
kindred. If all the Lords were summoned, it was certain that
even the most abandoned creature would find friends among
the number.[4] The refusal of the Commons to accept the
amendments was followed by the appointment by the Lords
of a committee to draw up reasons for insistence. The Commons had maintained that the new clause was foreign to the
general purport of the bill. The committee repudiated this
suggestion. The aim of the bill was the protection of innocent
men, accused of treason. Peers ought to be included among
the beneficiaries by this protection. Hence, if there was any
objection to the present method of trial of peers, this bill was

---

[1] *L. J.*, vol. xiv, p. 639.
[2] *Lords' MSS. 1690–1*, No. 442, pp. 319–27.
[3] See Torbeck's *Parl. Debates*, vol. ii, p. 351.
[4] Grey's *Debates*, vol. x, p. 213.

the proper place for its remedy.[1]   And unless a remedy were
forthcoming—this seems to be implied—the peer was more
exposed than the meanest subject. The statement prepared
by the committee closed with a rebuke to the Commons. The
Lords conceived that nothing conduced more to the preservation of the constitution than a good correspondence between
the Houses. As they would ever do their best to promote the
interests of the Commons, so they could not doubt that the
latter would be equally ready to comply with the Lords in any
instance in which they had so good a case as in the present.
The Commons, despite this exhortation, resolved by 136 to 120
to persist in their attitude. The Lords, said Dolben, already
had a power of overruling the courts of Westminster ; and by
accepting the clause the Commons would be completing the
work, overthrowing the King's prerogative and establishing
that of the Upper House in its place.[2]   There were, however,
defenders of the Lords, such as Finch and Colonel Granville,
who considered that so far as argument went all was in favour
of the amendments. There was only an obstinacy—excuse the
expression—against them.[3] Eventually, after further conference, the Commons agreed to accept the obnoxious clause with
certain amendments. Its application was to be restricted to
temporal peers only.[4] The provision that all the Lords should
be summoned was altered into a stipulation that there should
never be less than thirty-six present at a treason trial. This
was as far as the Commons would go as regards concessions ;
so that despite the prolonged discussion the bill was ultimately
lost.

This was the beginning of an attempt, several times repeated,
of the Commons to pass a treason bill which should not have
special reference to the Lords. The different measures they
introduced were fundamentally the same, varying only in such
small details as the number of the defendant's counsel, &c.
The bills of February 1693/4 and December 1864 met with the

---

[1] *L. J.*, vol. xvi, pp. 3-4, December 29.
[2] Grey's *Debates*, vol. x, p. 220.
[3] Ibid., p. 223.
[4] *L. J.*, vol. xv, p. 40. The Lords on January 20 agreed to accept this
amendment. They would not accept the other.

same fate. The first was summarily rejected by the Upper House at its second reading.[1] Speaking of the second bill, Burnet acidly remarks that 'the design seemed to be, to make people as safe in all treasonable conspiracies and practices as possible.'[2] The two most important amendments made by the Lords were, first, the inevitable addition about trial of peers, and secondly, the stipulation that if there were one witness to each of two separate treasons, charged in a single indictment, it was not to be considered that the two necessary witnesses were thereby provided. The Lower House agreed to the changes suggested by the peers with three exceptions. But it was only about the trial of Peers that no agreement was possible ; and it was again upon this rock of offence that the attempt at reform met with disaster.

The first session of William's third parliament was rendered memorable by the fact that a Treason Bill, originating in the Commons, actually passed both Houses and became law. As usual, the Lords added their favourite clause. Burnet tells us that the amendment was only passed by a small majority and with difficulty, 'for those who wished well to the bill looked on this as a device to lose it, as no doubt it was.'[3] The Bishop himself strenuously opposed the amendment, 'with all his impotent might,' sneers Dartmouth,[4] 'having never been in reality for liberty, but that of his own being impertinent, which by his being no peer, could have no benefit of this bill.' Whether the conduct of the majority in the Lords was dictated, as Burnet suggests, simply by a wish to wreck the bill, or whether—as is much more likely—it was the result of the perfectly genuine wish to safeguard the position of the peerage, at any rate the bill actually passed with the Lords' amendment incorporated in it. The obduracy of the Lower House had indeed by this time been worn out, and it was forced into acquiescence. The reform of treason trials—which it has to be remembered is

[1] *Lords' MSS. 1693-5*, No. 798, pp. 343-4.
[2] Burnet, vol. ii, p. 141.
[3] Ibid., p. 161.
[4] See Dartmouth's note on the above passage. Spiritual Lords had from the first laid no claim to trial by their peers owing to the fact that since the Conquest they had been so persistent in their determination to acknowledge no lay jurisdiction. See Pike, pp. 179-208.

aimed at in the original Trial of Peers Bill of the Lords—was much needed, and rather than suffer a further period of useless delay, the Commons assented to a clause which the majority among them cordially disliked.

The manner of procedure in peerage trials is exemplified in the various trials of Lord Mohun or in those of the Junto. Upon such occasions special efforts were usually made to secure a full attendance of peers. They were indeed finable if they failed to attend. If the charge were a capital charge the Bishops would deliver a protestation and withdraw. The opinion of the judges on different points of law would in the event of any difficulty be freely asked.[1] The actual trial took place not in the House but in Westminster Hall, which had to be suitably prepared for the occasion. The Lord Steward asked the opinion of the peers assembled severally, beginning with the junior baron, and each, when his name was called, stood up and declared whether he was content or non-content. Immediately he had pronounced the sentence of the House and the trial was over, the office of the Lord Steward came to an end, and he would openly break the white staff which was the symbol of his authority.

No discussion of the judicial powers of the House of Lords in our period would be complete which did not include some reference to the divorce proceedings with which it was from time to time occupied. Up till 1857 marriage could not be dissolved save by act of parliament. As the petitioner was required in the first place to petition for a separation and to bring an action against the co-respondent for damages, it required both time and money to obtain a divorce, and in consequence divorce bills were very infrequent. Indeed, before the accession of William III there are only two acts mentioned in the *Journals*, viz. those of the Marquis of Northampton in 1552 and of Lord Roos in 1670. Charles II had taken considerable interest in the latter, and had attended the debates of the Upper House when it was under discussion, for he had some thought at the time of obtaining a divorce from Catherine

---

[1] See, for example, the questions asked of the judges in connexion with the first Mohun trial. *Lords' MSS. 1692–3*, No. 658, p. 296.

of Braganza. In the reign of William there were several divorce acts passed. At about the time when the Duke of Norfolk at length succeeded in his celebrated suit against the Duchess, there were two other divorce bills before the House, viz. those of a certain Ralph Box and of Sir John Dillon, and the proposal was made that the precedent of naturalization bills should be followed and all divorce bills under consideration at a given time be merged into one.[1] A topical poem written in 1701 testifies to the greater freedom which is gradually being introduced.

> Farewell Church-juggle, that enslaved my Life,
> But bless the Powers that rid me of my Wife ;
> And now the Laws once more have set me free,
> If Woman can again prevail with me,
> My Flesh and Bones shall make my Wedding-Feast,
> And none shall be invited as my guest,
> But my good Bride, the Devil and the Priest.[2]

The famous *cause célèbre* of the reign was that of the Duke of Norfolk, which was first brought before the House in January 1691/2, and was not settled until April 1700. There were three different bills, and during the time in which they were under consideration the House had to listen to the repetition of much the same sordid evidence, which it was noticed on one occasion sent the Duke himself to sleep.[3] There were several different reasons why the first two bills were unsuccessful. Burnet saw in the support afforded to the Duchess the tokens of Jacobite activity. He was, as Dartmouth says, ever in apprehension of a halter, and so found 'a Jacobite influence predominant in all transactions'.[4] It might have been added that the Bishop of Salisbury was also in constant and fanatical apprehension of popery, and the Duchess was a Roman Catholic. The Duke himself could scarcely win the sympathy of virtue, as he was a notoriously vicious man, and had been the means of introducing his wife

---

[1] F. L. Bonet, D. p. 89, March 9/19, 1699/1700.
[2] 'On Divorce by Parliament', in the collection *Poems on Affairs of State* (4 vols., London, 1707), vol. ii, p. 272.
[3] F. L. Bonet, D. p. 72, February 27/March 9, 1699/1700.
[4] Burnet, vol. ii, p. 127, and Dartmouth's foot-note.

into the bad company which had depraved her.[1] He had also to contend with the strong Peterborough influence which was exerted on behalf of the Duchess, who was a cousin of the Earl. Indeed, the ultimate success of the Duke's suit in 1700 is to be explained by the fact that the Duchess' conduct in the Fenwick case had alienated the sympathies of her family. But altogether apart from these personal considerations, there was an obstacle against the Norfolk Divorce Bills in the shape of a principle. It was the custom that all divorce and separation suits should in the first instance go before an ecclesiastical court. The passing of a divorce bill in Parliament should only follow upon the decision of the spiritual authority. The first Norfolk Bill was therefore regarded as unprecedented, since it was not founded upon any ecclesiastical sentence.[2]

In March 1697/8 there was passed the Macclesfield Divorce Bill. It excited the greatest interest at the time, as may be gathered from a perusal of the dispatches of L'Hermitage, which abound in references to it. From January 16 until March 2 not a day passed in the Lords but this case came up before the House. The bill is remarkable by reason of its being the first divorce bill to become law although no judgment had been first given in an ecclesiastical court. During the hearing of the case counsel for the Countess made much of the point that the procedure was irregular. 'We say it is in the nature of the legislature to be an aid to other courts and not to take it from them.'[3] The Earl's answer was that his efforts to proceed with the case in a spiritual court had been frustrated by the persistent delays made by his wife. The case was without remedy save in Parliament. When the bill did eventually pass, a protest was made against it by Rochester and Halifax, 'because we conceive this is the first bill of this nature that hath passed, where there was not a divorce first

[1] *MSS. of the Earl of Denbigh*, p. 211 (*Hist. MSS. Comm. Rep.* 7, pt. i, app. Third Rep. on Denbigh Papers).
[2] For first two bills see *Lords' MSS. 1622–93*, Nos. 524, 642; see especially p. 18.
[3] *Lords' MSS. 1697–9*, No. 1197; see pp. 57–8. The Macclesfield Divorce Suit is of some general interest because Richard Savage claimed to be the illegitimate offspring of the Countess of Macclesfield and Earl Rivers.

obtained in the spiritual court, which we look upon as an ill precedent, and may be of dangerous consequence for the future.'[1] A similar objection was also raised to the passing of the Norfolk Bill in 1700, for in this case not only had no ecclesiastical judgment been obtained, but the bill was brought into Parliament when its ' subject matter had not first been proceeded on in the ecclesiastical courts '. Moreover, ' it may be of dangerous consequence to the settlement of families, to subject the dissolution of marriages to so short and summary a way of proceeding.'[2]

A year after the formal dissolution of the Duke of Norfolk's marriage, Lady Anglesey succeeded in obtaining a separation from her husband. She had previously failed in her petition to the Lords that her husband should be compelled to waive his privilege in order that she might institute a cause of separation against him in ecclesiastical courts.[3] As she was debarred from obtaining relief from this source, the Countess presented a petition for a separation bill.[4] The House made fruitless endeavours to reconcile husband and wife. The bill was introduced, evidence of gross cruelty was forthcoming, and as a result the bill was passed. Lord Haversham protested against a measure which gave not absolute divorce but perpetual separation.[5] He explained that ' marriage being looked upon in the Church of Rome as a sacrament always and in all cases indissoluble, but by the pretended authority of the infallible vicar, and there being, in some cases, an absolute necessity for a divorce, the Roman courts of judicature, fearing to expose the weakness of the infallibility, contrived this trick of a separate maintenance ; which practice of theirs, I humbly conceive, such a bill would give too much countenance to '. He also considered that a perpetual separation was a much heavier judgment upon the Earl of Anglesey than a divorce

---

[1] Thorold Rogers, vol. i, pp. 131-2, and *L. J.*, vol. xvi, p. 204.

[2] Thorold Rogers, vol. i, pp. 143-4, and *L. J.*, vol. xvi, p. 540 on second reading; p. 545 on third reading. This protest was signed by Rochester, Halifax, Montague, the Bishops of London, Exeter, Lincoln, and Rochester, and twelve other lords.

[3] *Lords' MSS. 1699-1702*, No. 1564, pp. 149-51.

[4] Ibid., No. 1571, pp. 188-205.

[5] Thorold Rogers, vol. i, pp. 143-4 ; *L. J.*, vol. xvi, p. 611.

itself would have been. It was a punishment for him and nothing more.

A short survey of such proceedings in the House of Lords as those in connexion with divorce bills or separation bills, impeachments or attainders serves to strengthen the impression of the judicial atmosphere prevalent in the House of Lords. It was assuredly not only in its exercise of its peculiar authority over its own members or in its jurisdiction as a court of appeal that the House performed judicial functions. Much of its legislation had a judicial colouring. The same may certainly be said of the Commons. Still, judicial characteristics belonged to the Lords in a particular degree even in the sphere of legislation. It was in the Upper House that the great divorce cases originated; it was there that they were carefully examined and decided. The part which the Lords played in connexion with attainders was essentially the same as that which they undertook in cases of impeachment. The Peers very openly assumed an attitude of superiority. They stood very much upon their dignity when the Commons impeached the Whig Junto. When Goudet and others were impeached in 1698, the Commons claimed the right to have seats provided for them. It was reasonable that they should be seated, for, as certain sympathizers in the Upper House pleaded, the managers of the Commons would have papers and records, 'which they could not conveniently make use of in a crowd'.[1] The Lords, however, contented themselves with the bald statement that the Commons 'have always come to the bar of the House without any other provision for them, and their Lordships intend to proceed in the same manner as hath been usual in all trials within their House'. The Peers once sent a message to the Commons summoning Sir Robert Clayton and Sir George Treby to attend concerning an alteration in the Lieutenancy of London. Upon the receipt of the message, Sir Thomas Clarges declared that it was an unfortunate thing; it affected him very deeply. He feared its consequence would be a rift between the two Houses. 'Is not this', he asked,

---

[1] Thorold Rogers, vol. i, pp. 132-3.

'a sort of bringing of original causes before the Lords'?[1] So prone were the sensitive Commons to see in actions of the Peers an attempt to extend the sphere of their judicial powers.

It should be remembered that the Lords made use of their peculiar position to attempt some noteworthy legal and judicial reforms. In consequence of complaints of grave abuses in the administration of justice the House, in November 1689, appointed a committee to inquire into irregularities in the Court of Westminster Hall.[2] Subsequently the inquiry was extended to the Court of Chancery, the Courts of the Grand Sessions in Wales and the Courts of the Counties Palatine. A great many scandals were brought to light in the course of the investigation. In April 1690 an attempt was made to remedy the abuses discovered by the committee by a Law Reform Bill,[3] which was intended to put an end to the buying and selling of offices. The penalties of former acts were to be made to extend to all ministers of state, judges, and justices. The fees of counsel were to be regulated, and all barristers when admitted to practice were to take an oath not to give presents to judges. If they failed to appear for a client or in such case did not return their fee, they were to incur the penalty of £100. The bill included a number of other provisions to regulate proceedings in Chancery, &c. This bill dropped with the session. It was followed by another measure of similar character, but restricted in scope, which sought to reform abuses in Chancery and other courts of equity.[4] It was marked by the jealousy which the common lawyer in those days always felt for the Court of Chancery. This bill also dropped, but a committee was appointed to draw up another for preventing unnecessary delays in Chancery, for regulating extravagant fees and expenses and restraining Chancery from giving relief after judgment in cases not properly equitable after judgment.[5] Only the initial proceedings of the committee are recorded, and no bill was produced.

[1] Grey's *Debates*, vol. x, pp. 133–4.
[2] *Lords' MSS. 1689–90*, No. 160, pp. 313–32.
[3] Ibid., No. 244, pp. 17–25.
[4] *Lords' MSS. 1690–1*, No. 304, pp. 128–41.
[5] Ibid., p. 138.

In November 1691 the Lords framed another measure dealing with Chancery.[1]   Its object was to put an end to the proceedings of the courts of equity upon bills of review, upon the very reasonable grounds that such bills were brought before the same persons who had decreed in the same cause before, so that nothing was gained and time was wasted.   Causes were to be reheard by five common law judges.   This bill passed in the Upper House, but was rejected by the Commons.   In February 1692/3 a severe bill to prevent the buying and selling of judicial offices appeared in the Lords, but disappeared after it had been committed.   In 1692 and 1693 a number of measures were introduced in the Lords dealing with such questions as clandestine mortgage frauds, abuses on procedure on outlawries.   Two attempts were made to limit the number of attorneys and to insure their proper qualifications.[2]   The former, made in a bill of 1698, was thrown out in the Commons.   The second, a less ambitious scheme, failed in a similar way in February 1699/1700.   The Lords also lost in the Lower House a Vexatious Suits Bill, in which they had sought to apply to the inferior courts of record the principle of an act, which had originated in the Commons, for checking such suits in the courts of Wales and the Counties Palatine.[3]   By the end of the reign not a great deal had been accomplished, but the constant endeavours made by the Upper House to remedy undoubted abuses in the administration of justice ought not to be forgotten.

[1] *Lords' MSS. 1690–1*, No. 438, pp. 308–13.
[2] Ibid., *1697–9*, No. 1200, pp. 69–88; *1699–1702*, No. 1482, pp. 62–4.
[3] Ibid., *1699–1702*, No. 1636, pp. 356–9.

CHAPTER VI

THE ARISTOCRATIC REVOLUTION—THE INTERREGNUM

THE English Revolution has been termed a conservative movement. Burke loved to demonstrate that the Revolution of 1689 did not formulate new rights, but maintained the old. As the movement was largely conservative, so also was it largely aristocratic. It was not effected by the howling mob of a revengeful populace; nor was it really accomplished by the victory of an invading army, or the prowess of a foreign champion. The Revolution was undeniably a national movement. Yet it was the work primarily of certain leading peers, not all of whom shared the same political views, but who were all actuated by a sense of the necessity of taking decisive steps to deliver their country from a despotic king. That such should be the case might well at the first glance appear surprising, the presumption being that the peerage would upon the whole tend to side with, and not against, the crown in emergency. The fall of monarchy and the nobility in 1649 seemed to be proof of the identity of their interests. In 1660 they had been restored together, and the peerage creations of Charles II had been very lavish. The answer to the enigma lies in the fatal perversity of James II. He needed the combined adherence of all the normal supporters of monarchical prerogative, and he succeeded in alienating all. Obviously there was nothing in his policy which was calculated to please the Whigs. It was disastrous that there was really nothing in it which was calculated to please the Tories. The Anglican clergy had supported James despite his Roman Catholicism. Perhaps acting partly under the muddled notion that there was some affinity between High Church Anglicanism and Roman Catholicism, the King exasperated the English clergy by openly flouting them and endeavouring to establish his own religion.

But it was not only the clergy, and particularly the bishops, that were roused by the Romanizing policy of the sovereign. What was just as serious, the temporal peers were aroused also. The Lords as a whole did not like popery; some of them were probably as much infected by anti-papist fanaticism as the ' mobile '. But they specially disliked popery when they saw it leading their King into courses which were wholly subversive of their cherished principles of government. The Peers regarded themselves as the hereditary councillors of the realm ; they considered that they ought to enjoy the full confidence of the sovereign. But as early as March 1686, James had begun to surround himself with a few chosen and kindred spirits, to whom alone he revealed his purposes, such as Father Petre, the Jesuit, who was as much disliked by James's truest friends as he was by his foes, Tyrconnel and Jermyn, Lord Dover. Barillon informs Louis XIV that the Earl of Powys has joined 'the other Catholic lords, whom the King of England consults, and who often meet at Lord Sunderland's to deliberate upon matters that offer ; it is a sort of council, independent of any other, and in which the most important resolutions are taken ; that is to say, those which relate to religion '.[1]   Such a small Catholic caucus as this was not calculated to be popular with any class, least of all with the courtiers. Even the devoted Ailesbury declared of Sunderland that ' pen cannot describe worse of him than he deserved '.[2] His opinion of Father Petre was equally unfavourable. Ailesbury also saw the unwisdom of the King's infatuation for so unworthy an object as Lord Dover ; but as he confesses, ' those the King loved had no faults '.[3]   Meanwhile the accredited leaders of the nation were treated with contumely. His opposition in Parliament to the royal policy led to the dismissal of the Bishop of London from the Privy Council. The objection of Sancroft to serve as an ecclesiastical com-

---

[1] Barillon to Louis XIV, March 26, 1686; Dalrymple, Part I, App. to Book IV, p. 107.
[2] *Memoirs of Ailesbury*, p. 127.   [3] *Ailesbury*, p. 130.

missioner was punished in the same way. Room was soon found in the Council for Catholic peers.[1] A further blow came when the two Hydes were dismissed from their posts. It was made clear to Rochester that he could only retain the treasurership on condition of his embracing Roman Catholicism. He preferred to abandon his office. At the same time Clarendon was recalled from Ireland, his place as lord-lieutenant being taken by Tyrconnel. The treasurership was put into commission, at its head being the trusty Belasyse with Dover as a colleague. Arundell of Wardour became Lord Privy Seal. In fact by the summer of 1687 it had become quite plain that the best qualification for political office was conversion to Romanism; and that in comparison with this experience in statecraft, administrative ability, the prestige of rank and tradition were in James's eyes negligible quantities.[2] The papal nuncio arrived in June at St. James's. The haughty Duke of Somerset refused to conduct him in solemn procession to court, and fell into disgrace in consequence. There is, no doubt, much that is absurd in the pomposity of Somerset. Still, it was an ill thing for James when he came in conflict with the pride of race of the English nobility.[3]

For the consummation of his designs, to secure Catholic indulgence, it was necessary to bring influence to bear upon Parliament. No properly representative House of Commons was likely to be favourable. Neither could the good will of the Lords be reckoned upon. Macaulay quotes three interesting lists which show the state of feeling in the Upper House on the question of the repeal of the Test.[4] According to one list, the number of those who would be in favour was 31, of those against 86, of those doubtful 20. According to the second computation, the numbers were—for, 33; against, 87; doubtful, 19. In the third, the numbers are, 33, 87, and 10 respectively. We should probably be justified in reckoning that the opposition would be three times as strong as the

[1] Belasyse, Powys, Arundell of Wardour, and Dover were made members of the Privy Council in July, 1686. Luttrell, vol. i, p. 383.
[2] Burnet, vol. i, p. 683.
[3] Macaulay, vol. ii, p. 271-3.
[4] Ibid., vol. ii, p. 316, foot-note.

King's party. How did James intend to deal with the opposition? When it was suggested that the Peers might prove recalcitrant, Sunderland turned to Churchill with the words, ' Oh, silly, your troop of horse shall be called up to the House of Lords.'[1] But for the present the main thing was to secure the subservience of a new House of Commons : it would not be necessary to deal with the other Chamber till later. In order to control the Commons, James, practically speaking, tried to make use of the Peers, when he commanded the lords-lieutenants of the counties to make all ready for the next election conformably with the King's wishes.[2] A number of the lieutenants absolutely refused to do so. Accordingly it rained dismissals. Prominent among those who were turned out was the Earl of Oxford, who told James very plainly that he would ' not persuade that to others which he was averse to in his own conscience '.[3] He was deprived both of his lieutenancy and his regiment. Owing to similar circumstances the lieutenancy of the West Riding of Yorkshire passed from the hands of the Earl of Burlington into those of a brother of the Duke of Norfolk.[4] The new lord-lieutenant was an ardent papist. The Earl of Shrewsbury lost both his lord-lieutenancy and his regiment. Indeed the list of those who were punished for their non-compliance is a lengthy one, and includes the Duke of Somerset, the Earls of Pembroke, Derby, Bridgwater, Thanet, Northampton, Abingdon, Scarsdale, and Gainsborough, and the Viscounts Fauconberg and Newport. Their places were taken by Roman Catholics.

It was not surprising that the nobility were as a whole discontented. They felt that they were being thrust out of their legitimate places to make room for a small ring of popish upstarts. Such circumstances as the Delamere trial and the seizure of the Earl of Stamford persuaded them that the King had no

---

[1] Dartmouth's note to Burnet, vol. i, p. 755.
[2] See *King James II's Proposed Repeal of the Penal Laws and Test Act in 1688; His Questions to the Magistracy and Corporations; with their answers thereto, in the three Ridings of Yorkshire*, by Sir George Duckett, Bart., 1879. The King's Instructions are printed on p. 4.
[3] *Memoirs of Sir John Reresby* (ed. J. J. Cartwright, 1875), p. 390.
[4] Ibid., p. 391.

respect for them. Some at court were complaining that their salaries were being unwarrantably diminished owing to some ill-advised retrenchments in the Treasury. Little wonder if, as Mulgrave says in his account of the Revolution, 'the general dislike of the King's management had like an infection reach'd some of the Ministers themselves, as the Earls of Mulgrave and Middleton, never the least tainted with being either false or factious.'[1] Active opposition from the disaffected leaders of the Peers was encouraged by the fact that William of Orange was so obvious a protector. It must be admitted that the love of intrigue was firmly rooted in many a noble heart in the late years of the seventeenth century. It was no part of the character of the man of affairs to act the part of a resigned Stoic. From the beginning of 1687 William was receiving letters of attachment from prominent leaders of the nobility, and fruitful work was done during the missions of Dykvelt and Zuilestein in England.

The first English nobleman to visit Holland was Mordaunt, subsequently notorious as Earl of Peterborough. He pressed William to undertake an expedition to England; but Mordaunt was not the type of man to win confidence or to succeed in carrying out secret enterprises. He was a noisy person, who courted the popularity of coffee-houses and talked very loudly there; and his excessive vanity might at any time render him a prey to an inquisition.[2] In 1687 the place of Mordaunt was taken by a man of very different stamp, the Earl of Shrewsbury,[3] the acknowledged leader of the Whigs. The remarkable diffidence, the shrinking

[1] *Works of John Sheffield, Duke of Buckinghamshire* (2 vols., 1729), vol. i, p. iii: Some Account of the Revolution.
[2] See H. C. Foxcroft's *Supplement to Burnet's History of His Own Time* (Oxford, 1902), p. 284.
[3] Burnet, vol. i, pp. 762-3: 'He seemed a man of great probity, and to have a high sense of honour. He had no ordinary measure of learning, a correct judgment, with a sweetness of temper that charmed all who knew him. He had at that time just notions of government; and so great a command of himself that, during all the time that he continued in the ministry, I never heard any one complaint of him, but for his silent and reserved answers with which his friends were not always well pleased. His modest deportment gave him such an interest in the prince, that he never seemed so fond of any of his ministers as he was of him.' Cf. Foxcroft's *Supplement*, p. 288.

from political life which too often robbed the country of the services of one of the most cultured and ablest men of his day, did not prevent Shrewsbury in the critical days of the Revolution from playing as important a part as any of the other notable actors in the drama.[1] In the early scenes indeed it was Shrewsbury that took the lead, and it was at his house that the conspirators used to meet. Russell and Sidney followed Shrewsbury, and by them the matter of the Prince's intervention was brought nearer to a head. The intriguers sounded a number of the principal peers with varying degrees of success. There was no man in England whose influence would carry greater weight than Halifax, but he did not regard the scheme as practicable. He was only tentatively approached and the lack of response did not encourage more intimate advances.[2] The confederates found him 'backward in all this matter'. He was never one prematurely to burn his boats. Besides, as a letter of his written in May 1687 shows, he thought that the situation was not really very serious. He considered there was little fear that popery would prevail.[3] Nottingham proved just as unsatisfactory.[4] He had stood very much aloof from the court of late, and at first he entertained the proposals of the intriguers favourably. Then he began to doubt. In his case High Church principles, though they necessarily alienated him from James, yet weighed heavily in the balance against resistance. Sidney probably does him an injustice, when he writes to the Prince: 'He has gone very far, but now his heart fails him, and he will go no further: he saith 'tis scruple of conscience, but we all conclude 'tis another passion.'[5] Nottingham, like Halifax, persuaded himself that things would come right of themselves.[6]

---

[1] See a remarkable letter from Shrewsbury to Somers, quoted in John, Lord Campbell's *Lives of the Lord Chancellors* (8 vols., 1846–69), vol. iv, p. 166: 'I cannot help referring to my old opinion, which is now supported by more weight than I ever expected, and wonder that a man can be found in England who has bread, that will be concerned in public business. Had I a son, I would sooner breed him a cobbler, than a courtier, and a hangman than a statesman.'

[2] Burnet, vol. i, p. 754.   [3] Dalrymple, Part I, App. to Book V, p. 69.
[4] Burnet, vol. i, p. 764.
[5] Dalrymple, Part I, App. to Book V, p. 112.
[6] Ibid., p. 118. Nottingham writes: 'The birth of a Prince of Wales,

A very different spirit was found in the Earl of Devonshire, like Shrewsbury a Whig leader. He was not a man of great mark, and William thought slightingly of him, averring that he had never heard him give a reason for anything.[1] Now, however, Devonshire made up his mind with great decision and threw himself zealously into the business. A yet more important adherent was secured in the person of Danby, who showed the same keenness as Devonshire. He had had no place in the administration during the reign of James, and he bitterly hated the entire policy of the King. Once won over, Danby became himself a propagandist ; and it was to his persuasion that the Prince's party owed the adherence of Compton.[2] Later, he made an appeal to the Earl of Chesterfield. ' I had rather lose my life in the field ', he writes, ' than live under an arbitrary power, and see our laws and religion changed, which is now visibly the King's intention.'[3] But Chesterfield could not approve. He had always had an aversion against taking arms against his sovereign, ' which the law justly terms compassing the King's death.'[4] He tried to dissuade Danby. Ambition, revenge, even patriotism might counsel resistance, yet no man could foresee what the issue would be of what at the time could only be a tragedy. Though backward himself, Chesterfield regarded success as certain. The King had committed his crowning blunder in the trial of the Seven Bishops, and the birth of the Prince of Wales which should have given him joy proved a dire misfortune. For the situation was at once profoundly changed. There was no prospect of the accession of the Protestant Mary. The menace was no longer temporary, but perpetual. The nobility would be submerged not for one single reign only, but indefinitely. The schemers saw that the time was ripe for immediate and

---

and the designs of a further prosecution of the bishops and of new modelling the army and calling of a parliament, are matters that afford various reflections. But I cannot apprehend from them such ill consequences to our religion, or the just interests of your Highness, that a little time will not effectually remedy, nor can I imagine that the Papists are able to make any further considerable progress.'

[1] Foxcroft's *Life of Halifax*, vol. ii, p. 236.
[2] Burnet, vol. i, p. 764.
[3] *Letters of Chesterfield*, p. 336.   [4] Ibid., p. 338.

decisive action. The famous seven, Shrewsbury, Devonshire, Danby, Lumley, Compton, Russell, and Sidney, met at Shrewsbury's house and drew up the Association, which contained a definite invitation to William of Orange.[1] They besought His Highness to find a remedy for the country's deliverance before it was too late; assured him that the populace were desirous of a change and that the greatest part both of the nobility and gentry were as dissatisfied as the populace; and that many of the most conspicuous among them would join the Prince on his landing.

This is no place for a full account of the events which followed upon the Prince's landing at Torbay on November 5, 1688. William expressed some disappointment at not finding as much immediate support as he had anticipated. It took some little time for risings to be organized; but organized they were. Delamere rose in Cheshire; Devonshire in Derbyshire; Shrewsbury secured Bristol; the Duke of Norfolk declared for a free parliament in his own county; Lord Herbert of Cherbury raised Worcestershire; Danby and Lumley together took the lead in Yorkshire.[2] Danby indeed was indefatigable.[3] He had hoped with many others of his supporters that William would land in the north. The Prince's failure to do so occasioned some disappointment, and in some perhaps even consternation. In these circumstances Danby showed the greatest dexterity in keeping up the spirits of his adherents. He made it clear to them that their position was now irretrievable; they could not go back and therefore they must advance. He assured them that they had already done enough to ensure their condemnation for treason; they could only escape by success in their present enterprise. When they heard a report that the King was willing to pardon all who would now secede from the Prince, Danby concocted a letter

---

[1] The text of the Association is printed in Dalrymple, Part I, App. to Book V, p. 107 *et seq.*; also in the appendix to Sir James Mackintosh's *History of the Revolution* (1834), pp. 690-2.

[2] Luttrell, vol. i, pp. 476-485, November 29 to December 9, 1688.

[3] See *MSS. of the Earl of Lindsey*, p. 449 (Hist. MSS. Comm., Rep. XIV, pt. ix), and also Laurence Echard's *History of the Revolution* (1725), pp. 149, 170-2.

which purported to give authoritative assurance that the King had in reality no intention of clemency.

In the hour of his distress James most signally failed to deal with the situation. He heard of the departure of the Dutch fleet for England, and was instantly all concession. He heard of its discomfiture in a storm and straightway abandoned compromise until he heard that the disaster to the Prince's fleet had been greatly exaggerated. At one moment he was seeking reconciliation with the bishops; at another he was trying to bully them into signing a special repudiation of the Prince of Orange's undertaking.[1] In his declaration William had stated that he entered the country on the invitation of the Lords Spiritual and Temporal. The bishops made the very reasonable objection that as the statement was made of the temporal peers as well as of themselves there was no reason to single them out. The King was enraged, but he could make no impression on Sancroft. He had to listen to a good deal of advice from his nobility. He was presented with a petition by the two archbishops and two bishops, signed by nineteen peers, in which he was asked to call a free parliament. There had been difficulties with regard to this document. It was intended that it should be signed only by those who had not made themselves obnoxious to the general welfare during the reign. On this ground Rochester was excluded. This annoyed his brother, who saw in the exclusion only the pique of Halifax. But as Nottingham, who was at this time very much at one with Savile, perceived, there were good reasons for the stipulation. Of what use was it to seek to gain the confidence of the country by a petition, in which there would be seen the strange picture of men asking for the repudiation of their own acts, and even for their own punishment?[2] The result of the quarrel was that Halifax, Nottingham, Kent, Pembroke, Weymouth, Fauconberg, Carlisle, and Paget abstained. James's answer to the petition was petulant. How, he ex-

[1] Diary of Henry Hyde, Earl of Clarendon, in vol. ii of his *Correspondence* (ed. S. W. Singer, 1828), vol. ii, pp. 493-7.
[2] *Hatton Correspondence* (Camden Society, 1878), vol. ii, pp. 103, 105. See also Foxcroft's *Life of Halifax*, vol. ii, p. 10.

claimed, could he summon a free parliament, so long as the Prince of Orange remained in the country? He told the bishops that they would do better by praying and preaching for him, and the temporal lords by appearing with swords in their hands, than by petitioning. Even now, though circumstances forced him to hearken to the voice of his hereditary councillors, he could not be prevailed upon to act in accordance with their advice.

At Salisbury James's ineffectiveness became more pronounced than ever. The advance of the Prince of Orange had been prospering. At Exeter the first important recruits began to arrive. There came Lord Colchester, Lord Wharton, and the Earl of Abingdon. Shrewsbury had predicted that once the ice was broken, all would be well.[1] Then the fear of being the first to join would give way to the fear of being last. James was abandoned by Churchill and Grafton, by Ormonde and Drumlanrig, eldest son of the Duke of Queensberry, and by Prince George of Denmark himself. They all entered the Prince's camp. Events prospered also in other parts of the kingdom. Newcastle, in whom the King had placed much confidence, failed to hold Yorkshire for him. Danby proved completely successful, and a declaration signed by six peers and a number of prominent gentlemen was issued at York. Another concourse of peers assembled at Nottingham—Devonshire, Manchester, Rutland, Stamford, Cholmondeley, Grey de Ruthyn, and even the reluctant Chesterfield.[2] There is a short but interesting essay by the Earl of Warrington in which he discusses the reason why the King fled from Salisbury.[3]

---

[1] Burnet, vol. i, p. 790.

[2] Luttrell, vol. i, p. 479; *Hatton Correspondence*, vol. ii, p. 105.

[3] *Works of Hy. Booth, Earl of Warrington*, p. 63 and sq., 'Reasons why King James fled from Salisbury.' James, says Warrington, could see plainly that the peers 'had thrown away the scabbard, and contemned the thought of asking quarter, for as they could never hope for another opportunity to recover their liberties if they failed in this, so they very well knew the inexorable temper of King James, that it would be to no good purpose to sue for his mercy, whereby being made desperate, and abetted moreover by the whole nation; he must expect the utmost that could be done by the united vigour of courage, revenge, the recovery of liberty, and despair, all of which would make up too strong a composition for King James his tender stomach, and turn his thoughts from fighting,

He concludes that it cannot have been the trifling desertions from the army. But he lays great stress upon the importance of the declarations of the nobility for the Prince. They would march through the country, boldly proclaiming their deliverer. Thus five hundred would speedily become forty thousand, and what was at first sight a cloud no bigger than a man's hand would quickly overspread the entire heavens. In other words, it was the menace of the leading discontented peers that caused James to throw away all his chances by his flight from Salisbury; it was the instrumentality of the peers in forming the nucleus of rebellion that caused the success of the Revolution. This is not a complete explanation of the situation; nevertheless it rightly emphasizes what was certainly a most important factor in it.

Upon his return to London on November 16 James once more had recourse to the Lords.[1] He summoned those who were in the capital and set before them the prospect of affairs, asked their advice and at the same time apologized for his failure to call a free parliament. There were some forty lords present, including Clarendon, Rochester, Nottingham, Halifax, Godolphin, and Oxford. A somewhat acrimonious discussion took place; James once more showing unwillingness to accept the advice that he had sought, particularly as regards the granting of a complete amnesty.[2] He failed to see that his welfare lay not in making examples but in making amends. Halifax, in Clarendon's phrase, spoke 'flatteringly'. But whether couched in terms too deferential or not, the advice he gave was thoroughly sound. As for Clarendon, he made a speech which

to contrive the best way to save his life, and this was the storm that drove him away from Salisbury.'

[1] *MSS. of the Earl of Dartmouth*, p. 216 (Hist. MSS. Comm., Rep. XI, App., pt. v); *MSS. of Lord Kenyon*, p. 209 (Hist. MSS. Comm., Rep. XIV, App., pt. iv).

[2] Macaulay quotes Van Citters, who he says had evidently obtained his information from some of those present. 'I cannot do it,' said James, 'I must make examples, Churchill above all; Churchill whom I raised so high. He and he alone has done all this. He has corrupted my army. He has corrupted my child. He would have put me into the hands of the Prince of Orange, but for God's special providence. My Lords, you are strangely anxious for the safety of traitors. None of you troubles himself about my safety.'—Macaulay, vol. ii, pp. 526–7.

was notable for the complete lack of deference shown in it.
He admits himself that he spoke with 'great freedom'.[1]
Ailesbury declares that the Earl 'behaved like a pedagogue
to a pupil';[2] and James's own vèrsion is 'My Lord Clarendon
flew into an indiscreet and seditious railing, exaggerating fears
and jealousies, and blaspheming the King's conduct, so that
nobody wondered at his going a day or two later to meet the
Prince of Orange at Salisbury'.[3] Such a proceeding is
certainly remarkable from one who so short a time before had
been filled with intense horror on learning that his son, Lord
Cornbury, had been amongst the first to go over to William.
'O God!' he had written, 'that my son should be a rebel!
The Lord in His mercy look upon me, and enable me to
support myself under this most grievous calamity! I made
haste home, and as soon as I could recollect myself a little, I
wrote to Lord Middleton to obtain leave for me to throw
myself at the King's feet.'[4] Less than three weeks later the
writer of these words had himself joined the Prince and his
own son. In the interval he had signed the petition to the
King on the subject of the summoning of a free parliament,
had been soundly rated by the Queen for doing so, and had
made his outspoken speech. There can be little doubt that
ever since James's dismissal of the two Hydes there had been
smouldering dissatisfaction in Clarendon's heart, and that it
only needed familiarization with the idea of William's mission
and possibly some small affront at Court to separate him from
his master.

James was now contemplating flight. Disregarding the
bold advice tendered by the loyal Ailesbury, he was once
more falling back upon the counsels of those Catholic advisers,
who saw that there could be no safety for them in a settlement.[5] We cannot doubt that to James it appeared that it

---

[1] Clarendon's *Diary*, vol. ii, pp. 206–10.
[2] *Ailesbury*, p. 192.
[3] *Memoirs of James II* in Dr. J. S. Clarke's *Life* (London, 1816), vol. ii,
p. 239. Even Burnet speaks of Clarendon's 'indecent and insolent
words, which were generally condemned '.
[4] *Diary*, vol. ii, p. 204.
[5] *Ailesbury*, pp. 195–6.

was not alone the peers who had openly sided with William that were against him, but also those who would speak so freely to him as his own supporters had been doing.[1] It was clear that they had no sympathy whatever for his cause; it was only their attachment to the monarchical principle that kept them at his side. And when even a Clarendon could find this consideration outweighed, it was not possible for the King to feel confidence in any but a very few of his adherents. Again, the conditions brought back from Hungerford by James's representatives, Halifax, Nottingham, and Godolphin, were far from reassuring.[2] In short, the tone taken by the Prince, the continuance of insurrections in the country, the attitude adopted by the prominent peers, together with the fearful warnings of his private advisers, convinced James that he was in peril not merely of losing his crown, but of losing his life as well. Having first sent his wife and child out of the country, he took flight himself.

What was to be done in this conjuncture? The King was gone; the promised parliament had not yet come into being; the writs had not even been issued; there was no recognized legal authority existing. Once more the Peers came forward to take the lead. Twenty-nine of them met together at the Guildhall and assumed the functions of government. Their first idea had been to consult with the magistrates, but the latter proved themselves quite incapable of rising to the occasion.[3] The Lords therefore arrogated to themselves the supreme authority in the country. Their meeting was fortified by the precedent of 1640, when Charles I had summoned the Peers together at York, though Parliament was not sitting.

---

[1] It is typical of the point of view taken by the peers—it was not James's—that Dartmouth refused to send the Prince of Wales to France or to hand over his fleet to Tyrconnel.

[2] The terms were: 'That papists should be disarmed, and removed from employments, the Tower of London and Tilbury fort put into the hands of the city, and Portsmouth into those of persons chosen by both Princes; that no more foreign forces should be brought into the kingdom; and that, if the King chose to reside at London during the sitting of parliament, the Prince might reside there likewise, attended with an equal number of guards.'—Foxcroft's *Life of Halifax*, vol. ii, pp. 16-24. See Burnet, vol. i, pp. 794-5.

[3] Ralph, vol. i, p. 1061.

This assembly of peers at the Guildhall is, therefore, of some constitutional interest.[1] But its importance at the time was severely practical. In all great national crises such as that which overtook the country when the King took flight, immediate action must be taken in order that the anarchical forces in society, ever prone to make their appearance on such occasions, may be kept in check. In such circumstances forms and ceremonies are apt to be swept away and the fundamental forces in the political system will stand revealed. It would be going too far to say that the Peers were thus proved to be the predominant power in England at the end of the year 1689.[2] Yet the way in which time and again they came to the fore in these critical weeks reveals them as leaders of the people, and amply justifies the use of the phrase, 'the Aristocratic Revolution.'

The proceedings at the Guildhall were such as might have been expected in the emergency.[3] In the first place, on December 11 a letter was dispatched to Lord Feversham, ordering him to remove his troops to distant quarters. Another letter was sent to Lord Dartmouth, who was in command of the fleet. As His Majesty had that morning privily withdrawn himself, their lordships wrote, they being desirous to prevent effusion of blood in this juncture desired him to see to it that there should be no acts of hostility between his own fleet and that of the Prince of Orange, should they happen to meet. They likewise required him to remove forthwith all Popish officers from their commands.[4] To the Earl of Rochester and Lord Weymouth and the Bishop of Ely and Rochester was

---

[1] Pike, p. 254.

[2] The following attended : The Archbishops of Canterbury and York ; the Bishops of Winchester, St. Asaph, Ely, Rochester, Peterborough ; the Earls of Pembroke, Dorset, Mulgrave, Thanet, Carlisle, Craven, Ailesbury, Burlington, Berkeley, Rochester ; Viscounts Newport and Weymouth ; the Lords Wharton, North & Grey, Chandos, Montague, Jermyn, Culpepper, Carbery, Crew, Ossulstune.—*The Parliamentary History* (Cobbett and Wright), vol. v, p. 19.

[3] For proceedings at Guildhall and the subsequent proceedings at Whitehall see Foxcroft's *Life of Halifax*, vol. ii, pp. 37–57 (*passim*). Miss Foxcroft uses the Lansdowne MSS. in the British Museum (MSS. 255, f. 40).

[4] *Dartmouth MSS.*, p. 229.

entrusted the task of drawing up a declaration of the reasons for the Peers' action.[1] In the declaration they stated that anxious as they had been for the Protestant religion, the laws of the land and the liberties of the subject, they had hoped to see the assembling of a free parliament ; but His Majesty having withdrawn himself, they could not be silent in these calamities. They had therefore unanimously resolved to apply to the Prince of Orange, whose kindness in helping by his presence to secure a free parliament they acknowledged, in order that he might rescue them with the least possible effusion of blood from slavery and popery. They stated that they for their part would do their utmost to assist His Highness in bringing together a parliament, ' wherein our laws, our liberties and properties may be secured, and the Church of England in particular with a due liberty to Protestant Dissenters.' In the meantime they would do their best to preserve peace in London and Westminster by disarming Papists and securing all Jesuit priests on whom they could lay hands. Whatever else might be necessary for the public good they would do as occasion required. This document was dispatched to the Prince by the hands of Pembroke, Weymouth, Culpepper, and the Bishop of Ely.[2] Finally, the assembled Peers sent to the Tower, demanding that the keys should be delivered up to them, and this being done, appointed Lord Lucas governor in place of Skelton.

December 11 closed in riot and fury within London. The mob broke out ; the opportunity for disturbance afforded by the uncertain state of events was too good to be let slip by the thieves and ruffians who infested the slums of the metropolis.[3] Next day the Peers again met, this time at Whitehall, in the endeavour to preserve order, Halifax now presiding in place of Sancroft.[4] Lord Montague moved that Oates might be discharged from prison, but nothing was done in the matter.

[1] For full text of this declaration see *Parl. Hist.* vol. v, pp. 19-20.
[2] Luttrell, vol. i, p. 485, December 9.
[3] *Works of Buckinghamshire*, vol. i, p. xv.
[4] Ralph suggests that it was the mere accident of the Prince's finding Halifax presiding over the Peers at Whitehall that brought him into favour with William subsequently.

Orders were given to fire upon the rabble should necessity again arise. The Queen Dowager sent to ask for thirty horse to be drawn up before Somerset House to disperse the mob ; whereupon the Lords desired Feversham to meet them, but the latter sent an excuse to the effect that the Queen Dowager desired him to stay and defend her. The night of December 12 saw a repetition of the previous excesses, but on the second occasion they were yet more outrageous and alarming.[1] The terrors of the Irish Night were long remembered. Next day the Peers resumed their sittings. They had been occupied with the question of Feversham's conduct when the unwelcome news was brought that James had been captured. When the messenger arrived, Halifax would have adjourned the meeting, but Mulgrave by calling attention to the messenger's presence forestalled him. Feversham was dispatched to attend upon the King ; the instructions to receive his commands and to protect him from insolence being added at Feversham's own request.[2]

On the 14th a reply to the Lords' declaration was brought from the Prince by Pembroke and the other deputies. He told them he intended to be in London in a few days' time. His presence was indeed urgently needed. It had to be admitted that the assemblage of Peers had not succeeded in its primary object of maintaining order. An armed force was necessary. In the meantime business continued to be transacted at Whitehall. On the 15th an examination was made of Lord Jeffreys, who had been attacked by the mob in their fury and had at his own request been removed to the Tower for safety's sake. For this service he humbly thanked his examiners, whose chief purpose with him was to ascertain what had happened to the Great Seal and the writs. William's chief anxiety now was to be rid of his father-in-law. He held a consultation with some of the leading peers at Windsor, and it was decided that the King should be advised to leave London whither he had returned. This advice was conveyed to James by Shrewsbury, Delamere, and Halifax, who was

---

[1] *Hatton Correspondence*, vol. i, p. 124.
[2] Foxcroft's *Life of Halifax*, vol. ii, p. 58.

now thoroughly in the Prince's interests.[1] William on December 21 summoned all the peers in London to meet him at St. James's. Some seventy appeared.[2] Having thanked His Highness for his assistance, they withdrew to Westminster. It is interesting to note that they resolved that in their address tenderness might be used in thanking the Prince for having called the Lords together, as they had a birthright which might be prejudiced.[3] Nothing of consequence occurred on the 22nd, except that Halifax took the chair by desire; but that evening James made good his flight out of England. The next day was a Sunday. On the 24th the Lords had to consider a new situation. An application was drawn up asking that the Prince should take upon himself the administration. This was formulated by Nottingham, Culpepper, Delamere, and the Bishops of London and Ely. The Prince was asked to summon a parliament by means of circular letters.[4] But upon this point there was less unanimity, for Nottingham, clinging to his Tory principles, still wished that the King should be asked for a legal writ, a proposal which was wholly impracticable, but which soothed the consciences of those who as yet did not see that they were already well embarked on revolution.

The Convention met on January 22. In the meantime the elections had returned to Parliament a House of Commons with a very strong Whig majority, and there could be little doubt what sort of line it would adopt. But what the Lords would do was doubtful. Would that assembly show sympathy with the sort of contractual doctrine which pamphleteers were disseminating?[5] How far could the more backward of

---

[1] Burnet, vol. i, pp. 800-1.

[2] The numbers are variously given. Chandler (vol. ii, p. 90) says there were 92. The *Parliamentary History* (vol. v, p. 23), probably following Chandler, says 'about 90'. Reresby says 'about 50' (*Memoirs*, p. 420). Macaulay accepts the computation in Dalrymple (Part I, Book VI, p. 216), i.e. 70.

[3] Foxcroft's *Life of Halifax*, vol. ii, p. 59. The fact that the Peers did not meet again after the 15th until summoned by the Prince is considered by Ralph to imply that they tacitly resigned all authority to him (vol. i, p. 1074).

[4] Foxcroft's *Life of Halifax*, vol. ii, p. 44.

[5] See Bartholomew Pamphlets for 1689, vol. i, in Bodleian: *The*

William's supporters be induced on mature reflection to accept the principle of a new system whose introduction they had unconsciously helped to effect? There were some who, like Somerset, Burlington, and Scarsdale, had been active in bringing in the Prince, but had never dreamed that he would contend for the crown.[1] Matters had gone much further than they had ever anticipated. In the House the Tories had a small but decided majority. In his account of the state of parties among the Peers, Mulgrave divided them into three classes, of which those who inclined to the King were much the smallest.[2] Some of these were actuated by motives of conscience; more, according to this authority, by despair of ever receiving any favour from William. But the bulk of the Tories were not well-affected towards James personally in the least. Some of them, like Danby, had taken a foremost part against him. They were attached not to the monarch, but to monarchy; and the distinction is one of vital importance. They had not exerted themselves to maintain the *status quo*; but now the horror of the thing which had been done, the sense that despite all that might be said about voluntary abdication and so forth, the sovereign had really been turned out of his own kingdom, weighed heavily upon them. In particular a number of the bishops, chief among them Sancroft, found themselves in a most unfortunate position, because their theory of government was semi-religious.[3] The

Breviate, or Advice before it is too Late. Also a pamphlet *On Magistracy, Laws and Obedience*:

'There is no natural obligation, whereby one man is bound to yield obedience to another, but what is founded on patriarchal authority.

All the subjects of a patriarchal monarch are princes of the blood.

All the people of England are not princes of the blood.

No man who is naturally free can be bound but by his own consent.

Public laws are made by public consent, and they therefore bind every man, because every man's consent is involved in them,' &c., &c.

[1] Reresby, p. 435.

[2] *Works of Buckinghamshire*, vol. i, p. xxxiv.

[3] The High Church principles of government are summarized in a pamphlet, which purports to be a *Speech of a Noble Lord against Deposing Kings for Male-administration* (Bartholomew Pamphlets, 1689): 'The law of God commands that the child should be put to death for any contumely done unto the parents. But what if the father be a robber? If a murderer? If for all excess of villainies, odious and execrable both to God and man? Surely he deserves the highest degree

position in which the Archbishop was placed was certainly
one of extreme perplexity ; but in virtue of his great position
and because, by his resistance to James, he had been voluntarily
or involuntarily an important agent in bringing about the
crisis, it behoved him to take some part in bringing about
a settlement of the country. He was the natural leader of
the Tories, yet he would not lead them, and refused so much
as to take his seat in the Convention.

The explanation given by Dalrymple of the greater strength
of the Tories in the Upper House when the Convention met
is probably the correct one.[1] The Lords had continued in
London ever since the arrival of the Prince. But the members
of the Lower House came from all parts of the country. To
the excitement occasioned by the appearance of a Dutch
army, the risings in the different counties, the dramatic success
of William and the disappearance of the King, there had
succeeded all the bustle of elections fought under conditions
of high pressure. When the Commons assembled, therefore,
they were still in the whirl of excitement ; they had had no
time to cool down, to think dispassionately, to remember old
prejudices, or personal predilections. They realized that a
momentous problem had arisen ; that it was their function
to solve it with as little delay as possible, so that their
attention was focussed exclusively upon the immediate question.
As the inevitable result of the state of high feeling throughout
the country it had followed that very strong and decided

---

of punishment, and yet must not the son lift up his hand against him, for
no offence is so great as to be punished by parricide. But our country
is dearer unto us than our parents ; and the prince is *pater patriae*, the
father of our country ; and therefore more sacred and dear unto us than
our parents by nature, and must not be violated, how injurious, how
impious soever he may be. Doth he command or demand our person or
our persons, we must not shun the one, nor shrink from the other.
For (as Nehemiah saith) Kings have dominion over the bodies or over
the cattle of their subjects at their pleasure. Doth he enjoin those actions
which are contrary to the law of God ? We must neither wholly obey nor
violently resist, but with a constant courage submit ourselves to all
manner of punishment, and show our submission by enduring and not
performing ; yea the Church hath declared it to be heresy to hold that
a prince may be slain, or deposed by subjects, for any disorder, or default,
either in life, or else in government.'

[1] Dalrymple, Part I, Book VII, p. 273.

Whigs had for the most part been returned. There can be
no doubt that there was a fairly large number of republicans,
who were glad to find that a constitutional crisis had arisen to
which they could apply their favourite theories. Some there
were who were anxious to prove that the English monarchy
was actually elective, though such ardent archæologists were
kept in the background. The case of the Peers was very
different from that of the Commons. They had for the past
few weeks been enjoying a period of comparative quiet after
the tumult. Electioneering frenzy did not trouble them.
They had therefore an opportunity to look around them, to
take stock of the situation, to regain their equilibrium and to
remember old attachments. In order to escape from an
intolerable position they had launched a boat in dangerous
waters. It was essential that they themselves should as far
as possible control its navigation, and not allow themselves
under pressure of a reckless crew to be swept away upon the
flood tide. Their minds were open once more to historic
principles ; their hearts assailed by ancient sentiments. After
all need there be any great upheaval? Certain changes were
inevitable, but it was necessary to retain the old system and
to beware of the new-fangled doctrines of an impertinent
generation, eager to make all things new.

Unfortunately for themselves the Tories were not united.
They had all the same end in view, but they differed greatly
as to the means by which it was to be attained. Some, such
as the Archbishop of Canterbury, would not commit themselves to any course of action. In a private meeting with
the bishops he had agreed that a regency was the best
expedient, but he would not come to Westminster to propose
the plan. That task was left to Nottingham, who led the
main body of the Tories in the House. There were again,
no doubt, others who would have liked to see the restoration of
James on certain conditions. Lastly, there were the followers
of Danby, who though prepared to go much further than the
orthodox Tory and determined that James should not be
allowed to return, yet felt that William had no good claim
to the English Crown, which ought to devolve upon Mary

singly. Thus the Tories, despite their majority in the Upper
House, were unable to present a united front to the solid
Whig phalanx, which, as events proved, possessed a great
advantage in the favour of Halifax, who presided in the
Lords.

The early proceedings of the Upper House in the Convention were of a non-contentious character.[1] It was resolved
that the 31st inst. should be celebrated as a thanksgiving day,
and that a special prayer for the occasion should be drawn up
by the bishops. There being no judges present, a number of
legal assistants were appointed, including Dolben and Holt.
It was determined that an address of thanks should be sent
to the Prince; that he should be requested to undertake the
administration; that the disposal of the public revenue should
be placed in his hands, and that he should be asked to have
an especial care for the present condition of Ireland. It was
resolved that no Papist should be permitted to enter the
lobby, the Painted Chamber, the Court of Requests, or Westminster Hall during the sitting of the Convention. The
appointment of Halifax as Speaker *pro tempore* closed the
first day's' proceedings. The Tory lords were anxious to
come into contact with the vital question at issue without
any delay. They realized how desirable it was for the success
of their own interests that the House in which their party had
a majority, the House which up to this point had taken the
lead, should take the initiative now. Accordingly Nottingham
tried to arrange that the Chamber should enter into consideration of the state of the nation at the earliest opportunity,
before ' any extravagant votes should be taken below'. The
Tory plan was upset very largely by the influence of Halifax,
who, trimmer as he was, had now entirely gone over to the
Prince's side and had no doubt come to the conclusion that
no other satisfactory solution was possible than that which
lay in the full recognition of the existing conditions.[2] He
declared, therefore, that any discussion of affairs at this stage

---

[1] Luttrell, vol. i, p. 485; *L.J.*, vol. xiv, pp. 101–6; Clarendon's *Diary*,
vol. ii, p. 252.

[2] Clarendon's *Diary*, vol. ii, p. 253.

'was just as much time lost; for the Lords should not proceed upon any business, till they saw what the Commons did'. The formal proposal for delay was made by Devonshire who, speaking on Friday the 25th, suggested that as the Lower House was to discuss the state of the nation next Monday, the Lords should postpone their consideration of that subject till the Tuesday, by which time, as he said, 'we shall be able to gather some lights from below, which might be of use to us.' The motion was carried, though (to use Clarendon's phrase) 'The lights from below did not pass without animadversions'.

In the Commons the Whigs were easily triumphant.[1] Finch and Musgrave might insist upon the republican tendency displayed in the arguments of the majority; the arguments embodied the widespread popular philosophy of the day. The King had virtually demised. A prince ceasing to administer justice ceases to be a king. James had overturned all the foundations of government, and a sovereign who acts against his own laws is a tyrant. The contractual theory, at the back of the Whig doctrine, was finally formulated in the celebrated motion, which was easily carried, 'that King James, having endeavoured to subvert the constitution of the kingdom by breaking the original contract between King and people, and by the advice of Jesuits, and other wicked persons, having violated the fundamental laws, and withdrawn himself out of the kingdom, hath abdicated the government, and the throne is thereby vacant.'[2] When this motion was brought up to the Lords it was laid aside for the time being. But another which accompanied it to the effect 'that it hath been found by experience to be inconsistent with the safety and welfare of this Protestant kingdom to be governed by a popish prince' was instantly accepted by the Lords without a division. It was evidently taken as an irrefutable statement of lamentable fact, and the Lords did not regard themselves as having by

---

[1] For an account of the debates in the Commons see *Original Papers of Philip Yorke, first Earl of Hardwicke* (London, 1785), vol. ii, pp. 399–401 for January 28, and pp. 413–25 for January 29.

[2] *C.J.*, vol. x, p. 14, January 28, 1688/9.

their acceptance of it committed themselves to the contractual creed. But in reality there was no fundamental difference between the two motions. The immediate inference to be drawn from the second resolution was that sovereignty was based rather upon national expediency than upon hereditary right. Either resolution involved a breaking away from the hereditary principle; the one explained it by a fiction, the other justified it by the verdict of experience.

Before embarking upon the intricate questions raised by the House of Commons, the House, being in committee with Danby as chairman, discussed the question whether without necessarily agreeing that the throne was vacant, the problem could not be better met by the expedient of a regency than by that of making a new king. If the proposal of a regency were adopted, then the old system might in essentials be retained and uncomfortable questions be banished. Nottingham took the lead and made a long and able speech in which he discussed the question apparently for the most part from the historical point of view.[1] In the reign of Edward III it had been resolved that the King had no peer in the kingdom; no one could judge him. It had also been resolved that he could not abdicate his kingdom. The conclusion which Nottingham drew from these and other similar arguments was that a regency was the best remedy and came nearest to the law. Ailesbury objected to the manner of the speech as being too lawyer-like; he confessed that he had not felt edified by it.[2] Clarendon supported the motion, speaking in a peevish strain.[3] Rochester also spoke, and spoke well,

[1] For rough notes of this speech see *Lords' MSS. 1689-90*, No. 10, p. 14.

[2] The following particulars are taken from Ailesbury, p. 232. Ailesbury says a good deal that is of interest about the proceedings in the Upper House during the sitting of the Convention; and it is unfortunate that more extensive use cannot safely be made of his accounts of debates. But he is so often inaccurate, so often speaks clearly from imperfect recollections of events in the past, that it is impossible to rely on him implicitly. His avoidance of dates makes it at times very difficult to be sure to which debate he is referring. No doubt can, however, exist in the present instance.

[3] His attitude now, in view of his having gone over to the Prince's side, greatly irritated William. It is suggested that he was actuated by resentment at not receiving the lord-lieutenancy of Ireland upon which he had set his heart.

but as usual with too much passion.[1]   He was very apt to
lose his self-control in debate, so that the force of his rhetorical
skill and knowledge was in large measure lost.   Still, the
case for a regency was put so ably that some thought,
especially after Nottingham's speech, that the motion would
be carried.   It was two exceedingly forceful speeches by
Halifax and Danby, who were on the present subject quite
united, that altered the complexion of affairs.   As it was the
motion was lost by the narrow margin of 51 to 49.[2]   Only
two of the fourteen bishops present voted against the motion,
viz. London and Bristol.

Next day, January 30, the Lords examined the principal
resolution from the Commons clause by clause.   Although
many maintained the complete divine right theory, still the
clause which spoke of the original contract between king and
people, which James had broken, was passed by 54 voices to
43.[3]   But even after the acceptance of so revolutionary a
doctrine as this, the Tories were not yet beaten.   Their chance
came in the discussion of verbal questions, where it was possible to indulge in the intricacies of sophistic argument.   They
took exception to the word ' abdicate '.   James might have
broken a compact, but abdicated he had not.   The Tories
triumphed ; they carried a resolution for the substitution of
the word ' deserted '.   The debate was resumed next day
when the question of the vacancy of the throne was considered.   The Whigs perceived as the result of the previous
day's discussion that they were in danger of being again
defeated.   Danby, who had taken upon himself the rôle of

---

[1] See Macky, p. 45.
[2] So Clarendon's *Diary*, vol. ii, p. 256. In *Lords' MSS. 1689-90*, No. 10,
p. 15, the numbers are given as 51 and 48.   Clarendon, however, gives
a precise list: Dukes of Somerset, Southampton, Grafton, Ormonde,
Northumberland, Beaufort ; Earls of Kent, Pembroke, Exeter, Scarsdale,
Chesterfield, Westmoreland, Thanet, Clarendon, Craven, Nottingham,
Feversham, Berkeley, Rochester, Abingdon, Ailesbury, Lichfield,
Yarmouth ; Viscount Weymouth ; Lords de la Warr, Ferrers, Chandos,
Brooke, Leigh, Coventry, Jermyn, Dartmouth, Crew, Godolphin, Griffin,
Maynard, Arundell of Trerice ; the Archbishop of York ; the Bishops of
Winchester, Norwich, Lincoln, Llandaff, Ely, Chichester, Bath and
Wells, Peterborough, Rochester, Gloucester, St. David's.
[3] *Lords' MSS. 1689-90*, No. 10, p. 16.

protector of the Princess Mary's interests, would not accept the theory of vacancy, as he held that Mary was already Queen by right. The Whigs, abandoned by their former ally, in their predicament moved that instead of the words 'the throne is thereby vacant' there should be inserted the conclusion 'the Prince and Princess of Orange be declared King and Queen'. But the previous question was moved and the 'vacancy' clause rejected by eleven votes.

The situation created by the divergence between the two Houses was complex. Various expedients were being canvassed throughout the country, for crowning the Prince and Princess jointly, for crowning the Prince alone.[1] The Lords' treatment of the Commons' motion did not admit of either of them. So keen did popular feeling in London become that an attempt was made to influence the Peers by petitions, and during the debates crowds would assemble in the neighbourhood of St. Stephen's and insult the Tory lords as they made their way either to or from parliament.[2] William took measures to put a stop to these proceedings. Although the Lords had stood out against the Commons, the cause of James personally was not thereby advanced in any way. Not content with agreeing to the resolution that the security of the Protestant religion was incompatible with the rule of a popish prince, they commanded that a special thanksgiving for delivery from popery and arbitrary power should be drawn up together with a prayer for the deliverer. A letter for the Convention from James was read by neither House.[3]

When the Lords' amendments to their resolution was brought into the House of Commons, no hesitation was shown in dis-

[1] See Bartholomew Pamphlets for 1688: (1) *Reasons for placing the Prince of Wales on the Throne, singly during Life.* (2) *Reasons for crowning the Prince and Princess of Orange jointly.*

[2] *A History of Political Transactions and of Parties from the Restoration to the death of William III*, by Thomas Somerville (1792), p. 232.

[3] The text of the letter is given in *Lords' MSS. 1689-90*, No. 11, pp. 18-22. It might seem scarcely credible in after days, thought Mulgrave, that a full House of nobles should not so much as open what might be reckoned the last words of a dying sovereign. The reason he gives is that it was thought the recital of the letter might prove too moving.— *Works of Buckinghamshire*, vol. i, p. xxvi.

missing them. The Commons did not agree because they considered that the word 'deserted' did not express the conclusion to be inferred from the premises to which their lordships had agreed, viz. that James II had violated the original contract between king and people. Nor could they accept the Lords' amendment of leaving out the clause referring to the vacancy of the throne. Vacancy, in their opinion, was the corollary of abdication, just as abdication was of royal subversion of the fundamental laws of the constitution.[1] In other words, the Lords were arraigned for inconsistency and illogicality. A free conference was asked for by the Lower House and agreed to. It took place, but led to no solution of the difficulty, for the Lords stood their ground. Nottingham, who was their chief representative, explained that they insisted upon the substitution of the word 'deserted' for 'abdicated', because the latter was a word unknown to the common law of England, and secondly, because abdication was a voluntary renunciation; and James had made no voluntary renunciation. In the second place, the Lords insisted upon their second amendment, because the monarchy was hereditary and not elective, and because no act of a king could invalidate the right of his heirs, and therefore allegiance was due 'to such person as the right of succession doth belong to'. When the result of the conference was made known to them, the Commons once more rejected the Lords' amendments, but only by the small majority of 181 to 151.

It had been William's intention not to interfere with the deliberations of the Convention, but he now lost patience with its dilatoriness and determined to settle the question at once by definitely stating what his own wishes were. When Mary made it quite plain that she would never consent to be Queen save in conjunction with her husband, and he that he would never be tied to his wife's apron-strings, Danby realized that his scheme was doomed. This put an end to the schism between his party and the Whigs and rendered the acquiescence of the House of Lords inevitable. There took place, however,

---

[1] *C. J.*, vol. x, p. 18, February 2.

a second conference between the Houses on February 6, at which the Tory peers once again explained their position.[1] Probably most readers of the account of this discussion share with Macaulay his feeling of disappointment. It is not merely that the conference was practically unimportant, as the actual result was not affected by it, but that the arguments adduced appear so very puerile. But, though the discussion resolved itself into a haggling about the precise meaning of words, and though no general statements of principle are to be found, still questions of principle were involved and underlay the quibbling. Over and over again the Tories were twitted with their inability to answer the question, ' If the throne is not vacant, by whom then is it filled ? ' They objected that ' abdicated ' was a word unknown to the English law ; so for that matter was the word 'deserted'. 'Abdicate', Mr. Sergeant Holt solemnly explained, was a word frequently met with in the best Latin authors, such as Cicero. The retort made by Nottingham and his fellow managers was that the language used by the Commons seemed to suggest that the English Crown was elective. The Bishop of Ely was responsible for the distinction between the exercise of government and the right to govern. The King might have abdicated the former, he could not abdicate the latter. Clarendon objected to the contract theory that allegiance to the sovereign was owed immediately upon the Crown's devolving upon him, before ever he had taken the Coronation Oath. The question whether, granted that James had renounced, he could renounce for more than himself occasioned some acrimonious discussion. Pembroke and Clarendon would have it that the throne being hereditary, it must in default of James be occupied by his heir, to be met by the legal retort, ' Nemo est haeres viventis.' ' I say, no man can be his heir while he lives,' exclaimed Maynard. ' If he has any he is *in nubibus*, our law knows none ; and what shall we do till he be dead ? ' Later on the debate in the hands of the Hydes wandered off into a disquisition on the subject of the deposition of Richard II. Nottingham in the last words he spoke

---

[1] A full account of the conference is given in Torbeck's *Parl. Debates*, vol. i, pp. 189 *et seq.*, and also in the *Parl. Hist.*, vol. v, pp. 67–107.

at the conference made an appeal to the Commons' representatives to reflect lest in getting the established government they wished for in their own way, 'they should overturn all our legal foundations.' Of the sincerity of Nottingham there can be no question. He knew that the time spent in the conference had been so much time wasted; he knew what was destined to take place, and though he himself could not conscientiously agree, he actually confessed that he was glad that the fact of others being less scrupulous rendered an escape from the deadlock possible.

Clarendon had been very well satisfied with the conference. ' I think ', he wrote, ' that all impartial men who were present will own that the Lords had by far the better of the argument, both upon the point of reason, and according as the law now stands.'[1] It was therefore a terrible disappointment to him that upon his return to the House after so successful a meeting it was only to find defeat for his party. He laments that ' such was the strength of the malicious (I think I may so call them) contrary to all law and right reason, the question was put whether to agree with the House of Commons'. Halifax, he complained, ' drove furiously.' His chief argument was that of necessity. The crown was only made elective *pro hac vice*, and then reverted to its ordinary hereditary channel. Nottingham made ' a substantial reply '. Nevertheless the motion was carried by a majority of twenty.[2] Authorities differ as to the exact numbers. Several of the Tory peers absented themselves—Chesterfield, Weymouth, Ferrers, Godolphin, the Bishop of Oxford. Grafton, Southampton, and Northumberland, who had all three voted for the regency, saw fit to side with the majority, whose ranks were also swelled by the inclusion of several peers who were but rarely to be seen within the walls of the House, such as the Earls of Lincoln and Carlisle. Another of the contents was the Bishop of Durham, who had previously absconded and was actually waiting for a ship to convey him out of England, when he was

---

[1] Clarendon's *Diary*, vol. ii, p. 260.
[2] Clarendon gives the numbers as 62 to 47 ; but the more trustworthy computation is that given in *Lords' MSS. 1689-90*, No. 10, p. 18, viz. 65 to 45.

prevailed upon to buy at least a pardon by giving his vote for the new settlement. Thirty-eight peers recorded their dissents. Then the decisive question was put ' whether the Prince and Princess of Orange shall be declared King and Queen of England and of all the dominions thereunto belonging '.[1] It was not thought fit to divide the House upon this question, which was therefore counted as being unanimously carried ; but Clarendon believed that there were really forty who would have been for the negative. In his diary for this day, February 6, he recorded, ' I think this was the most dismal day I ever saw in my life. God help us ; we are certainly a miserable, undone people.'[2]

The interregnum was now, for better or worse, over ; and the Lords had to bear their share of responsibility for the Revolution which had been accomplished. It was not alone the Whig leaders like Shrewsbury that had brought about the downfall of James II, and so prepared the way for a new régime. The Seven Bishops by their opposition to the King's ecclesiastical policy, Tories like Danby and Clarendon by their dislike of the King's governmental methods, had also contributed to the result. Had they in November 1688 come to the conclusion that the sacred cause of monarchy was bound up with that of James himself, had they in that belief subordinated their personal feelings to the cause of a principle, it is conceivable that the course of events would have been quite different. In point of fact, though James was given sound advice from a few of the peers, he was not supported by the peerage, firm prop and stay of monarchy as it was supposed to be. The divergence between the grandeur of the hereditary principle and the littleness of its embodiment, between the principles of its adherents and their personal interests, resulted in the curiously illogical attitude of the conservative-minded members of the Upper House, who, while they were prevailed

[1] The phraseology 'are and are declared to be' was adopted with a view to propitiate the Tories. As the time at which their Majesties began to be is not specified, it was not absolutely essential to adopt the vacancy theory in order to subscribe to the resolution. See *L. J.*, vol. xiv, p. 126, February 12.

[2] Clarendon's *Diary*, vol. ii, p. 262.

upon to acquiesce in the fact, would not accept the theory of the new settlement. But this very illogicality is typical of the Revolution settlement, as it has been typical of all our constitutional settlements ; moreover, it was certainly a cause of its success and its stability, for illogicality is often a necessary condition of compromise and reconciliation.

CHAPTER VII

THE ARISTOCRATIC REVOLUTION—THE SETTLEMENT

THE period in which the Revolution Settlement was established synchronizes, roughly speaking, with the duration of the first parliament of the reign of William and Mary. The conduct of the Upper House throughout this period is a continuous illustration of its intention to preserve as many conservative elements as possible in the Revolution, in which it had willingly or unwillingly become involved. Much of the history of the first parliament indeed resolves itself into a struggle between an extreme party, whose strength lay in the House of Commons, and a party of compromise, which was predominant in the House of Lords. It was inevitable that the triumphant Whigs, strong in their Commons' majority and the success of their policy in the Convention, should be anxious to press their advantage and to establish their supremacy. They regarded the Revolution as peculiarly their own work. The King owed his kingship to them. He should, therefore, act as their perpetual ally and aggrandize them at the expense of their rivals. This was not William's policy at all. The number of Tories given high office in the state, and more particularly the high degree of confidence enjoyed by Nottingham in the royal closet, gave very great umbrage to the Whigs. Hence the attitude of the Whig majority in the Commons is found to be characterized by considerable party bitterness against their opponents and not a little resentment against the King.

When once the succession had been formally settled and the Convention had escaped a somewhat puzzling dilemma by solemnly declaring itself a parliament, there was no more pressing problem before it than that afforded by the religious question. It was not a tolerant age according to our modern standards, and it never occurred to any Protestant that anything could be gained by attempting a reconciliation with the hated Papists. They had had their hour ; they were considered to have imperilled the security of the country; they had been worsted and they must bear the consequences of their defeat. *Vae victis !* The Lords had during the Interregnum ordered that all Papists should be compelled to leave London. When the Convention met they had obtained detailed information as to the number of Roman Catholic householders of less than three years' standing resident in the different parishes of the City and Westminster.[1] On March 1 they followed up these proceedings by introducing a bill for the removal of Papists from London.[2] The bill became law on April 24. The case of the Protestant dissenters was very different. Despite the persecutions which they had suffered under Test Act and Clarendon Code, they had repudiated the advances made by James II in the name of religious liberty, and had staunchly supported the Anglican cause. Justice demanded that their conduct should meet with its reward. William, himself a Calvinist, did his best to assist the very remarkable attempt which was made at the Revolution to unite all his Protestant subjects.

When the Peers were called upon to take the oaths of allegiance to their new sovereign a small number refused, including Clarendon and eight of the bishops, among whom were five of the famous Seven. 'But in the meantime', says Burnet rather uncharitably, 'that they might recommend themselves by a show of moderation, some of them moved the House of Lords, before they withdrew from it, for a bill of toleration, and another of comprehension.'[3] As a matter of fact both proposals were introduced by the high-church Nottingham at the urgent request of William. The two bills were closely connected with another, viz. that for abrogating the old oaths of supremacy and allegiance and substituting new ones. This measure, which determined the oaths to be taken

---

[1] *Lords' MSS. 1689–90*, No. 6, pp. 2–11.
[2] Ibid., No. 20, pp. 36–7.   [3] Burnet, vol. ii, p. 6.

by office-holders, has to be distinguished from the former
measure which applied only to members of the two Houses.
In consequence of the abstention of the non-juring bishops, the
second bill was pushed on with great acrimony by a certain
anti-clerical section in the Commons, who imagined that the
majority of the lower clergy would probably follow the example
of these bishops, and would thereby be discredited. The bill
was brought up from the Commons on March 18, was read
twice and committed, but not further proceeded with, as the
Lords abandoned it in favour of a bill of their own.[1] This,
which purported to be 'for the better discovery of Popish
recusants and repressing all usurped and foreign power and
preserving the King and Queen's Majesties in their persons,
and the more assured support of the government ',[2] was read for
the first time on March 14. The following day it was referred
to a select committee to draw clauses for making the abrogation of the oaths clearer and for removing the necessity of
receiving the Sacrament as a test for holding office. Here, in
the attempted abolition of the hateful test, was the making of
a great reform. It was one which the King had very much at
heart. He came down to Parliament, and in the Upper House
made a speech dealing mainly with Irish affairs, in which he
expressed the hope 'that they would leave room for the admission of all Protestants that were willing and able to serve '.
But the proposal was too advanced and too bold for the time.
The question being put whether to agree to the clause for
repealing so much of the Test Act as concerns the receiving of
the Sacrament, it was resolved in the negative. Leave was,
however, granted to dissentient peers to record their reasons for
dissent, and eight peers did so.[3] They argued very properly
that a hearty union among Protestants was a greater security
to the Church than any test which could possibly be invented ;
that the obligation to receive the Sacrament was a test on
Protestants rather than on Papists ; that so long as it continued
there could not possibly be that thorough union amongst Pro-

---

[1] *Lords' MSS. 1689-90*, No. 38, pp. 63-6.
[2] Ibid., No. 33, pp. 52-5.
[3] See Thorold Rogers, vol. i, pp. 71-2.

testants which had always been desired, and which was at that time indisputably necessary; finally, that a greater caution 'ought not to be required from such as were admitted into offices, than from the members of the two Houses of Parliament, who were not obliged to receive the Sacrament in order to enable them to sit'. When the bill came up for its third reading, a rider was offered, providing that no officer should incur the penalties of the Test Act in case he should receive the Sacrament in any Protestant congregation within a year before or after his admission. This also was rejected.

Although the abrogation of the test proved too great a demand upon the conservatism of the Peers, there was one important proviso in the cause of leniency which they wished to have carried. They agreed that all persons, who should in the future enter upon any office, civil or ecclesiastical, such as in the past would have necessitated the taking of the oaths of supremacy and allegiance, must be required to take the new oaths; but, on the other hand, they were anxious that those who were already in the enjoyment of such office should only be required to take the oaths if they were particularly and individually tendered to them. That is to say, any such person would not necessarily, because of the new succession, be compelled to take the oaths, but he would always be liable to be called upon to do so, should suspicion arise as to his loyalty. This conciliatory scheme aimed at the protection of the uneasy conscience of High-Church Anglicanism.

Burnet, who had just been created Bishop of Salisbury, happened to make his first appearance in the House when the debates on this question were proceeding.[1] He immediately began to take a prominent part in the activities of the Chamber, and as he is careful to inform us, to take the lead in favour of the clergy. The arguments for and against the cause of leniency have been summarized by him. In favour of the motion it was argued that the liability to be called upon to swear and to be punished in the ordinary way upon failure to do so would be a sufficient restraint, whereas the peremptory demand with the present threat of deprivation would only

---

[1] Burnet, vol. ii, pp. 7-9.

cause desperation among many conspicuous clergy, and this would be dangerous to the government. Moreover, in the very offices of the Church the clergy owned their allegiance to God, and this was a more solemn obligation than any other could be. If they failed to fulfil the Church's offices the clergy could be proceeded against in accordance with the ordinary law of the land. It was urged on the other side that it was not fitting that any government should entrust so sacred a function as that of the clergy to men who would not give any security for their loyalty to it, especially since the oath already required was too wide and too loose. The day fixed for the new oaths to be taken was some months distant, and allowed ample time for men to consider their position and examine their consciences. If by that time they were still unable to convince themselves of the propriety of acknowledging the legitimacy of the new régime, it was not right for them any longer to fill posts in the Church. The arguments in favour of conciliation carried the day in the Upper House, as was only to be expected from its character and composition at the time. The majority sympathized profoundly with the uneasy scruples of the believers in divine right. But that this sympathy was not confined to high Tories is shown by the fact that the majority were led by the Whig, Burnet. The latter confesses, however, that his feelings changed somewhat by reason of certain discoveries concerning the conduct of the non-juring clergy. When the tolerant proviso of the Lords reached the Commons, the latter would have none of it. They were resolved that they would not be baulked of their prey. Two conférences proved unavailing to produce any agreement, and eventually the Lords gave way altogether even upon the question of the maintenance of the non-juring clergy. The only mitigation which they succeeded in obtaining was that the King should be empowered to reserve the third part of the revenues of twelve benefices for such clergy as should be deprived in consequence of the act.

Over the Toleration Bill no such difficulty arose, for it did not necessarily mean more than the unavoidable reward of party services. It affirmed no principle; it gave no recognition to dissenters. The rule still remained that of intolerance, and there was nothing in the measure to prevent a speedy return to intolerant practice, should it prove desirable. Thus the exemption from the penalties of certain persecuting laws, though entailing substantial benefit to dissenters, was not too startling a change for the scruples of the rigid and uncompromising Anglican. Moreover, the bill was fathered by the chief lay representative of the party most calculated to oppose it. Two proposals, brought forward in the two Houses respectively, whose object was to make the operation of the bill temporary and so to put dissenters upon their good behaviour, though thoroughly in harmony with the spirit of the measure, were both defeated.

The incomplete and perhaps somewhat grudging nature of the benefits bestowed by the Toleration Bill is typical of a good deal of our most successful legislation. It was certainly in keeping with the temper of the time, and to that fact the measure owed its success. But it has long been recognized that many of the encomiums bestowed upon it as marking the dawn of a tolerant spirit have been misplaced. A much more interesting attempt to give effect to the most enlightened ideals of the day is shown in the Comprehension Bill, which suffered a less happy fate.[1] Although there was much nobility in the idea of comprehension, still there was an element of bargaining in it. If only the test is retained, the High Church party suggest, we will then see what can be done to make it possible for the dissenter of to-day to take the Sacrament in accordance with the usage of the Church of England to-morrow. Some of the provisions of the bill are most remarkable. For example, it is proposed that in place of assent to the Thirty-nine Articles the taking of an oath only should be required. The terms of the oath, it was originally suggested, should be as follows : ' I, A.B., do approve of the doctrine and worship and government of the Church of England by law established, as containing all things necessary to salvation, and I promise in the exercise of

---

[1] For the text of this most important and interesting bill see *Lords' MSS. 1689-90*, No. 32, pp. 49-52. The complete text of both the original measure and the amendments is given ; so that it is possible to trace its full history in the House of Lords.

my ministry to preach and practice according thereunto.' That
such a concession as the permission to take so loosely worded an
undertaking should have been suggested is sufficiently extraordinary. Still more so is the fact that, when Burnet proposed
that the words ' submit to ' should be substituted for ' approve ',
the amendment was accepted by thirty-five voices to three. An
interesting clause, which appears in the original draft, but was
subsequently omitted in committee, was to the effect that any
person who had been ordained by the Presbytery, and not by
a bishop, should notwithstanding upon his desire to be admitted
into the ministry of the Church at once be so admitted by the
laying on of hands of a bishop in a certain form, and that
henceforth he should be regarded as capable of performing
offices and enjoying benefices exactly as if he had been
examined and ordained according to the ordinary form of
the Church of England. Other clauses permitted the omission
of the surplice, of the sign of the cross in baptism, of kneeling
when receiving the Sacrament.[1] On the last point there was
some vehement debate, as it was thought that dissenters' chief
objection to taking the Communion according to the usage of
the Church of England was the necessity of taking it kneeling.
Hence this exemption would mean that all employments
would instantly be besieged. Despite opposition, however,
this clause was eventually carried, Burnet being particularly
zealous on behalf of it. The last clause in the bill gave rise to
difficulties owing to the question of machinery. It is particularly striking as it admits that the liturgy is capable of certain
alterations and improvements. For the purpose of making
them it was proposed that a commission should be set up. On
report it was moved that this commission should contain laymen as well as clergy. It is interesting to note that this motion
was only lost in accordance with the ancient custom *semper
praesumitur pro negante*, the votes being equal. A vigorous
argument, drawn up by the dissenting peers, claimed that the

[1] The use of the surplice was still to be compulsory in the Chapels
Royal, all Cathedrals, collegiate churches and chapels; and when it was
not used a black gown suitable to the degree of the wearer was to be
worn in its place.

Church was acknowledged and defined as consisting of both clerics and laymen; that the matters to be considered were of human, and even of parliamentary institution, and were therefore the concern of one party as much as of the other. It would, besides, facilitate matters to have members on the commission who could satisfy both Houses, Commons as well as Lords, as to the reasons for which alterations were made.[1]

The fact of the inception of so bold and so arresting a scheme as is contained in the Comprehension Bill in the House of Lords, the interest of the arguments brought forward concerning it in the Chamber, justify and indeed necessitate somewhat fuller treatment than need be given to the majority of the measures with which the first of William's parliaments was concerned. The brilliant attempt failed, and it is not difficult to understand why it did so. Conservative feeling was satisfied by the measure of relief granted by the Toleration Bill, and regarded the second measure as superfluous. There were those who, while Whig in secular matters, approached to Toryism where the Church was concerned. The Revolution Settlement had not altered fundamental religious sympathies and aversions. But, on the other hand, Whig lords such as Mordaunt and Macclesfield took the opportunity to indulge in fiery and contemptuous language against the Church. Another agency working against the bill was of a particularly discreditable character. There was a maxim, says Burnet, even amongst those apparently most zealous for the dissenters, 'that it was fit to keep up a strong faction both in Church and State,'[2] the idea being that not only was dissent in itself a valuable asset, but toleration would be better maintained if the number of those who needed it was large. The Comprehension Bill, the work of the Lords, in spite of difficulties, passed through the Upper House. But in the House of Commons, having been read only once, it ceased to be.

There is reason to believe that William had the welfare of the measure very much at heart. But it was not in religious matters only that his wishes were meeting with opposition.

[1] Thorold Rogers, vol. i, pp. 74-6.
[2] Burnet, vol. ii, p. 12.

There was a section of the Whigs in the Commons who were determined to press the sovereign as much as possible.[1] This could best be done in connexion with their control of revenue. It was felt to be desirable that supplies should be granted annually, or at any rate for only a short term of years at a time. It has to be admitted that opposition came also from the Lords in financial matters. The Tory peers brought strong opposition to bear against the bill to discontinue the hearth tax, opposition which was probably prompted very largely by ordinary conservative feeling. The reason assigned for the Tories' action by the Whigs was that the Tories feared lest the King should win too great favour with the nation by the removal of so unpopular a burden. The reason they themselves gave was that the tax was the only one upon which certain reliance could be placed in time of war.[2]

Parliament was necessarily occupied very largely in the passing of such defensive legislation as is required by great political emergencies. No opposition was made to two Habeas Corpus Suspension Bills. But a Treasonable Correspondence Bill, originating in the Lords, was rejected in the Lower House. The Peers did not take very kindly to the Militia Bill, introduced by the Commons, and brought to the Lords on July 16, 1689. This measure was based upon the Act of 1662, but some important changes were made, whereby a good deal of authority originally in the hands of the Crown and the lords-lieutenants was taken away.[3] Thus the peerage was robbed of a certain measure of influence. The bill was considerably amended both in the committee and report stages. But it is not true to say, as Burnet does, that it was allowed to lie upon the table owing to the Lords' opposition; its further progress being in fact blocked by the prorogation in August, of which no doubt the King and the Upper House were both glad to take advantage. The other important military enactment of

---

[1] So Burnet, vol. ii, p. 13.

[2] This was a very strong argument, there being so very little direct taxation in these days; and it was particularly desirable in time of war that there should be some direct impost which could be reckoned upon.

[3] See the two measures compared in *Lords' MSS. 1689–90*, No. 12c, pp. 206–17.

the parliament—the Mutiny Act—was not of a very controversial character, and the amendments made by the Lords
were only on points of detail.

Both Houses showed activity in the punishment of past
offenders. Jacobites such as Salisbury and Peterborough were
committed to the Tower, the Commons having resolved that
in joining the Church of Rome during the late reign they had
committed high treason. The Lords appointed a so-called
Murder Committee to investigate the circumstances surrounding the death of Lord Russell.[1] But it was in the Commons
that the greatest animosity was shown, where the Whigs made
violent attacks upon Halifax and Danby, now Marquis of
Caermarthen. In the case of Halifax, the attack was opened
in the Upper House, where the Whigs had a vehement
champion in Mordaunt. The proposal that the King should
be asked to appoint another speaker was unsuccessful and
the motion for the previous question was carried. In the
Commons a more sweeping motion was brought forward, that
it was advisable that Halifax should be dismissed from the
services of the Crown. The friends of Halifax found themselves in a majority of not more than eleven or fourteen.[2]
Strong partisan and quarrelsome feeling became more and
more marked, especially after a prorogation. The most acrimonious question arising before that date was occasioned by
the devotion shown by the Whig House of Commons for
a man whom they regarded as their friend and champion,
Titus Oates.

The whole of the Oates case is complicated, and the issues
primarily at stake were of no great consequence: they merely
concerned the fate of a singularly loathsome informer. Their
importance lies in their having been the cause of the first of
the critical ruptures which took place between the two Houses
during the reign. On March 11, 1688/9, Oates sent in a
petition to the Upper House in which he set forth in detail
the abominable treatment to which he had been subjected,
and begged their lordships to discharge him from his unjust

---

[1] *Lords' MSS.*, No. 154, pp. 283-310.
[2] See Macaulay, vol. iii, pp. 409-10.

imprisonment.[1] The case was taken into full consideration on April 26, when the judges who had tried Oates were called upon to justify their sentence. The other nine judges, the best legal authorities of the day, were unanimous in condemning in the strongest terms the punishment to which the petitioner had been subjected. Nevertheless, when the main question was put, whether the judgment should be reversed, it was resolved in the negative by 35 votes to 23. A protest was signed, in which it was argued that the whole matter had been outside the power of the King's Bench; the judgment had been barbarous, inhumane, unchristian; the vote of the Lords would encourage similar judgments in the future; Holt, Pollexfen, and Atkyns had declared the sentence to be contrary to law and precedent.[2] Only a few days previous to the sitting at which the Peers resolved not to reverse the sentence, a printed paper circulated by Oates had been brought into the House. It had been resolved that it contained matter tending to a breach of the privilege of the House, and this motion had been carried by 29 votes to 18. There were weighty objections to this action as to the other. It did not appear in what respect the paper had infringed privilege. It had been addressed to both Houses, and therefore the vote of the Lords was likely to breed dissension between the Chambers.

The truth is that considerations of policy or prudence, and even considerations of justice, were silenced at the sight of the man who had brought misery upon some of the highest families in the land. Nottingham for one made the exceedingly injudicious speech which so exasperated his sovereign. He declared that as Oates had been whipped from Aldgate to Tyburn, the best way to reverse his sentence was to have him whipped again from Tyburn to Aldgate.[3] All the latent prejudice of the Peers, all their class feeling, all their natural

[1] For the Oates case see the following papers in *Lords' MSS. 1689-90*: No. 31, Oates' Petition; No. 49, Oates *v.* Rex (Writ of Error); No. 50, Oates *v.* Rex (continued); No. 51, Oates *v.* Duke of York (Writ of Error); No. 54, Petition of Titus Oates (pp. 76–84); No. 138, Oates, Reversal of Sentence Bill. See also Chandler's *Lords' Debates*, vol. i, pp. 364–85, and Torbeck's *Parl. Debates*, pp. 453–6, 457–65.

[2] *L. J.*, vol. xiv, p. 228.

[3] See Foxcroft's *Life of Halifax*, vol. ii, p. 218.

repugnances were aroused. The sufferings of the wretched petitioner might indeed have been terrible: they could not have been as great as those which he had gratuitously brought upon the nation. Instead of showing mercy the noble lords cavilled at the informer's assumption of the title of Doctor of Divinity. But they had placed themselves in an untenable position. They had shown that their attitude was the result simply and solely of sentiment. They refused to bow the knee to the besmirched idol of a perverse and wicked generation, the Whigs in the House of Commons. Even to grant justice seemed humiliation. But they proceeded to make their position still more indefensible when they petitioned the King to grant a pardon to Oates. The retort was obvious. What was wanted was not mercy, but justice. The petition was in fact a confession of weakness. The Commons proceeded with a bill of their own for the reversal of the sentence against Oates. In the preamble they stated that the verdicts against the Doctor had been corrupt. When the bill was discussed in the Lords, it was decided to omit this statement. The debate was adjourned till next day, when the preamble to the enacting clause was considered. Objection was now taken to a clause asserting that the verdict of the King's Bench had been 'erroneous, cruel, and illegal, and ... of evil example to future ages'. When the question was put whether to agree to the preamble, it was resolved in the negative, but only by six votes (41 to 35). Eventually two terminological amendments were agreed to,[1] and a proviso was introduced to the effect that Oates should never again be allowed to appear as a witness. With these amendments the Commons refused to agree. A free conference, at which the case for the Lower House was led by Somers, proved unavailing. The Lords determined to adhere to their amendments by 48 to 38, and the bill had accordingly to be dropped.

Macaulay has suggested, probably with truth, that the conduct of the Lords in the Oates case was responsible for

---

[1] Instead of *erroneous* to read *unprecedented*; after *illegal and of evil example for future ages* to read *that the practice thereof ought to be prevented for the time to come.*

the way in which the Commons treated the Bill of Rights. The famous Declaration had passed through the Convention without any difficulty and with no important alteration. But when the bill which incorporated the terms of the Declaration came up for discussion, the Lords added four notable amendments. The first, which was proposed by Burnet at William's own request, settled the crown in default of issue to Anne on the Princess Sophia, 'as being the next Protestant in the lineal succession of the royal family, and to the heirs of her body.'[1] The second amendment added to the clause disabling Papists from succeeding to the crown, the words 'or such as shall marry Papists'. Burnet proposed the insertion of still a third clause, absolving subjects from their allegiance should any such marriage take place. The last of these four amendments was to leave out entirely the last portion of the bill, which related to the *non-obstantes*, i. e. put strictures on the dispensing power of the Crown. With these amendments the Bill of Rights was returned to the Commons, who rejected the first without a dissentient voice, and also negatived the fourth. Conferences proved useless to produce agreement, and the bill had to be dropped. The reason for the opposition of the Lower House to the very prudent and reasonable first amendment regarding the succession is doubtful. Burnet, ever on the alert to detect republican machinations, sees in it nothing less than a design to extinguish monarchy and to bring the succession to a speedy end. There was undoubtedly a strong republican following among the Commons, but this fact supplies no sufficient explanation of the united action of the House. The reason suggested by Macaulay is much more plausible: that the House was actuated by resentment against what it considered the scandalous conduct of the Peers in connexion with Oates's petition.

As time went on, the relations between the two Chambers had been growing more and more strained. The friction came to burning-point on the question which had proved the bone of contention all through the sitting of this first parliament: the

[1] See *Lords' MSS. 1689-90*, No. 174, pp. 345-9; Burnet, vol. ii, p. 15; *L. J.*, vol. xiv, pp. 215, 218, May 22 and 24.

question of vengeance or pardon for political foes. The Whig majority in the Lower House made plain their dislike of William's expedient of indemnity.[1] It was insinuated that the King's desire for mild courses revealed undue fondness for his prerogative; that he wished to grant pardon to all the ministers of the late reigns simply in order that he might have servants in his employ as obsequious as the servants of former princes. The Whigs showed great keenness in drawing up a long list of exceptions from the indemnity, so as to nullify the effect of the Indemnity Bill as far as possible. The whole of the Lower House evinced an incomparable zeal for inquiring into abuses. They annoyed the sovereign by drawing up a resolution for making a settlement upon Anne before they had settled one upon him.

It is not to be wondered at that William lost patience. His efforts to tranquillize the country were proving unsuccessful owing mainly to the animosities of that party which might have been expected to be his greatest assistance. It was already clear that William's policy of maintaining an equipoise between parties was faced with two great obstacles. The first was the intensity of party feeling, the second the inherent spirit of opposition subsisting between the two Houses of Parliament. To quote Dalrymple, whose remarks upon the political situation are often very illuminating, 'the state of mutual opposition in which these assemblies had stood for half a century, the antipathy of individuals against each other in the last two reigns, some present jealousies in the Peers of the interests of their own order, together with a belief they entertained, that the present House of Commons had hostile intentions against monarchy itself, mingled private passions with political divisions.'[2] With the intention of preventing the Commons from proceeding with the dangerously controversial subjects upon which they had been engaged, the King first adjourned and then prorogued parliament.

But when the House reassembled, it was at once proved that the Commons would not allow themselves to be baulked

[1] See Grey's *Debates*, vol. ix, p. 253.
[2] Dalrymple, Part II, Book III, p. 103.

so easily. Not even the case of Oates itself had occasioned such friction as was aroused by the Corporation Bill. It being rumoured that the Tories were making headway at court, and that they were pressing for a speedy dissolution, the Whigs determined upon a decisive stroke which should result in the establishment of a permanent ascendancy of their party in all future parliaments.[1] The primary purpose of the bill was perfectly just and necessary. Parliament had been corrupted by the Crown's tampering with corporations. It was therefore to be enacted that all surrenders of customs and franchises to the Crown had been illegal and should henceforth be regarded as null and void. So far there could be no legitimate objection to the measure. But in the report stage in the Commons, a further clause was proposed by Sacheverell, that all who had been concerned in delivering up of charters without the consent of the whole municipal body should be turned out of all corporations, and be incapable of holding office in them for six years. The Tories realized the ulterior purpose of Sacheverell : that it sought to make the House of Commons no better than a Whig monopoly, at any rate for the period specified in the clause. Both parties understood that the fight upon which they were engaged was critical. The Tories brought up their full strength and fought so well that in the end the Whigs yielded, and it was shorn of its most objectionable clause that the Corporation Bill reached the Upper House.[2] They took into consideration the declaratory part, and asked the opinion of the judges as to the legality of the practice of surrendering charters. Here they found disagreement. The opinion of the committee which sat upon the question was exactly divided as to the desirability of retaining the first clause. According to rule, therefore, it was omitted, i.e. the word 'declared' was left out, as also the phrase 'were and are illegal and void'. When the committee reported it was resolved to agree by 51 votes to 43. A protest was signed by nine peers, including the staunch Whigs—Herbert,

[1] Burnet, vol. ii, p. 38.
[2] For the proceedings of the Lords on the Corporation Bill see *Lords'*
MSS. 1689-90, No. 208, pp. 422-33.

Macclesfield, Montague, and Sidney. The bill dropped with the prorogation with which William put an end to the parliament.

William had indeed grown tired of his first parliament with very good reason. The Commons, besides prosecuting such schemes as the Corporation Bill, had occupied their time chiefly in attacking their enemies, especially Caermarthen and Halifax, in critical inquiry into the conduct of the Irish war, and in diligently proceeding with their bill of Pains and Penalties. William's position was difficult. He wanted to side with neither party; but events seemed to show that he must side with one or the other. Tory principles were not Revolution principles. Yet it was from the Whig stronghold in the House of Commons that William had met with the greatest opposition to his wishes. He complained that the Commons treated him like a dog. Their usage 'boiled upon his stomach'.[1] The prorogation was in effect a blow struck by the King for the Tories. They were being hard pressed at the time; their opponents were growing more and more urgent against them. The Sacheverell clause in the Corporation Bill might be followed up by similar expedients, and the whole position of the Tories jeopardized.

But the crisis concerned not only the relations of the two parties; it concerned also the relations between the two Houses. The attempt to form a Whig oligarchy in the Lower House involved an attempt to aggrandize the powers of that House. The triumph of the election at the opening of the reign had given an impetus to the Whig majority to enhance the influence of the Chamber in which they were collected. Their attempt to settle the succession in the first place had met with opposition in the Lords. From that time right through the two sessions of the parliament they had carried on an attack upon the citadel of conservatism, an attack which might with almost equal truth be termed a Commons' attack as a Whig attack. Partly, of course, because the Tories were stronger in the Lords and they were on the defensive, there was much less animosity shown in

[1] Foxcroft's *Life of Halifax*, vol. ii, p. 207.

the Upper than in the Lower House. Not that it was by any means absent, as the Oates case proves. But on the whole it may certainly be said that the Peers showed more of the spirit of conciliation, entered more into the King's desire for peace, than did the Commons. It was only natural that the House of Lords, with its sympathy for the Church and for legitimist doctrine should seek to do its best for the non-jurors. But it was the House of Lords also in which the endeavour originated to bind together all the Protestant subjects of the Crown. There were not wanting in the House ardent Whigs to support the proceedings of their brethren in another place. Yet the ardour which breeds factiousness was tempered and controlled by the more solemn atmosphere which belongs to the Upper House in the legislature. The tradition of the House impelled to peace in times of political crisis. There were in it forces which served in some degree to counteract extravagant tendencies in the Commons. In the Commons there was the desire to make of the Revolution a party triumph, to consider it as only the stepping-stone to some further consummation, which should be in favour of the Whigs. The conservative forces in the Upper House were directed to the end of making the Revolution as far as possible acceptable to all parties, of making of it a permanent settlement.

CHAPTER VIII

THE LORDS AND THE CONSTITUTION

THE House of Lords had been party to a revolution which was at once dynastic and constitutional. To the average peer perhaps the first aspect was the more apparent. He was probably much more interested in his own personal relations with the new sovereign than in those of his class with the new constitution. The very manner in which legislators attacked their problem attracted more attention to the dynastic than to the constitutional aspect. Primarily their efforts were directed to securing the Protestant succession. That at the same time they should seek to make certain constitutional changes was made to appear almost haphazard. For future generations the important fact was to be that the English throne had ceased to be strictly hereditary ; that the Crown had become not divine but parliamentary in origin ; that in this change the philosophic basis of a despotic system of government had been given the death-blow ; that henceforward what we term specifically constitutional government would progress more smoothly. But contemporaries were compelled by the exigencies of their position to fix a great deal of their attention upon the problem of how to maintain the dynasty, whose security alone would enable them to reap the constitutional benefits which had been rendered possible. Tory nobles found themselves required to join associations for the defence of their Majesties, to take oaths of allegiance or to abjure solemnly their late sovereign and all machinations in his behalf. They were asked to swallow the phrase 'rightful and lawful' as applied to the present settlement. The Whigs took delight in endeavouring to force them from their position of illogical compromise. But even among Whig peers there was a feeling that being required to take oaths at frequent intervals was

a thing obnoxious in itself. Philip, Lord Wharton, said that
he had taken abundance of oaths in his time. He hoped God
would forgive him if he had not kept them all. He could not
pretend to remember them all.[1] Even the ardent Macclesfield
was of opinion that the ' chief effect of demanding oaths was
to make men desperate against the government '. The wisdom
and the efficacy of the expedient of demanding declarations of
allegiance may alike be doubted.[2] Certain it was, however,
that means of security had to be taken to guard a constitutional and dynastic settlement which was constantly being
exposed to fresh perils. The Act of Settlement is a great
constitutional measure ; but it was in the first place simply
an expedient, just as the Abjuration Bills were, to deal with
the immediate exigencies of the situation.

Had the proposal made by the Lords in connexion with
the Bill of Rights been accepted by the Commons, the death
of the Duke of Gloucester in July 1701, the only surviving
son of the Princess Anne, would not have called for any fresh
legislation. As it was, a further settlement of the succession
was rendered immediately imperative. As new regulations
with regard to the succession had to be made, so it was
resolved to take the opportunity to make new regulations
with regard to the constitution, on the lines laid down in the
Bill of Rights. The account given by Bonet of the Act of
Settlement makes somewhat curious reading. To him it was
not surprising that it should be the Tories that were responsible
for the bill.[3] He was only apprehensive of the opposition of
the Whigs, of the republican party, who might take the opportunity to introduce their anti-monarchical schemes. His chief
hope for the passing of the measure without objectionable
features was in the intervention of the House of Lords. It
was they, in Bonet's opinion, that would prove most zealous

---

[1] Burnet, vol. ii, pp. 43-4.
[2] A favourite argument was that all new impositions were, so to speak,
a breach of the original oath tendered at the beginning of the reign.
' Things of that kind ought to be fixed and certain, and not mutable and
endless.'
[3] F. L. Bonet, D. pp. 241, 273 : July 30/August 10, September 6/17
1701.

for the security of the succession ; at the same time the very motives which would make them zealous for this would also urge them to oppose the constitutional provisions of the bill. Yet in point of fact the Act of Settlement passed quite easily through the Upper House without amendment.

It was indeed generally anticipated at the time that the measure would meet with opposition in the Upper Chamber.[1] Could the peerage be expected to view with equanimity the new regulations, which entrenched on royal authority? Did not these limitations mean that the ultimate power was devolving upon the people, or rather upon the leaders of the House of Commons, who ruled by faction and interest? Monarchy and peerage alike would suffer. In a word, was not the balance of power about to be changed? It would be difficult for the Upper House to keep the Lower within bounds. It was expected that the Peers would insist upon certain stipulations concerning their privileges, and that there would consequently ensue a quarrel between the two Houses, which were already embittered on the subject of the Whig impeachments. These prognostications were not fulfilled, although one or two interesting proposals with regard to the peerage were made during the passage of the bill through the Upper House. Devonshire advised that a clause should be inserted to prevent the reckless creation of peerages. It was absurd, he insisted, that men might be made peers, even though their fathers were tailors. The most important motion was one brought forward by Longueville, who revived a scheme which had been mooted before. It was that those persons who should henceforward be created peers must possess a certain amount of landed property—for example, £3,000 for a baron, £4,000 for a viscount, and so forth—and that this property should be inalienable from the peerage. The idea was a favourite one with their lordships, who, however, rejected all these suggestions, and the bill was passed in its original shape. At the

---

[1] It is interesting to contrast the earlier passages in Bonet's *Dispatches* where the question of securing the succession after the death of the Duke of Gloucester is first discussed with the passage dealing with the actual Succession Act, E. 80 : March 11/22, 1700/1.

third reading there were five peers who recorded their protests, Huntingdon, Plymouth, Scarsdale, Guilford, and Jeffreys.

The acquiescence of the Lords in the Act of Settlement does not want for an explanation. Some light is thrown upon the subject by Burnet in his somewhat partisan account.[1] He is anxious to throw discredit upon the promoters of the bill. He admits that the new ministers spoke of the project with much zeal. But he adds ' those who were still jealous of their sincerity' looked on their conduct as a blind. He considered that the whole manner in which the act was managed was suspicious and showed no tokens of sincerity on its authors' part. The affair was, he complains, put off from day to day and gave place to the most trifling matters. But it is not of delay merely that the Bishop complains ; it is of indifference as well. ' The committee', he tells us, ' once or twice sat upon it, but all the members ran out of the House with so much indecency, that the contrivers seemed ashamed of this management.' Upon this passage it has been justly commented, ' If this be true, neither party seems to have given themselves concern, at this time at least, about the Hanoverian Succession.'[2] Burnet, in his eagerness to prove his point, has proved a great deal too much. But he has probably revealed the truth. Neither party was immensely interested in the Act of Settlement. In comparison with the Impeachments, the great subject of contention which had been exciting the political world, all else became insignificant. Unless the whole question of the Revolution state was to be fought out afresh, unless the Tories were definitely to declare themselves Jacobite, the Succession Act must be regarded as a non-party measure in its primary provisions at all events. The Lords may not have liked the new constitutional clauses ; on the other hand, they knew that the

---

[1] Burnet, vol. ii, pp. 270–1.

[2] Dartmouth's comment upon the above passage in Burnet. Cf. Dalrymple, Part III, Book II, p. 217 : ' When the Whig party in England assumes the credit of placing the family of Hanover on the throne, they belie all history to serve themselves. For they opposed and defeated the settlement, soon after the revolution, and gave themselves no trouble about it at the end.'

succession must be secured, that circumstances would not brook delay.[1]   Thus they hesitated to introduce amendments in view of the already serious state of friction existing between the Houses, lest the bill should be lost altogether.

One other consideration had no doubt weight with the Lords, as it certainly had with William himself.   The constitutional clauses of the measure after all referred to a future date, to the time when the new Hanoverian dynasty should sit upon the throne of England.   Of what use was it to risk the loss of a bill which was of instant necessity by quarrelling over stipulations which might after all never take effect?[2] The truth is that the Act of Settlement is not altogether such a commanding landmark in our constitutional history as at first sight it appears.   It was to a very large extent abortive.[3]   And although contemporaries could not forsee this, still it seems clear that it did not arouse the keen interest usually devoted to a measure of first-class importance. Practically considered, the act ranked at the time not so much with the Bill of Rights as with the numerous expedients by which the government sought from time to time to secure the Protestant succession.   If this interpretation of the Act of Settlement be the correct one, it then becomes clear that from their attitude towards this measure we can obtain no certain light as to the attitude of the House of Lords on constitutional questions.   It would at all events be very rash and premature to imagine that because they passed the act, they had necessarily any sympathy with the spirit of its constitutional clauses. We are on much firmer ground when we proceed to consider the attitude of the Upper House in regard to other constitutional legislation of the reign, notably that which concerns the powers and influence of the House of Commons.

We find during our period a persistent attempt to purify the House of Commons by the introduction of two main schemes of reform, viz. those embodied in the Triennial Bills and Place

---

[1] F. L. Bonet, E, p. 205 : May 20/31, 1701.

[2] See Émile G. Boutmy's *Études sur Droit Constitutionnel* (Paris, 1885), p. 54.

[3] The two great constitutional clauses, i. e. those referring to the Privy Council and to Office-holders under the Crown, were both abortive.

Bills with which we are frequently meeting. The Triennial
Bills have to be distinguished from the abortive Triennial Act
Revival Bill of November 1689, which sought to revive the
act of Charles I for Preventing of Inconveniences happening
by the Long Intermission of Parliaments.[1] The object of the
later bills was quite different from this. They dealt with the
duration of parliaments, and not with the intervals between
them.[2] The first of these was introduced in January 1692/3,
and in the Upper House.[3] It was brought forward by
Shrewsbury and was entitled ' an act for the frequent meeting
of parliaments '. What it stipulated for was not triennial, but
annual parliaments. Parliament must be held at least once
every year. In the second place, should the sovereign fail to
issue writs, the Lord Chancellor is to do so upon his own
authority. Such was the original scheme of the measure
which subsequently ripened into the Triennial Bill. As re-
drafted by Mr. Justice Rokeby it assumed a very different
guise. The compulsory clause was dropped altogether; the
whole baldness of the original draft disappeared. Now for the
first time the idea of the triennial duration of a single parliament was introduced. By a very strange oversight, although
the first section of the bill still required that Parliament should
sit every year, there followed a stipulation that there should
not be a longer interval than three years between different
parliaments. This curious inconsistency was removed by
an amendment of the Commons, which the Lords accepted ;
and the bill then became a Triennial Bill in the modern sense
simply and solely.

The arguments used in the debates on the bill in the Upper
House were such as might be expected. Those who feared
the influence of the electorate held that short parliaments,
involving as they did frequent appeals to the country, were

---

[1] *Lords' MSS. 1689–90*, Nos. 171, 191, pp. 343–4 and 364–77.

[2] The Triennial Act of 1664 is one in the same sense as that of 1641,
from which it differed only in the absence of the compulsory clauses
which distinguished the enactment of the Long Parliament.

[3] For the first Triennial Bill see the following: Burnet, vol. ii, pp.
106–7 ; Torbeck's *Parl. Debates*, vol. ii, p. 359 ; *Lords' MSS. 1692–3*,
No. 660, pp. 299–302.

dangerous. On the other hand, it could be urged that long parliaments produced staleness ; members tended to grow out of touch with their constituents. Some were of opinion that members who had sat together for a long time were apt to treat their sovereign without due respect. Others with perhaps greater force argued that the result of long parliaments was precisely the contrary ; that members were prone to come under royal influence, if the court were given sufficient time in which to exercise its powers of bribery. Whichever argument may have been the better one, it is clear at all events that both court and opposition persuaded themselves that they had reason to dislike lengthy parliaments and to support the Triennial Bill.

The measure, having passed the Lords, was carried in the Commons by 200 voices to 161. But it met with stalwart opposition there. The conduct of the Peers was viewed with considerable suspicion. Their object, asserted Sir Edward Seymour, though ostensibly frequent parliaments, was in reality the dissolution of the present parliament. 'By this bill ', he continued, ' you will take off the dependency of the people on the Crown, and set up the Lords, that have no right, and turn the Commons out of doors. Is it reasonable that the Lords, who only represent themselves, should turn you out that represent the people ? '[1] The Peers had in fact been guilty of unwarrantable presumption in meddling with affairs which did not concern them. It was maintained on somewhat shaky premises, that as the Lords were themselves firm and secure, questions relating to the duration of parliament were the province of the Lower House only. The Peers were denounced as being engaged in a nefarious attempt to draw ' all our causes and fortunes to their bar, where relations and friends decide matters '. Nay, more, in assuming the right to dissolve the House of Commons they were guilty of arrogating to themselves a prerogative of the Crown. In short, according to Sir Richard Temple, the Commons had never been con-

[1] Grey's *Debates*, vol. x, p. 300. See in Grey not only the account of the proceedings on the first reading on January 28, but also of the second reading February 20, pp. 304 *et seq.*

fronted with a greater danger than that which the Triennial
Bill presented. The jealous suspicions of the Commons were,
it must be admitted, quite natural. But if the merits of the
proposition were considered, apart from the question of its
origin, the case for the bill was to the majority a clear one.
Harley harangued against the Lords as much as any one, but
he thoroughly approved of the provisions of the bill. There
were others again who, like Sir William Strickland, confessed
that they thought more charitably of their lordships' intentions, and asked whether it was in any case reasonable to
examine into the motives of those who were performing a real
kindness.[1] To all who had the purification of the House at heart
the bill clearly had great attractions. To the King, however, it
was altogether obnoxious, and he had recourse to the royal
veto. A second bill was introduced in the House of Commons
in the following November. It was lost there by ten votes,
not without suspicion of royal manipulation.[2] Then in
December Monmouth introduced a third bill in the Upper
House identical with the re-drafted measure of January
1692/3.[3] Some record of the ensuing debates has come down
to us, but it cannot be said that they are of especial interest.
Discussion centred very much upon questions of phraseology,
viz. the relative merits of the words 'to hold' and 'to
assemble'. What was really being aimed at was the definition
of a session. Could it be said that a parliament had been
'held' if no act had been passed in it? A proviso was added

---

[1] Grey's *Debates*, vol. x, p. 306.

[2] See *Lords' MSS. 1693-5*, Introd., p. xxi. '"This result", says
Macaulay, on the authority of numerous pamphlets, "confounded all the
calculations of the best politicians of the time." But the *Hush Money*
pamphlet, which he quotes as making Seymour the contriver of its
unexpected rejection, adds in another passage cited by Ralph (vol. ii,
p. 475 note) that Seymour himself had predicted and promised in the
Cabinet, at the time when the King had vetoed the previous Bill, that
the next one would share the same fate and that this had stolen out
as a Cabinet secret. Perhaps the best explanation of the result lies in
the words of Caermarthen in his memorial to the King (Dalrymple,
Part III, Book II, p. 32) that "his ministers agreed in opinion, that
nobody knew one day what the House of Commons would do the next." '

[3] For this bill see *Lords' MSS. 1693-5*, No. 759, pp. 51-3. For an
account of the debates in the Upper House see *MSS. of the Earl of
Denbigh* (Hist. MSS. Comm., Rep. XII, App., pt. v, pp. 215-8).

explaining 'that a parliament shall be understood to be holden, although no act or judgement shall pass within the time of the assembly'. The Tories, Somerset, Nottingham, and Abingdon, would have liked to see the bill rejected *in toto*. All the bishops with the exception of Dr. Watson were, we are told, in favour of the measure, which passed in the Upper House, only to be rejected in the Commons by the considerable majority of 197 to 127. No doubt the arguments which had weighed so heavily against the Lords' interference before were responsible in large measure for the rejection of the bill on this occasion.

It was not long before the measure was once more revived, in 1694. This time it passed through both Houses and received the royal assent.[1] Nothing was said about annual sessions; and as the act was finally framed it was possible that as much as three years might elapse between the dissolution of one parliament and the assembly of the next. This being so, the act did involve theoretically a diminution in the power of the House of Lords, seeing that it was established that there could be no parliament without a House of Commons.

---

[1] Pike, p. 333 : 'This was of greater consequence in relation to the House of Commons than in relation to the House of Lords because it set a limit, for the first time, to the period during which representatives could sit in the House of Commons without re-election. It was, however, of very great constitutional importance, and indirectly affected even the House of Lords. As the principle was now established that there could be no 'Parliament' without representatives of the Commons, a dissolution precluded the Lords from sitting in any Parliament until the writs for the summons of a new House of Commons had been returned, and there was nothing to compel the issue of the writs until three years had elapsed after a dissolution. The Parliamentary functions of the Lords, being now dependent on the existence of a House of Commons, might thus legally be dormant for no less than three years. Practically no inconvenience followed, because there has never been a year in which a Parliament has not met, but, theoretically at least, the power of the House of Lords was curtailed.' Two contradictory views may be taken on the subject of the influence of the Triennial Act on the authority of the Upper House. On the one hand, it may be maintained that a House of Commons which sits only a short time has no opportunity to consolidate its power. On the other hand, it may be said that the Upper House might take a much freer hand with a House of Commons which had sat for a long period and might be regarded as out of touch with the constituencies. The argument that frequent elections must necessarily strengthen the hands of members of the Lower House is weakened by the consideration that the influence of the peerage at elections was in these days so considerable.

When we remember that next to the King's own opposition the greatest obstacle to the passing of the Triennial Bill was the House of Commons' dread of the unwarranted interference of the other assembly in their affairs, it seems at first sight surprising that we do not come across more protests against the Peers' open and persistent interference in what the Commons might very justly consider peculiarly their own affair, viz. parliamentary elections. Yet the pamphlets and broadsides of the day are not full of invectives directed against the Peers on this ground. The very silence of the publicist is indeed evidence of the wide extent of the practice. That the Lords should endeavour to maintain a preponderating influence in the Lower House by obtaining the election of their own nominees was accepted as being so inevitable a part of the prevailing political system that it did not call for particular comment or animadversion. But though we do not discover traces of the system in the pages of the indignant reformer, we find frequent references to it in the correspondence of the day. There are many, for example, in the Portland Papers. Simon Harcourt, wishing to obtain a seat at the elections in 1700, finds that it is too late to attempt any place where there is not 'a commanding interest'. He therefore appeals to the Duke of Newcastle. Will not his Grace come to the rescue, and thereby render a service, not only to Harcourt himself, but to the Church party also?[1] The Duke had special influence in the borough of Westminster. In 1695 he is being appealed to by the Chancellor of the Exchequer to give his agents instructions to assist Montague himself and Sir Stephen Fox, who are joining together to stand for the borough.[2] Fifteen years later we find Newcastle contriving the return of General Stanhope for the same constituency.[3] If we turn to the Vernon Correspondence we find sundry passing references to the electioneering activities of Wharton and Macclesfield in August 1698.[4]

The machinery of electioneering is made very plain in some passages in the Coke Correspondence, contained in the papers

[1] *Portland MSS.*, vol. ii, p. 177.   [2] Ibid., p. 173.
[3] Ibid., p. 222.   [4] *Vernon Corr.*, vol. ii, pp. 145, 152.

of Earl Cowper.[1]   It is not difficult to interpret such a letter,
for example, as the following: Sir Gilbert Clarke writes to
Thomas Coke in February 1700/1, desiring that he may be
allowed a view of the poll-book.   'I am told', says he, 'my
Lady Halifax's letter was stopped by the way a fortnight, till
most of her interest was made against you.   And notwithstanding my Lord Ferrers' orders, you had but a small part
of his interest about Shirley, Bralsford, and that angle belonging to him in those parts.   Mr. Wills, the Duke of Newcastle's
agent, came to Derby with a body of freeholders for both
Lords.'   Evidently in this instance the peers' manoeuvres
have not been as successful as usual, but the Duke of Newcastle may accomplish much.   Another letter to Coke about
this time gives him advice with regard to his own candidature.
It is necessary that he should speak to Lord Roos (son of
the Earl of Rutland), to Lord Hartington, and Lord James
Cavendish.   It is essential that Lord Stamford should either
be actively on Coke's side, or at all events not against him.
His opposition would be fatal.   As a matter of fact Coke was
unsuccessful.   So three weeks after the receipt of the last
letter there comes another, one from Lord Stanhope, who
offers to procure a vacant seat in Lancashire for him, without

---

[1] *MSS. of Earl Cowper at Melbourne House, Derbyshire*, vol. ii,
p. 417 (Hist. MSS. Comm., Rep. XII, App., pt. i).   See also a letter in
Buccleuch Papers (*MSS. of Duke of Buccleuch at Montague House*, vol. ii,
p. 1).   Pp. 245-6, Letter of Sir J. Somers, Ld. Keeper, to Shrewsbury:
'If I am not misinformed, Mr. Penn makes but an ill use of what he
obtained from your Grace, for he is got to Bristol and makes all the
interest he can for Sir J. Knight.   But of this I may perhaps give your
Grace a more certain information.   The business of the Countess of
Middlesex is in such a posture that I am very much troubled that your
Grace is not here to direct us.   The Duke of Bedford is disturbed at the
apprehension of changes, but his agents have endeavoured to make an
interest, and that actually before any notice of the Cambridgeshire
election.   Besides this, so many persons have been engaged for him and
Sir John Wolstenholme, and the appearance is such and it is so universally
understood that your Grace and I gave the first motion in this thing that
I am afraid it cannot be desisted from without a good deal of reflection.
'Let me beg your Grace's opinion in this matter.   Mr. Montague is very
earnest to have the thing proceed, so is Baron Broadbury.   If it does go
on, the under-sheriff (who is a friend) says it would be of great
consequence if the poll might be in Hide Park.   You can best tell if that
may be obtained, and in what manner.   The Duke of Leeds gives a good
deal of roast beef against Mr. Montague.'

the latter's even coming down or taking the slightest trouble in the matter. Illustrations might be multiplied.[1] Perhaps none are more striking than those of the Earl of Rutland's influence. No candidate was very likely to be returned for Leicester unless he enjoyed the Earl's support.[2] There is an interesting letter in the correspondence from Lord Roos to his father, asking leave to stand for Leicestershire, which would be a safe seat. He adds the secret intelligence that the King has been pleased to signify 'he hopes that those who are his friends and have interest will use it for such as are of opinion we were of last session'. King and peerage were often in alliance in order to secure a tractable House of Commons. But this is not the only interest of Lord Roos' letter. It reminds us of the important part played by the sons of peers. The most convenient way in which the Lords could maintain an influence in the Lower House was to send their sons into that House. The practice was widely prevalent; and an examination of lists of the nation's representatives will show that quite a considerable proportion among them were intimately connected with the peerage by family ties. Indeed many of the ablest members of the Upper House had served a novitiate in the Commons before they succeeded to their titles.[3]

In one way or another the task of influencing the House of Commons was not a difficult one for the peer at the end of the seventeenth century. For a man of Thomas, Lord Wharton's tastes the pursuit afforded an agreeable pastime. But it was not necessary to possess sons to act as representatives of the father's interests or to have large sums of money, in order to exert influence.[4] In the days of a feudal aristocracy it was inexpedient for the dependent voter to offend the landed potentate. From time to time the Commons protested against

---

[1] An account of the method of bribing a borough will be found in Lord Campbell's *Lives of the Lord Chancellors* (the biography of Cowper), vol. iv, pp. 283-5. The Duke of Bolton was anxious to secure the seat of Totnes for Cowper, when the latter contemplated entering Parliament.

[2] *MSS. of Earl of Rutland at Belvoir*, vol. iii, pp. 162, 167, 169.

[3] Such, for example, were Savile, Marquis of Halifax, Clarendon, Nottingham, Pembroke, Rochester, Wharton.

[4] See E. Porritt's *The Unreformed House of Commons*, vol. i, p. 547.

the electioneering practice of the Peers. They drew up a series of resolutions in 1691 condemning it; but after the Restoration it was as rampant as ever. A point was, however, gained soon after William's accession, when by act of parliament the Lord Warden of the Cinque Ports was deprived of the right of 'nominating and recommending to each of the said Cinque Ports, the two ancient towns and their respective members, one person whom they ought to elect to serve as baron or member of Parliament for each respective port, ancient town or member'.[1]

The interests of the Peers being what they were, it followed that the different efforts made in the Commons to obtain greater independence did not meet with the co-operation of the Upper House. The question of the determination of disputed elections remained a difficulty. The Commons not unnaturally wanted to be the sole arbiters in such cases, and to exclude the Peers altogether. In January 1690 they sent up a bill to the Lords on this subject.[2] It was stated that there had of late been a great increase in the number of disputes, many of them being entirely unfounded. It had been found that the decision of so many cases by a committee was a hindrance to the business of the House, and that the method of procedure was really an encouragement to the abuse. The remedy proposed was that in the future, instead of being dealt with by a committee, all double returns and 'other matters relating to elections of members to serve in Parliament' should be heard and determined at the bar of the House of Commons, before they proceeded to any other business save the necessary taking of the oaths. This bill was negatived in the Lords on its third reading. The Commons made another, and this time a successful, attempt to settle the problem of unlawful and double returns in 1695.[3] The solution then proposed was that all returns should be made according to the last determination of the House of Commons. In a very thin House the bill passed in the Lords by 27 votes

---

[1] 2 W. and M. c 7.
[2] *Lords' MSS. 1690-91*, No. 377, pp. 251-2.
[3] See Burnet, vol. ii, p. 162; Chandler's *Lords' Debates*, vol. ii, p. 450.

to 20. From their protest we know what were the arguments of the minority, who on this subject may well have represented the opinion of most of their absent brethren. They objected that 'the confirming, by act of parliament, the proceedings in another place, which have never been examined here, is derogatory to the dignity, and inconsistent with the justice of the House of Peers'.[1] They felt—and here clearly the bill touched a very sore point—that the arrangement was tantamount to the creation in the Commons of a court of judicature, an expedient which they declared to be contrary to the constitution of the government and to the practice of all previous ages, and likely to 'contribute to the introduction of evil precedents, and be of dangerous consequence hereafter'. As a matter of fact, the promulgation of the act did not afford a complete solution of the difficulty. There is evidence that the Lords were in the habit of whipping up their nominees and directing how they should vote whenever petitions were presented, and that this practice continued unabated until the passing of the Grenville Act in 1770.[2]

It cannot be said that during the reign of William any great progress was made in freeing elections from noble influence. In 1699, in consequence of the Earl of Manchester's having given a vote at an election in Huntingdon, the Commons resolved 'that no peer of this kingdom hath any right to give his vote at an election of any member to serve in Parliament';[3] and this Standing Order was certainly effective, as there is no further instance of a peer's actually voting at an election. But a subsequent Order of the House, of a more general character, remained a dead letter. It was declared to be 'a high infringement of the liberties and privileges of Great Britain for any lord of parliament, or any lord-lieutenant of any county, to concern himself in the election of members to serve for the Commons in Parliament'.[4] This Standing Order was completely disregarded

---

[1] Thorold Rogers, vol. i, pp. 125-6.
[2] See Porritt, vol. ii, p. 450.
[3] C. J., vol. xiii, p. 64, December 14, 1699.
[4] C. J., vol. ix, p. 654, January 3, 1701/2.

by the peerage; and noble influence at elections was probably even greater in the eighteenth than it had been in the seventeenth century.

As important as the determination of election disputes was the question of the composition of the House of Commons, of the qualifications necessary for membership. In 1696 a bill was introduced, excluding from the House all but natural-born subjects of the realm; providing that every knight of the shire must possess property worth £500 and every burgess property worth £200; and lastly, putting severe penalties on bribery and corruption.[1] This measure had to meet the opposition of the merchant class,[2] of the King himself, who used his vote to defeat it, and also to a certain extent of the House of Lords, who nevertheless passed it. The indignation of the Commons at the fate of their bill found vent in a motion to the effect that whoever had advised His Majesty not to give his consent to it was an enemy to the King and the kingdom. The motion was defeated by a large majority, but this did not betoken acquiescence in defeat. Very soon another bill, similar to the last and retaining the same figures as property qualifications, was introduced.[3] But in order to meet what was considered a legitimate objection to the former proposal, a clause was added, providing that any merchant or trader of seven years' standing, who had resided in a borough for the space of twelve months before the date of election and possessed property of £5,000 total value, might sit as a borough member. This measure contained no such provision against bribery as the former had. The concession in favour of the traders evidently did not give satisfaction, for a number of petitions were presented against the bill by different towns. The bill did not

[1] See the following: L. J., vol. xv, pp. 677, 699, 713; Lords' MSS. 1695-7, Nos. 1016, 1028, i.e. pp. 199-201 and 216-17; Burnet, vol. ii, p. 161; Torbeck's Parl. Debates, vol. iii, p. 164.

[2] The Lord Mayor presented a petition against the bill, representing that it would incapacitate from membership of the House of Commons many 'very eminent merchants and traders of great estates and knowledge'.

[3] See Lords' MSS. 1695-7, No. 1093, pp. 375-8; Burnet, vol. ii, p. 181; Torbeck's Parl. Debates, vol. iii, p. 429.

survive its second reading in the Lords, being rejected by the substantial majority of 62 to 37. It may be asked why it was that the Lords, who had consented to its predecessor, threw out the present measure. No doubt the influence of the King had something to do with the action of the Peers, who would naturally gain increasing confidence in their opposition, as they perceived the extent of the urban feeling against the bill. It certainly is not necessary to see any token of democratic sympathy in their action. If we are to believe Bonet—and we may well do so—the argument which weighed most heavily with the Lords was a personal one.[1] The fact was that if the bill passed into law, it would involve the disqualification of practically all the younger sons of peers and many of their eldest sons, none of whom had as a rule much property of their own. The bill was therefore regarded as a menace to the political influence of the peerage.

Great as was the obstacle to complete independence on the part of the Commons presented by the House of Lords, still greater was the menace of court influence. At no time before or since has corruption been carried on with greater thoroughness than it was under William III.[2] In 1692 much discontent had been aroused by the flagrant misuse of preferment, and the opposition raised an outcry for free and impartial proceedings in Parliament. So many members of the House at this time were officers in the army that the assembly were nicknamed 'the officers' parliament'. This state of things gave rise at the end of the year 1692 to the first Place Bill

---

[1] F. L. Bonet, A, pp. 33 and 56-7: March 10/20, 1695/6.

[2] Burnet remonstrated with the King, who, while professing to refute the necessity of such methods of government, declared 'it was not possible, considering the corruption of the age, to avoid it, lest he should endanger the whole'. Burnet, vol. ii, pp. 42, 86, 105.

Cf. James Drake, *A History of the Last Session of Parliament* (1702), p. 87: 'By these means we have seen at one time in the House, near 300, who all held Places in the King's Pleasure; who together with those whom Secret Pensions, Future Hopes and other Private Engagements draw after 'em, made a Party so formidable, that some great courtiers by whose Inspiration they moved, grew insolent; and within Doors treated those Gentlemen with contempt, who came hither only to serve their country, without any separate regard to themselves; and without Doors, have the Hardiness to promise for the House, before they consulted it.'

of the reign.[1] Its provisions were simple. No member of the House of Commons was in the future to accept any place, office or employment under the Crown; if he did, he was to be declared incapable of sitting any longer. In every such case a new writ must be issued for the election of a new member. The only office excepted from the operation of the act was to be that of the Speaker. The bill passed in the Commons without much difficulty. Those who held offices had not the courage to oppose. On the other hand, those who did not enjoy any form of preferment feared that if they uttered any protest, it might appear that they were only recommending themselves to the Crown for office in the future.

In the House of Lords the Place Bill met with a different reception.[2] The motives which had silenced opposition in the other Chamber had no existence here. There was an exciting struggle, the discussion being protracted for several days. Six hours' debates were unusual, but they were found necessary in this case. As so often happened in the parliamentary history of this reign, the lines of party division were not at all closely adhered to. On the whole Whigs were for the bill and Tories against it; but there were notable exceptions. The Tories Halifax and Mulgrave were amongst the foremost advocates of the bill, which was also supported by such thinly-veiled Jacobites as Ailesbury, Scarsdale, and the Bishop of St. Davids. The Whigs Devonshire, Dorset, and the moderate Godolphin were against it. The fact is that with this Place Bill, as with so many other controversial questions of the day, the fundamental distinction was less one between Whig and Tory than one between Court and Opposition. Devonshire, Dorset, and Godolphin were members of the Cabinet. They with Portland knew well the King's wishes. They therefore joined the bulk of the moderate Tories, such as Caermarthen and Nottingham, Rochester and the great majority of the bishops, who held

---

[1] *Lords' MSS. 1692-3*, No. 643, pp. 279-81.
[2] For the proceedings in the Upper House see the following: *Lords' MSS.*, pp. 279-81; *MSS. of Earl of Denbigh*, p. 212; Despatches of Friedrich Bonet in Ranke, vol. vi, p. 198.

that the tendency of the bill was to sap the roots of monarchy
and to encourage the growth of republicanism. They argued
that it was hard to deprive the sovereign of the prerogative
which all his predecessors had enjoyed of rewarding the
fidelity of those who had served him best; especially hard
when this king was one to whom his subjects were particularly
indebted and from whom they had little to apprehend.[1]

Burnet tells us that the feeling which weighed most strongly
with the opponents of the measure was that it seemed to
establish an opposition between the Crown and the people.
It is notable that the Bishop during the debates on the bill
harangued eloquently in its favour, but when it came to the
point of voting, discreetly absented himself.[2] If he wished to
please both parties, it is clear that he only succeeded in annoy-
ing both. But Burnet was always unpleasantly faced by the
difficulty of reconciling his Whig views with his personal
allegiance to William.

One of the very few speeches delivered in the House of
Lords which have come down to us is one in which Mulgrave
argued very strenuously for the passing of the bill.[3] The
English constitution was, he said, the envy of other nations.
There was a king. Then there was a House of Lords, 'to
advise him on all important occasions about peace and war;
about all things that may concern the nation, the care of
which is very much entrusted to your lordships'. But as the
peerage could not in the nature of the case be very closely in
touch with the generality of the people, there was a House of
Commons, which was to record their grievances. In order
that the functions of the Lower House should be efficiently
performed it was necessary that particular care should be

---

[1] Cf. *Cursory Remarks upon some late Disloyal Proceedings in Several
Cabals*. This pamphlet is printed in *Somers Tracts*, vol. xi, pp. 149
et seq. P. 186: 'Every Protestant gentleman of England, under such
requisite qualifications as the law has established, hath a right to be
elected member of parliament, and nothing can look with a more arbitrary
countenance upon the gentry of England, than a design of this nature;
for it takes away their birthright, and sinks their honour in the esteem of
the nation, as it distinguishes them as men unfit to serve their country,
because they have the honour of serving their king.'

[2] Burnet, vol. ii, p. 106. He passes over this bill rather rapidly.

[3] *Works of Buckinghamshire*, vol. ii, p. 95 *et seq.*

taken of the representation in it. But how could this representation be satisfactory if, after they had been chosen, members 'changed their dependency', as he put it, by engaging in employments inconsistent with their trust? The general carelessness which was apparent in public business was, he argued, largely due to the fact that so many members of Parliament had other interests to attend to than those of the public. The danger was great in every case, greatest of all in the case of Parliament men who enjoyed places in the exchequer. 'Would any of your lordships', Mulgrave asked, 'send and entrust a man to make a bargain for you, whose very interest shall be to make you give as much as he can possibly?' That would be like playing a farce in which the actor holds a dialogue with himself. But really this was no farce, 'for 'tis no laughing matter to undo a nation. But 'tis altogether as unnatural for a member of parliament to ask first in the King's name for such a sort of supply, give an account for him how much is needful towards the paying such an army or such a fleet, and then immediately give by his ready vote what he had before asked by his master's order.' Mulgrave argued that the bill involved no disrespect to the King. 'All that we would prevent', he declared, 'is that a good rich corporation should not choose to entrust with all their liberties a plain honest country neighbour, and find him within six months changed into a preferred cunning courtier; who shall tie them to their choice, though he is no more the same man than if he were turned papist, which by the law as it stands already, puts an incapacity upon him.' With all reverence be it spoken, it was no less the King's duty than his true interest to allow to the nation entire freedom in the choice of his representatives. Mulgrave besought his hearers to reflect how much might turn upon a single vote, and counselled them not to suppose that because the bill did not concern them immediately, they need not be careful in the matter. Let them take warning by the state of the French nobility, who let things slide until the people should be quite mastered, only to find that they were mastered themselves. He considered that the people of this country were easily provoked. Let them not have a new provocation in being debarred from a sense of security in their representatives. There was a real danger that at a time when such vast sums were being expended on the war with France, the people might suppose that the money was not being given, but taken. ' I am sure ', Mulgrave concluded, ' whatever success this bill may have, there must needs come some good effect of it, for if it passes, it will give us security ; if it be obstructed, it will give us warning.'

Mulgrave was not a man of principle, and one cannot be sure how far his attitude on this question was the result of genuine conviction or personal pique against the King or the Court party. But whatever his motives, it is clear that there is a great deal in his argument that necessarily commends itself to readers of to-day. Some such measure as this Place Bill was imperative if the House of Commons was to perform its functions in full health and vigour, and be freed from the enervating atmosphere of jobbery and corruption. But the eloquence of Mulgrave proved vain. It could not carry the weight due to its intrinsic merits owing to the suspicions that unavoidably attached to one so volatile. The Court party spared no efforts to defeat the bill.[1] The different divisions were exceedingly close. On the third reading the bill was passed by 42 to 40. Then, however, a debate arose as to whether proxies entered that day should be allowed upon the question, and it was resolved in the affirmative. The Speaker then reported the proxies to be contents 3, non-contents 7 ; and the bill was accordingly rejected by two votes. The chagrin of the supporters of the measure was very great at finding victory thus snatched from them at the last moment. They consoled themselves, however, with the reflection that they had a majority in the Lower House and were on an equality with their opponents in the Upper. They had been unfortunate in the fact that Shrewsbury and

[1] The Earl of Scarborough inveigled Pembroke, one of the leading supporters of the bill, out of the House, and then returned bringing Schomberg, an opponent of the measure. Mulgrave unsuccessfully raised an objection to their being received at so late an hour in the debate.

several others of their number had been away in the country. They bitterly resented their betrayal by the Whig members of the Council and the perfidy of the Bishop of Salisbury and of the Earl of Macclesfield. They had been beaten only by chance, and they would have better fortune next time.

The next time proved to be a year later (December 1693), when a bill practically identical with the last was sent up to the Lords from the Commons. The former introduced several amendments. To the clause disabling an office-holder from sitting in the House of Commons they added the words 'unless he or they shall be afterwards elected to serve in the same parliament'. That is to say, appointment to an office was to necessitate not retirement from Parliament altogether, but simply re-election. Such a scheme had been offered in the Lords the year before, but had been rejected. In the second place the Peers omitted the clause exempting the Speaker of the House of Commons from the operation of the act. The Lower House accepted the first of these amendments, but not unnaturally rejected the second. A conference was held with the result that the Lords decided by 36 to 25 to give way. The Earl of Rochester and the Bishop of London protested against this decision, being no doubt prompted by their knowledge of the great influence for corrupt purposes possessed by so complete a master in the arts of bribery as Sir John Trevor. They declared with some justification that it was inconsistent that an act professing to provide against corruption should exempt from its operation the man who was calculated to do more mischief than any one else.[1] They did not, however, solve the dilemma as to what was to be done with a Speaker not exempted from the operation of the act. The bill had now passed both Houses. To William's chagrin the Lords had failed him. Once more he had recourse to his veto.

The Commons made another attempt to carry out their design in the House of Commons Officers Bill of March 1698/9.[2] The measure had but a short life, as the Lords

---

[1] Thorold Rogers, vol. i, p. 112 ; *L. J.*, vol. xv, p. 335, January 5, 1694.
[2] *Lords' MSS. 1697–9*, No. 1410, pp. 282–3.

postponed its serious consideration for a fortnight, until the day on which Parliament was prorogued. 'The Lords are much given to favouring the intentions of the court' is Bonet's comment.[1] This time they had not failed their sovereign. In the end the Commons had their way. The persistent demand of the reformers was engrafted in the Act of Settlement, and accepted together with all the other clauses by the Lords.

It must be clear from a review of the constitutional questions which affected the House of Commons during our period, that although there might sometimes be a nearly equal division of opinion in the Upper House, still on the whole that Chamber was distinctly opposed to the other. Generally speaking, it was not in the interest of the Peers any more than it was in that of the King that the House of Commons should become independent. On the other hand, the loyal House of Commons men complained that the Lords were constantly interfering in matters outside their province. This was felt, as we have seen, in connexion with all questions respecting the composition of the Lower House. It was felt, perhaps, even more strongly in connexion with the most cherished of all the powers of the Lower House—control over finance.

It was not until comparatively recent years that the House of Lords had come to be looked on as the enemy by the Commons, when the latter tried to make good their claim to sole control of taxation. In the Middle Ages it was by extra-parliamentary bodies such as the colloquies of merchants, whom Edward III had delighted to consult, that their right had been menaced. In the earlier years of the seventeenth century it was the Crown that was the danger. During the constitutional struggle which ended in the triumph of the Commonwealth the Lords had not been challenged upon the specific question of taxation ; and after the Restoration they made it plain they did not conceive that they had ever surrendered their control.[2] In 1661 they originated a bill for paving and repairing the streets in the neighbourhood of West-

---

[1] F. L. Bonet, C, p. 88; cf. p. 99: April 21/May 1; May 5/15, 1699.
[2] Porritt, vol. i, pp. 548–56.

minster. They were even anxious to provoke a controversy
with the Lower House, that they might demonstrate that
they did most emphatically claim the right to originate,
amend, or reject a money bill. Accordingly they made an
amendment to one. The Commons vehemently protested.
The Lords reasserted their claim. 'We find no footsteps',
they declared, 'in record or history for this new claim of the
House of Commons. We would see that charter or contract
produced by which the Lords divested themselves of the right
and appropriated it to the Commonwealth in exclusion of
themselves. Till then we cannot consent, or shake or renounce
foundations, in the laying whereof it will not be denied that
the Lords and Grandees of the realm had the greatest hand.'[1]
' The Peers appealed to law; the Commons in their answer
to custom. They averred that the Lords had forfeited their
privilege by non-usage. The constitution of the country, in
their view, was not founded simply upon a basis of statute and
ordinances, but upon one of customs and understandings as
well.[2] To which the Lords might well answer that they were
not responsible for the omissions of their predecessors; the
temporary discontinuance of a practice was no reason why it
should not be resumed, seeing that there had been no formal
renunciation in the past. Unfortunately for themselves the
Lords did not stand firm upon their principles. They did
indeed amend another money bill in 1678, but eventually
they surrendered in the dispute which inevitably ensued.
This year 1678 is generally regarded as marking a turning-
point in the history of the House of Lords' control of taxation.
It is from this time that we date the wording of bills of supply :
' We, your Majesty's most faithful Commons, have given and

---

[1] *L. J.*, vol. xi, p. 328, July 30, 1661. There were two precedents in
the reign of Elizabeth. See Pike, p. 343, foot-note.

[2] See Resolution of the Commons in 1671 : ' That in all Aids given to
the King, by the Commons, the Rate or Tax ought not to be altered by
the Lords.' *C. J.*, vol. ix, p. 235. A Resolution in 1678 runs: ' That all
Aids and Supplies, and Aids to his Majesty in Parliament, are the sole
gift of the Commons. And that it is the undoubted and sole right of the
Commons, to direct, limit and appoint in such Bills, the Ends, Purposes,
Considerations, Conditions, Limitations, and Qualifications of such
Grants; which ought not to be changed, or altered by the House of
Lords.' *C. J.*, vol. ix, p. 509.

granted to your Majesty.' The crucial struggle was perhaps fought and decided in the reign of Charles II ; yet there were serious quarrels between 1689 and 1702, which made it clear that the Lords still maintained it to be their right both to reject and amend money bills.

The earliest important dispute of this nature during the reign arose over the celebrated Land Tax Bill of 1692/3.[1] To put a tax of four shillings in the pound on land in any case marked a great innovation, and the bill is important in the history of the House of Lords, if for no other reason, because its members were the greatest landowners in the country. The proposal which the Lords made in connexion with the tax is of especial interest because the part they played has been somewhat misunderstood. Burnet's account of the matter follows upon his explanation of the ill-humour prevalent in the two Houses. He speaks of the factious opposition of Halifax and Mulgrave, who had contrived to win over Shrewsbury. These leaders were, says Burnet, supported by Jacobites and discontented Whigs. 'But', he continues, ' they knew that all their murmuring would signify little, unless they could stop a money bill, and since it was settled in the House of Commons as a maxim that the Lords could not make any alteration in money bills, when the bill for four shillings in the pound land-tax came up, they put their strength to carry a clause that the peers should tax themselves.'[2] It has been properly objected to Burnet's account that what the Peers wanted to do was not to tax themselves, but merely to assess their own property—a very different thing. It can only be said in partial justification of the historian that the phraseology of one of the motions is misleading. It runs, ' that a clause be added for the Peers to tax themselves for their personal estates '. As the question was put, however, there was no such ambiguity. What was to be decided was whether a clause should be added to the bill of the same nature as one in a former poll-tax.

The reference was to the Poll Bill of 1689. The Lords

---

[1] *Lords' MSS. 1692-3*, No. 665, pp. 305-7.
[2] Burnet, vol. ii, p. 104.

had then named commissioners from among themselves for purposes of assessment, and the Commons had made no objection. This was the precedent upon which the Lords acted upon the present occasion, and the Lower House showed inconsistency in refusing to admit the provisos added by the Peers to the Land Tax Bill. There appears some excuse for this, when we remember that although the Bishop of Salisbury had been himself one of the commissioners in 1689, he can now find no defence for the proposal to act upon the precedent. After a futile conference had taken place the Lords began to waver. It was actually moved to recede from their position, because there was more in the proviso than was intended by the House. Mulgrave, however, vehemently demanded delay, urging that a committee should be appointed to examine precedents. This he pressed for several hours, as Burnet confesses, 'with a force of argument and eloquence beyond anything that I ever heard in that House.'[1] It were better, he declared, to have property in Turkey than in England. If the Lords yielded in this, 'they divested themselves of their true greatness; and nothing would remain but the name and shadow of a peer, which was but a pageant.'[2] Burnet adds with evident satisfaction that despite this pomp of oratory, 'the Lords considered the safety of the nation more than the shadow of privilege,' and passed the bill without amendments. They contented themselves with making a solemn declaration of principle. To make amendments in a bill of supply they conceived to be 'a fundamental, inherent and undoubted right of the House of Peers, from which their Lordships can never depart'.[3] Considering, however, the inconveniences which arise should there be any delay in the granting of supplies, they would not insist at this time. Such lame conclusions to assertions of privilege in regard to matters of finance are to be met with not infrequently in the history of the House of Lords.

They showed a more determined front, however, not a month

[1] Burnet, vol. ii, p. 105.
[2] See Friedrich Bonet in Ranke, vol. vi, p. 205, January 17/27, 1692/3.
[3] L. J., vol. xv, p. 190, January 19.

later in connexion with a bill of minor consequence, viz. the
Duchy of Cornwall Bill, brought from the Commons in February
1692/3. The Lords introduced certain small amendments, to
which the Commons agreed with the exception of one, which
restored a former rate of fees. This was rejected because it
was held to involve the laying a tax upon the subject.[1] At
a conference between the Houses the Lords resolutely insisted
upon their amendments, and appointed a committee to prepare
a list of reasons for their firmness. There were no further
proceedings.

A very similar situation arose just four years later in connexion with a bill prohibiting the importation of all East India
silks with purpose to encourage the silk manufacture at home.[2]
A similar measure had been initiated in the Commons the
previous year, but it had aroused hostility and been laid aside
in the Upper House. In the present instance petitions were
heard against the bill. In committee the Lords extended its
operation to all wrought silks imported and all calicoes printed
and stained out of the realm. The Commons would not agree,
first, because they considered the amendment would be injurious
to the export trade; secondly—a more important reason—
because the amendment involved the imposition of additional
penalties, which might originate only with the Commons. The
Lords maintained in answer to the constitutional objection that
to impose pecuniary penalties was no charging of money upon
the people, because ' nothing can truly be called so, which is
within the people's choice not to pay if they please. And
their Lordships cannot imagine how the imposing a penalty in
a legislative way can well be denied to arise properly in this
House; when according to the Law of the Land their Lordships, in a judicial way, are in possession of that undoubted
right by themselves alone '.[3] Whatever may be thought of
the validity of this curious argument, it was obviously not to
be expected that the Commons would acquiesce in a constitu-

---

[1] C. J., vol. x, p. 895.
[2] For the two bills here referred to see Lords' MSS. 1695-7, Nos. 1050,
1051, 1121.
[3] L. J., vol. xvi, p. 121.

tional theory which gave the Lords control over all indirect taxation. Both parties remained obdurate, and the bill was lost.

The vexed question of the Lords and money bills found its way into the discussions on the exceedingly important problems connected with the Bank of England and the currency. There was a natural prejudice in the House of Lords against the Bank scheme, which was supposed to be inimical to the interests of the landed gentry, and a vigorous attempt to throw out the Tonnage Bill, by which the fund-holders were turned into a corporation, was made by the Tories Halifax, Rochester, and Nottingham, assisted by the Whig Monmouth.[1] Their arguments were that the scheme of the Commons was anti-monarchical; that it would make it very difficult in the future to raise money on the security of land; that the scheme would be prejudicial to commerce because money would be lying idle in a bank; that it was hazardous to have so large a sum in a single fund. It would appear that but little attempt was made to controvert these not very convincing objections. What carried the Tonnage Bill in the House were considerations quite extraneous from the merits of the bill. Lord Berkeley put the case thus. Supposing their lordships determined to wreck the bill, what must follow? The Commons being unwilling to allow the right of the Lords to touch a money bill, there would be endless and fruitless conferences, and a great waste of time, although the necessities of the war required that money should be raised instantly, and everything done to enable His Majesty to leave at once for the continent. Nottingham, for his part, was not afraid of a conflict with the Commons, who, he urged, were session by session entrenching upon the peculiar privileges of the House of Lords. The Lords, however, disregarded the appeal to their *amour-propre*, deeming it politic to yield to the pressure of circumstances. The majority upon the bill was 43 to 31, a majority, in Bonet's opinion, of heads rather than of arguments.

---

[1] For particulars of this important debate see Friedrich Bonet in Ranke, vol. vi, p. 247 ; L'Hermitage, O. O., pp. 243-4, April 24/May 4, 1694. The Lords' dislike of the Bank of England induced many of them to lend support to Harley's grandiose scheme for a Land Bank, which proved so complete a fiasco.

Both Houses gave their serious attention to the very pressing problem presented by the ill state of the coinage.[1] But clearly the Commons regarded the activities of the other House with suspicion. They agreed with Burnet's verdict that in the Lords' 'it was not possible to give the proper remedy'.[2] A measure, which aimed at the suppression of the practice of clipping, but which proved certainly unsuccessful in operation, was introduced in the Lords in February 1694/5, and after some haggling was accepted by the Commons. So bad did the state of the currency continue to be that the King in opening his third parliament drew very special attention to the subject. The Lords lost no time in considering the matter and resolved upon joint action with the Lower House. The Commons, for their part, showed no keenness for co-operation, but occupied themselves in formulating Montague's great reform scheme. When the bill reached them, the Lords made several amendments, including the addition of a clause to the effect that the deficiency on all clipped money whatever should be made good. They also objected strongly to the multiplication of mints, which they regarded as dangerous. The Commons would not accept the amendments, because in them 'is a charge, and there are pecuniary penalties laid upon the subject, which ought to have their commencement only from the House of Commons'. The Lords made answer that they regarded the Commons' allegation as highly derogatory to their House, but since the Commons had contented themselves with a bare statement, their lordships answered with as bare a denial of it. The situation produced a deadlock, and the bill was allowed to drop.

It was not long before a second bill with the same object was forthcoming. Although they thanked the other Chamber for its extraordinary solicitude in the subject of the coinage, the Commons were nevertheless determined upon having

---

[1] For the proceedings of the Lords on the coinage see *Lords' MSS. 1695–7*, No. 978, pp. 128–31 ; Chandler's *Lords' Debates*, vol. i, pp. 497–8 ; Torbeck's *Parl. Debates*, vol. iii, pp. 50–2, 423–4.
[2] See Burnet, vol. ii, pp. 140, 147.

their own way. The clause concerning the erection of mints reappeared. This aroused opposition not merely upon the ground of its supposed demerits, but because the Lords considered 'that it is contrary to the known and usual method of proceedings in Parliament that the same clause should by either House be brought into a new bill while it remains undetermined in the old'. Their lordships solemnly warned the Commons against all such innovations in the future, but in consideration of the importance of the coinage question were willing to give way.[1]

If the Lords objected strongly to the Commons' introducing in a new bill a provision to which they had taken exception in a previous measure, they had especially good cause for protest when such provisions were reintroduced in specific money bills, which the Commons defied them to alter. To this undeniable abuse of tacking the Lower House had recourse more than once during the reign. An early instance of it was afforded by the Poll Bill of February 1691/2.[2] Hereon was grafted a proviso for taking the accounts of the public moneys; this had formed a bill by itself earlier in the session, which had been lost owing to disagreement between the Houses. The action of the House of Commons was stigmatized as unparliamentary, highly prejudicial to the privileges of the Peers, and likely to be of dangerous consequence to the Crown.[3] Nevertheless the Lords surrendered owing to the immediate necessity for a bill of supply, contenting themselves with entering in their *Journals* a solemn record for all posterity to witness 'that they will not hereafter admit upon any occasion whatsoever, of a proceeding so contrary to rules and methods of Parliament'. Notwithstanding the emphatic nature of this declaration, they were destined more than once again during the reign of William III to submit to a House of Commons' tack, as in connexion with the great disputes over the Army Disbandment and the Irish

---

[1] The entries of these proceedings from the appointment of the select committee are expunged in the Minutes, and there is no record of them to be found in the *Journals*.

[2] *Lords' MSS. 1692–3*, No. 539, pp. 50–1.

[3] Thorold Rogers, vol. i, p. 104.

Forfeited Estates, which will be fully dealt with in their chronological order in the next chapter.

Indignant protestations, measured declarations of what the House considered its constitutional rights, availed very little when they were not accompanied by action of corresponding firmness. Objection was very reasonably taken by the Duke of St. Albans and others to the withdrawal of the House in the case of the aforementioned Poll Bill. Such pusillanimity they justly regarded as no better than an invitation to further aggression. The Lords were often sufficiently obstinate to bring matters to a temporary deadlock, but in all important cases they eventually submitted. The House of Commons never did. Thus while they made no formal surrender of their claim to intervene in money matters, but on the contrary lost no opportunity of reiterating it, the Peers' position grew weaker and weaker every year. It mattered not at all what the constitutional merits of the controversy might be so long as the House of Commons could appeal to pressing necessities of the state.

CHAPTER IX

THE GREAT QUARREL BETWEEN THE HOUSES

It might almost be said that the parliamentary history of
the reign of William III resolves itself into the record of a
series of quarrels between the two Houses. At the very
outset they made their appearance. The initial question
whether William should or should not be King of England
occasioned a dispute. The question of revenge or indemnity
drove the Chambers into hostile camps and made the tale of
the first parliament of the reign one of warfare. And from
that time onward the Houses were constantly coming into
collision, disagreeing in a way which rendered it increasingly
difficult for harmony to be restored after each successive
dispute. Now it was the privileges of the Lords, the exclusive
judicial powers they claimed—such questions as that of the
trial of peers—that gave occasion for ruptures; at another
time it was the rights of the Commons, their control of taxation or, again, their attempts at the reform of their own House.
Notable as is this state of discord between the Houses at all
times during the reign, it becomes especially acute in its later
years. After the Treaty of Ryswick there ensues a series of
disputes which has in it something so dramatic that it is best
considered in its entirety. This great quarrel becomes more
and more envenomed until it culminates in the story of the
Whig impeachments.

The Treaty of Ryswick marks an epoch in the history of
the reign. Up to then the country had been involved in
a great war, during part of which it had been in fear of
invasion. The national danger had inevitably had the effect
of uniting all sections of the community to a certain extent.
But now that there were no distractions abroad men had time
to think more of their own small enmities. For William

himself, forced henceforward to live more among a people whom he did not understand and did not like, the change from war to peace was not a happy one. Amid the general rejoicings, moreover, he alone clearly understood that the peace would not be permanent. He could not persuade the nation that preparation for war was still necessary.[1] A standing army and the taxes necessary to maintain it were alike unpopular. When the King expressed his opinion in favour of keeping up a land force the Commons seemed to regard it as an injury that he should offer advice to them, his advisers. William thought 15,000 troops necessary ; the Commons would only agree to 8,000. The army question was not yet over. The second parliament, remarkable for the dispute between Lords and Commons over the case of Charles Duncombe, came to an end. When the third assembled in 1698 the Commons proposed a further reduction in the forces. Thinking that the arena of foreign politics looked very peaceful they concluded that 7,000 troops, all of whom were to be natural-born subjects of the realm, were ample for the requirements of national security. Determined upon having their way, they introduced an army bill for the disbandment of a thousand troops, and tacked it on to a supply bill, as it was feared that the Lords might prove recalcitrant.[2]

There were not wanting in the Upper House champions willing to pick up the gauntlet so rudely flung in their faces. The Tories Leeds, Normanby, Rochester, and Nottingham, were expected to make a strenuous fight on behalf of the

---

[1] William's conduct was unfortunate. He showed perversity in not instructing his ministers as to his precise wishes. The Commons had given their verdict in favour of maintaining a force of 8,000 troops before the government made the official suggestion for 15,000. Burnet, vol. ii, p. 206. See note by Hardwicke on this passage.

[2] There is a severe attack on the conduct of the Commons in the pamphlet entitled, *Cursory Remarks upon some late Disloyal Proceedings in Several Cabals* (*Somers Tracts*, vol. xi, pp. 149–90) : ' Blush ! O heaven ! and let the earth be amazed and tremble ! Tell it not in Gath, proclaim it not in Ashkelon, lest the whole nation be condemned and included in the guilt of a few seditious and ungrateful members, that, having received the benefit of their deliverance from his goodness, durst not trust him with an army to defend their liberties.'

privileges of the Chamber. The situation was felt to be dangerous.[1] The Commons occupied themselves with business of little or no consequence in order that they might keep their attention fixed upon the proceedings of their adversaries. The effect of the anticipated struggle was seen in the sinking of the public funds ; and in consequence of the serious financial troubles which must follow upon a quarrel at this juncture, it was considered by many of the wisest and most influential peers that it would be better both for the nation and the court that the Lords should sacrifice their dignity, as they had done in similar circumstances before, and pass the bill.[2] They felt that it did not make requisite provision for the public safety ; and yet they could not see how matters would be in any way improved by a rupture with the House of Commons. These views were put forward, in particular, by Somers and Tankerville.[3] The latter urged that the King would gain more by conciliation than he lost. If he accepted the bill he would knit the hearts of the people closer to him, and the goodwill of the people was of incomparably greater value than a thousand troops. These two speeches represented the general feeling. Individuals might differ in their ways of looking at the matter, but they nearly all concluded by advising the passing of the bill. Nottingham and those who were most in the confidence of the court maintained silence. It was accordingly agreed that the bill should be read a third time, and it thus passed quietly without a division.

William disguised his anger and gave the royal assent, for which the Peers drew up an address of thanks, in which they assured His Majesty 'that at all times for the safety of the Kingdom and the preservation of the peace which God hath given us, this House will assist and defend your Majesty against all your enemies both at home and abroad '.[4] The incident was not yet quite over. The King could not bring himself to part with his Dutch Guards who had faithfully

---

[1] F. L. Bonet, C, p. 22 : January 27/February 6, 1698/9.
[2] *Vernon Corr.*, vol. ii, pp. 254-5.
[3] L'Hermitage, T.T., p. 83 : January 31/February 10.
[4] *L. J.*, vol. xvi, p. 372.

served him so many years. He was brought so low as actually to petition for pity.[1] He informed the Commons that he had made all arrangements for the transport of the Guards and would dispatch them immediately ' unless, out of consideration for him, the House be disposed to find a way for continuing them longer in his service, which His Majesty would take very kindly'. There was real pathos in this appeal, but it fell upon deaf ears. There is a tradition that when William heard of the refusal of the Commons to accede to his request, he paced up and down the room, at last exclaiming, ' If I had a son, by God, these Guards should not quit me.' There can be no doubt that in consequence of his treatment by the House he did seriously contemplate retirement from the country altogether.[2]

On this occasion the Lords showed a very different spirit from the Commons. They had at least expressed sympathy with their sovereign. A committee on February 8 reported a resolution to the effect that 'as a particular mark of their respect and duty to his Majesty, this committee hath thought fit to declare that they are ready and willing to enter into any expedient that shall be thought proper and consisting with the forms of Parliament for retaining near his Majesty for the year one thousand six hundred and ninety-nine those Guards who came over with his Majesty to our assistance and have constantly attended him in all the actions wherein he hath been engaged'.[3] In the debate on the subject the majority supported Godolphin in his proposal that the Guards should be retained. Normanby agreed that this was a compliment to His Majesty, but would have liked to hear more as to how the proposal was to be carried into effect. Leeds, Stamford,

---

[1] See Dalrymple, Part III, Book VII, p. 179.
[2] See the text of the remarkable speech which it is believed he intended to deliver in Parliament. Dalrymple, Part III, Book VII, pp. 180-1. That it was no idle threat on William's part seems to be proved conclusively by a letter from Somers to Shrewsbury. The former admits that he had found it difficult to believe that the King seriously contemplated retirement, but says that he has had such confirmation of the reality of the resolve that he is no longer able to disbelieve it. *Correspondence of Charles Talbot, Duke of Shrewsbury* (ed. W. Coxe, 1821), p. 572.
[3] *L. J.*, vol. xvi, p. 377.

Tankerville, and Rochester all spoke of the necessity of giving
satisfaction to the King, particularly as the nation was left so
exposed. But there were others who considered that it was
useless to attempt anything after the passing of the bill for
disbandment, from whose operation the Guards had not been
excepted. How could the Lords augment the number of the
troops when it was not in their power to grant the means for
their support ?[1] When the vote was taken there proved to
be 54 in favour of agreeing with the committee's recommenda-
tion, 38 who were not.[2] But as Normanby and others had
perceived, the favourable intentions of the Lords were of no
practical avail, when once the Commons had made up their
minds that the troops must go. The rebuff with which the
Lower House met the King's entreaties was at once followed
by the departure of the Guards.

The next important disagreement between the Houses
arose in 1700 in connexion with the question of the Forfeited
Irish Estates. It is impossible to understand this dispute
without first briefly reviewing the previous history of the Irish
difficulty. In order to do this it is necessary to go back
to the Rebels Attainder Bill in 1690, when Parliament was
busied in strengthening the Revolution state and improving
the conditions of Ireland after the war in that country.[3] The
Commons voted that the sum of one million pounds should be
raised by the forfeiture of the estates of rebels. They introduced a bill of attainder against all persons in rebellion in
England and Ireland, in which their confiscated property was
applied to the charges of the war. It was plain upon the face
of it that it would be difficult to manipulate such a measure
with equity. When the bill became public numerous petitions
were presented for exemption from its penalties upon one
ground or another. So numerous were they that the House
of Commons came to the conclusion that it would be simplest
not to deal with any. When, however, the bill came before

---

[1] *Lords' MSS. 1697-9*, No. 1357, pp. 284-5.
[2] All the thirty-eight joined in signing a protest.
[3] For this bill see *Lords' MSS. 1690-1*, Nos. 370, 374 ; Burnet, vol. ii,
p. 67, pp. 228-30 and 234-47.

the Lords, they determined that in common justice the petitions ought to be read, and proceeded to read them.   In consequence of this it was found necessary to add a great many provisos to the bill, which thus became exceedingly cumbrous, and in the end proved abortive.   In the course of the proceedings the Court party had succeeded in adding a clause to the effect that the Crown should have the disposal of a third of the forfeited estates.   When, however, the bill failed to pass, William promised that he would give no grants from estates confiscated in Ireland.   But at the same time he held himself free to grant such terms to the Irish as circumstances should necessitate.

Rather less than a year after this we find the Houses once more in collision on Irish affairs, this time in connexion with the act for abrogating the oath of supremacy in Ireland.[1] The intention of the bill was to disable all Irish Papists from public offices and from the professions of law and medicine. The Lords objected that the proposal infringed the rights granted by the Capitulation of Limerick, and, therefore, made certain amendments in order to safeguard the privileges of all who were in Limerick on October 3, 1691.   The Commons refused to accept these amendments, and it was only after a third conference with the other House that they at last yielded.   In February 1691/2 a new Irish Forfeited Estates Bill, together with a similar measure for England, came up from the Commons, who were anxious to revive the proposals of their unsuccessful Rebels Attainder Bill.[2]   They did not manage to do this, as the Lords calmly ignored both bills, though reminded of their existence by the Lower House.

After this the matter of the Irish estates did not again become a burning question until the year 1699.   William had disregarded the promise he had made in 1690, and had since rewarded a number of his friends, chiefly Dutchmen, with grants from the forfeited estates.[3]   The chief beneficiaries

---

[1] See *Lords' MSS. 1690-1*, No. 441, pp. 315-19; Murray's *Revolutionary Ireland and its Settlement*, p. 243.

[2] *Lords' MSS. 1692-3*, Nos. 558, 559, pp. 65-72.

[3] Acting on the theory that the estates of rebels became the King's property by the law of treason; and no doubt encouraged by the silence

were Portland, Albemarle, Rochford, Galway, Athlone, and
Lady Orkney, who had at one time been William's mistress.
The grants made to Portland and Lady Orkney were of great
extent and value.[1] In the first session of the fourth parliament the question of these forfeited lands was taken up by
the Commons. They appointed a commission to take an
account of the estates in Ireland ; the commission consisting of
seven persons, viz. the Earl of Drogheda, Sir Richard Levinz,
Sir Francis Brewster, Francis Annesley, John Trenchard,
James Hamilton, and Henry Langford. A clause appointing
these commissioners was tacked on to a Land Tax Bill, and in
this way it passed the Upper House, not without protest.[2]

In order to understand the rights and wrongs of the dispute
which subsequently arose, it is desirable to follow some of the
facts as set forth in the newly published Manuscripts of the
House of Lords concerning this commission. Of the seven
commissioners the first three were Whigs, the other four
Tories, of whom Trenchard, the leader, was a particularly
violent man. The conduct of the Tory members cannot be
too severely condemned. They made it their sole object to
use their opportunity so as to embarrass the sovereign. When
the report was produced, the Whig members of the commission
found that they could not agree with it *in toto*. Some clauses
in it they passed through with misgivings owing to the manner
in which they were expressed, others they could not sanction
at all either because they were not within the powers enforced
on the commissioners or because they were not warranted by
proof. They also complained of most unfair treatment at the
hands of the majority.[3] The report which the Tory com-

---

of Parliament to regard his promises as no longer binding. For a severe
criticism of William's action see J. E. Thorold Rogers's *The Economic
Interpretation of History* (1909), pp. 424-9. P. 428 : ' It was alleged by
Davenant, and alleged with historical truth, that it was not in the power
of the Crown to grant more than a life interest in any part of the Crown
estate, and the precedents for this construction of the law were numerous
and cogent.'

[1] There was no accurate knowledge of the extent of these estates
before the investigations of the commission. There were no maps.
See Murray's *Revolutionary Ireland and its Settlement*, p. 329.

[2] See Thorold Rogers's *Protests of the Lords*, vol. i, pp. 134-5.

[3] See *Lords' MSS. 1699-1702*, No. 1471. Pp. 14-15 contain the letter

missioners presented was eminently calculated to win them popularity, at so high a figure did they value the confiscated estates,[1] and such a rosy picture did they draw of the reduction in taxation which would be possible if the estates were utilized for public purposes.[2] Among the articles in the report to which the minority had objected[3] was one in which the King was accused of having gone beyond the Articles of Limerick in his indulgence, and another in which it was stated that the labours of investigation had been thwarted by men in high position 'from the fear of the grantees and the persons in power whose displeasure is not easily borne'. It should be noticed that the attention bestowed in the report on the Countess of Orkney's estate was a piece of sheer effrontery, as her lands were part of the Crown property, and, therefore, did not come within the cognizance of the commission.

The rancour of the Tory commissioners was equalled by that of the House of Commons when they started their proceedings after the presentation of the report.[4] On December 15, 1699, they resolved that a bill should be brought in for the application of the Irish estates to public purposes. They also resolved that they would not listen to any petitions on the subject,[5] and that they would take into consideration the great services performed by the commission. They followed up this by committing Levinz to the Tower. He accused a certain member of having written a letter to the commissioners recommending the separate reference to Lady Orkney 'because that might reflect upon somebody'. When the

of the Minority to the Chancellor. Attempts had been made to win them over by private letters and instructions which the Tory commissioners said they had received from the House of Commons. Finally, the majority had insisted that unless the minority were prepared to put their names to the whole report, they should not put their names to any part of it.

[1] They grossly exaggerated the value.

[2] Thorold Rogers, *The Economic Interpretation of History*, p. 429: 'If the Irish forfeitures could lighten this load of debt, it was not unreasonable for a people, smarting under novel taxes, irritated at a great direct tax on land, to claim for itself the repayment of those funds, the advance of which had made the Irish conquest alone possible.'

[3] The clauses were Nos. 8, 10, 25, 32, 66, 78, and 79.

[4] For proceedings of the Commons see Torbeck's *Parl. Debates*, vol. iii, pp. 134-9.

[5] Here they followed their own example of 1690.

accused denied the charge, Levinz was adjudged to be guilty
of a 'groundless and scandalous aspersion'. Two days later,
when the Court party proposed as an amendment that a proportion of the estates should be reserved for the disposal of
His Majesty, the proposal was indignantly rejected. On
January 15 a resolution was passed reprimanding all who
had advised the King's grants. The House communicated
the gist of their resolutions in an address to His Majesty, who
replied by coldly suggesting that the Commons had been
neglecting their public duty in not providing supplies. The
curt rebuke stung them to fury. Having dealt with their
King, they now directed their attack upon the Lords by
deliberately tacking their Resumption Bill on to the Land
Tax Bill.

It is well to realize precisely what was the attitude of the
House of Lords towards the bill. It is quite clear that they
were not opposed to the expedient of raising public moneys
from the Irish estates. The finances were not flourishing,
and the proposed expedient was a convenient method of over-
coming the serious difficulty of raising the necessary supplies.
It would at all events have been altogether impossible to
resist a measure so entirely popular in character, however
obnoxious it might be to all who had profited from the royal
grants. But the bill went far beyond the reasonable proposal
of utilizing the confiscated estates to ease the taxpayer.[1] It
provided for the resumption of more than the estates which
had been forfeited after the rebellion of 1689. It resumed
all grants made since 1685, and all property held by grantees
since that date was at a blow to be taken away from them.
The whole of the estates were vested in thirteen trustees,
who included among their number the four faithful Tory
commissioners. It is true that the rights of all except the
actual grantees were safeguarded, but these rights were really
at the mercy of the trustees, and if any unfortunate person

---

[1] See Murray's *Revolutionary Ireland and its Settlement*, pp. 328–32
on the effects of the scheme on Ireland. The Commons' scheme created
almost as great a revolution in real property in Ireland as the
Cromwellian and Caroline Settlements (p. 330).

claiming a right failed to make it plain to their satisfaction he was to be fined heavily for having wasted their time. As rewards were to be offered to any one who gave information as to estates yet undiscovered, which were liable to resumption under the act, it was extremely likely that the security of the poor Irish would be invaded, and their property subjected to an inquisition whose object was confiscation wherever possible. There was, moreover, to be no appeal. Upon that point the Commons were determined. There was, in short, a good deal to call for criticism in the Resumption Bill. It was just one of those pieces of impatient, in part vindictive, legislation which require the intervention of a revising tribunal. But it was not only on the score of its inherent vices that opposition to the bill in the House of Lords was to be anticipated. The animus of the House of Commons had been directed primarily against the sovereign: but it was certain that it would be directed against the House of Lords also, should they dare to take exception to the bill. The device of tacking showed contempt for the Peers. They had with comparative equanimity submitted to it in the last session. What they had then permitted they would have to permit again. They had shown themselves weak, and, therefore, they might be treated without respect. Thus the Resumption Bill distinctly involved an attack upon the powers and privileges of the Lords, and in this light the latter regarded it.

The obnoxious measure was ushered into the Upper House on April 3, 1700. After the first reading Haversham fired up against it, declaring it to be fit only for rejection.[1] This view was taken also by Stamford, Ferrers, and Anglesey; but the drastic expedient of rejecting the bill at so early a stage in the proceedings was not likely to find favour, and the second reading was carried by 70 to 23.[2] On April 8

[1] *Vernon Corr.*, vol. iii, p. 4.
[2] A protest was signed by Richmond, Bolton, Stamford, Anglesey, Mohun, Abergavenny, Audley, and Haversham, in which they gave as reasons for dissent (1) that the bill tended to the alteration, if not destruction, of the constitution, (2) that a tack was contrary to all rules of Parliament, and was dangerous both to the Crown and to the House of

there was an eager debate. Devonshire declared that with
their money bills the Commons were invading the prerogatives of the Lords, and implicitly those of the monarch, since
the peerage stood as a sort of barrier between King and people.
Normanby supported the House of Commons on this occasion.
Leeds delivered a somewhat lengthy harangue to show the
necessity for the bill, but concluded by opposing it. Sunderland,
through fear of affording occasion for his enemies, gave his
opinion in favour of the measure. So did Rochester, though
he insisted upon the privileges of the Chamber. Peterborough
delighted the assembly by a little analogue. He compared
the House to a man whose affairs are in disorder. Some one
proposes that he should take a rich wife. Although the
woman is a baggage the man prefers to take her and live
with a demon than to be exposed to the cruel necessities of
life. Peterborough thought that the man was a wise one,
and that the Lords would do well to follow his example and
obtain security even at the expense of so distasteful a burden
as a tack.[1] After the second reading the bill was returned
with sundry amendments to the Commons.[2]

There was an outburst of fury. The amendments were
unanimously rejected, and a conference clamorously called
for. It was ordered that a list of the Privy Council should
be laid before the House. An idea was abroad that the King
managed the Lords. 'They object to tacking,' cried one
excited member, 'let them take care that they do not provoke us to tack in earnest. How would they like to have bills
of supply with bills of attainder tacked to them?' Seymour,
Musgrave, and Harcourt dilated upon the misery which would
befall the nation owing to the Lords' obstinacy, all to preserve
the grants of those who would beggar the King.[3] At the
conference held on April 9/20 the Commons made it quite
clear that they would accept no amendment at all. Both

Lords, and (3) that the bill endangered the security of property. *L. J.*,
vol. xvi, p. 568.
 [1] F. L. Bonet, D, pp. 123–4; April 9/20, 1700.
 [2] The chief was the alteration of the clause whereby estates which had
not been forfeited were handed over to the trustees.
 [3] *Vernon Corr.*, vol. iii, pp. 12–13.

sides stood firm. Next day there took place a second conference, at which the Lord President produced a number of
reasons why the Houses insisted upon their amendments.

Among the reasons given was that 'though there be nothing
in the said amendments relating to aids and supplies granted
to His Majesty in Parliament, yet the Commons have thought
fit to take occasion thereupon to assert a claim to the sole
right, not only of granting all aids in Parliament, but that
such aids are to be raised by such methods, and with such
provisions as the Commons only think proper. If the said
assertions were exactly true (which their lordships cannot
allow) yet it could not, with good reason follow from thence
that the Lords may not alter or leave out, according to their
amendments, when the saving estates of innocent persons, and
of such as have been outlawed after their death, makes such
amendments necessary.'[1] They had amended a clause in the
bill which instituted outlawry after death. They could not
accept what was equivalent to condemning a man unheard.
Another clause to which they took grave exception was one
which disqualified the commissioners of assize from membership of Parliament. Such a rule, if it was to be made at all,
ought to have formed the substance of a separate enactment.
The Commons had as a matter of fact produced place bills
ere now. 'The joining together in a money bill', pursued
their lordships, 'things so totally foreign to the method of
collecting money, and to the quantity and qualification of the
sums to be raised, is wholly destructive of the freedom of
debates, dangerous to the privileges of the Lords, and to the
prerogatives of the Crown. For by this means things of
the last ill consequence to this nation may be brought into
money bills, and yet neither the Lords, nor the Crown, be
able to give their negative to them, without hazarding the
public peace and security.' Finally, the Lords vindicated
their own conduct in the case, lamenting the inconvenience
which must accompany the loss of the bill and a quarrel
between the Houses, but affirming that they had been desirous
of avoiding such ill consequences by every means in their

[1] *L. J.*, vol. xvi, p. 575.

power, as appeared by the fact that they had overlooked irregularities in former bills, although they had always protested against them. But they had found their kind intentions had had no other effect than to invite further attacks upon them. At no time had they entertained any designs to invade the least right of the Commons. All they wanted to do was to defend their own. Consequently, they regarded themselves as wholly discharged from the suspicion of being in any way accessory to such constitutional dangers as seemed likely to arise.

Neither these arguments nor further conferences produced any change for the better in the situation. Excitement prevailed everywhere. The Commons, having ordered the lobby of their House to be cleared of all strangers, that the back door of the Speaker's chamber should be kept locked, and that the sergeant should stand at the door and permit no one to leave, thus shut off from the outer world and in the heated atmosphere of exasperation, debated upon the obstinacy of the Upper House. Throughout London there was uproar. Westminster was thronged with crowds, so that it was only with great difficulty that any one could approach either House. A rumour was current that the King had come down to the Cockpit and had sent for his crown with the intention of dissolving Parliament immediately. There were many in the House of Lords, as Burnet says, who, though loyal supporters of the King, were yet for passing the bill. They feared that a dissolution would only make matters worse; that the unfriendly Tory majority in the Commons would only be increased in numbers thereby; that the bill would be reintroduced, possibly with even more disagreeable features than before.[1] Burnet himself urged these considerations; and he acknowledges that William was much displeased with him in consequence.[2] Sunderland was another who persistently

[1] Burnet was roused to much excitement during these debates. At one time he so far forgot himself as to shout out 'Stuff, stuff' at an observation made by the Earl of Anglesey. *Vernon Corr.*, vol. iii, p. 24.

[2] Burnet, vol. ii, p. 240. See Hardwicke's note. Burnet confesses that he gave his advice being under a misapprehension as regards the meaning of some clauses in the bill. He did not realize till afterwards how bad they were.

counselled retreat, and Portland and Albemarle sided with him, much as they must have hated the bill.[1]   At last Albemarle and Jersey had an interview with the King in which they counselled that means should be taken to secure the passage of the bill.   They understood that Leeds was aiming at forcing a dissolution.   This they considered could only result in disastrous consequences to the King owing to the state of ferment in the nation.   The scheme they advocated was that the Archbishop of Canterbury, who had been strongly against the bill, should be requested by the King to see that the opposition on the episcopal bench was removed.   There was a saying spread abroad that those who were in favour of the amendments were either bishops, beggars, or bastards. The report of the final conference with the Commons having been made to them, the Lords voted upon the fatal question of whether they should continue to stand firm.   The contents numbered 40, the non-contents 37.   The crisis seemed to be over.   But the tension was prolonged for a few minutes longer. Proxies were called for and were allowed.   The votes were found to be equal.   The Earl of Bridgwater, who presided in the absence of the Lord Chancellor, then gave his vote in the negative, as he was bound to do by rule, and declared the motion to abide by the amendments to be lost.   It was then resolved to agree with the Commons by 39 to 34.   That the crisis had been averted was due to the Archbishop, who, acting upon his instructions, had just before the critical moment risen and beckoned to his brethren on the episcopal bench to follow him outside the House.

The Commons, having won their great victory, now proceeded to turn their wrath upon a special object of execration to them—the Lord Chancellor, Somers, whom the King soon after found it advisable to dismiss in consequence of his unpopularity.   The unfortunate affair of Captain Kidd gave a handle to the enemies of Somers, but a far better opportunity was shortly afforded them when the details concerning the Partition Treaties came to light.

[1] F. L. Bonet, D, p. 137, April 12/23, 1700; *Vernon Corr.*, vol. iii, p. 17.

Englishmen in the days of William III had only hazy ideas about foreign affairs. Even statesmen were lamentably ignorant about them, and in order that the policy of the country should be carried on with understanding William had kept them under his own control, rarely consulting his ministers and only approaching Parliament upon the subject when he needed supplies with which to carry on the war. Except when the country was actually endangered Parliament showed no great zeal for hostilities, and when the Tories preponderated in the Commons there was not much sympathy shown with the King's policy. But, generally speaking, it may be said that apart from occasional outbursts of spleen against the Dutch, the story of parliamentary activity in foreign affairs is told in the customary expressions of loyal support with which communications from the sovereign on the subject were uniformly received. Their main interests being centred in things at home, both Houses of Parliament were content to give the King and his advisers a free hand.[1] Having enjoyed a considerable immunity from criticism William had really no right to complain when their ignorance of foreign affairs led to the Commons' resolve to reduce the forces, and when the revelation of the irregular way in which he had been wont to carry on negotiations on behalf of the realm of England created an outcry against such unconstitutional procedure.

The first step in the consideration of the Partition Treaties was taken by the Upper House in March 1700/1.[2] William's deliberate determination to rouse Parliament against Louis by revealing some of the machinations of the latter inevitably led to more prolonged and serious consideration of foreign affairs

---

[1] Somewhat different attitudes were adopted by the two Houses in 1701. The King maintained that both the safety of England and the existence of Holland were at stake. The Lords' reply was as satisfactory as even William could desire, since they requested His Majesty to set in operation the old treaties and renew the alliance of 1689. The Commons, though fully realizing the perils of the situation, were not willing to go as far as this. They did not consider that the project of alliance with the Emperor was at all warranted, and they were certain that it would be too expensive. See Von Ranke, vol. v, pp. 265–6.

[2] *Lords' MSS. 1699–1702*, No. 1559, pp. 220–73.

than had been at all customary.   In the course of its debates
the House obtained leave to examine all the documents relating
to treaties concluded since the Treaty of Ryswick.   As the
result of the investigation, Devonshire, although a privy
councillor and member of the cabinet, was moved to declare
that those who were responsible for the recent Partition Treaty
ought to answer for it with their heads.[1]   Another peer went
even further, and declared that their heads would not suffice,
though what precisely it was that he wanted besides does not
appear.   After a series of angry attacks upon ministers, which
lasted five hours, Godolphin and Marlborough intervened and
suggested that an address should be presented to His Majesty
to pray him that for the future treaties might be concluded
only in Privy Council.   It was resolved that this temperate
opinion should be expressed in the most decent and respectful
manner possible.[2]   While a committee, at whose head was
Nottingham, was drawing up the address, the Lord President Pembroke, Halifax, Portland, and Somers all made an
attempt to justify the conduct of ministers with regard to the
negotiations—conduct which, particularly in the Chancellor's
case, it is not possible to defend at all, when once the principle
of ministerial responsibility is admitted.[3]   The Lords' address,
reported on March 20, 1700/1, proved to be both firm and respectful.[4]   It was inevitable in the circumstances that it should
contain a reflection on His Majesty, but it was couched in terms
of ' deep humility'.   It was proposed to send to the Commons,
who also had been discussing the treaties, for their concurrence
in the address.   But the question being put, it was resolved in
the negative by 45 voices to 27.   The resolution is notable, as
it forms a sort of prelude to the ensuing quarrel.

The recent debates had occasioned a good deal of rather
violent talk.[5]   There was bickering on the question of the
respect due to royalty.   A peer who spoke disrespectfully of

---

[1] F. L. Bonet, E, p. 91 : March 17/28, 1700/1.
[2] *L. J.*, vol. xvi, p. 622.
[3] See, however, the attempt that Burnet does make, vol. ii, p. 261.
An answer to it is given in Onslow's note on the passage.
[4] *L. J.*, vol. xvi, pp. 628–9.
[5] Torbeck's *Parl. Debates*, vol. iii, p. 152.

the French King was rebuked by another peer, who declared that the King of France was not only to be respected, but also to be feared. A third noble lord retorted 'that he hoped no man in England needed to be afraid of the French King; much less the peer who spoke last, who he doubted was too much a friend to that monarch to fear anything from him'. Normanby spoke with his customary eloquence. He and the other Tories, as Burnet confesses, managed the debates with great dexterity.[1] The Bishop blames William for his neglect in not attending to the manipulation of matters in the House. 'No directions were given and we were involved in great difficulties, before the court was aware of it: the King either could not prevail with his new ministers to excuse the treaty, if they would not justify it; or he neglected them so far as not to speak to them at all about it.' Burnet thought that the Tory lords designed to set on the House of Commons to impeach some of the ministers concerned in the treaties. He sees evidence for this in the motion to send to the Commons for their concurrence in the Lords' address.

In the meantime the Lower House had been proceeding in the matter of the treaties, in a more bellicose fashion than the Lords had done. *They* also had drawn up an address; but it was remarked how different was its tone from that used by the Peers.[2] The latter had directed their attention chiefly to reform; the Commons thought chiefly of revenge. The 18th of April saw the impeachment of Somers. A conference, desired by the Lower House, took place between the Houses, and the Lords entrusted the papers which they had been examining to the Commons. It was well understood that although Portland had been first attacked, the animus of the Lower House was really against Somers, who endeavoured to meet his adversaries' charges in an apologia which he delivered actually in the other House,[3] but whose impeachment immediately followed, together with those of Halifax and

---

[1] Burnet, vol. ii, p. 260.
[2] F. L. Bonet, E, p. 110: March 25/April 5, 1701.
[3] The effect of this speech on its audience is disputed. See Burnet, vol. ii, p. 267, and cf. Dartmouth's note.

Orford. The decision to bring forward these impeachments was carried by only a small majority, and it became doubtful whether the angry party were strong enough to be able to carry through their project.

Up to this point the conduct of the Commons, though possibly marred by a show of personal animosity, had been perfectly justified. They were right in remonstrating against the method in which the recent Partition Treaties had been carried through; they had quite a good case in impeaching ministers for acquiescing in unconstitutional practice. Unfortunately, they now made a great blunder. Being aware of their weakness and diffident of their capacity to carry through their impeachments to a successful issue, the Tories secured the drawing-up of an address to His Majesty, in which they expressed their great satisfaction at having found in their recent investigations that His Majesty had shown great care of his people in not entering into negotiations without the advice of his English ministers. They found that Somers was chiefly responsible for the recent treaty, assisted by Orford and Halifax. These men, the Commons had discovered, had insinuated to the King that he might enter into the treaty without the advice of the Council. The Commons could not but resent such treatment of His Majesty. In order, therefore, that the delinquents might no longer be able to deceive their sovereign, they humbly besought His Majesty that he would be pleased to remove Somers, Orford, and Halifax from his council and presence for ever, as also the Earl of Portland, who had actually transacted the treaties.[1] This address, which amounted to a condemnation before trial, was passed through the Commons, and presented to William. It is not to be wondered at that the Lords were incensed by the action of the other Chamber. What the Commons were endeavouring to do was to render the jurisdiction of the Peers a nullity. What a farce must those impeachments be if the accused were to be punished before the cases were tried and before the victims had even had the chance to make a formal answer to the indictment! On April 16 after a protracted debate it was

[1] *C. J.*, vol. xiii, p. 497, April 16, 1701.

resolved by the substantial majority of 49 to 29 'that an address be made to His Majesty, that he will be pleased to pass no censure or punishment against the four noble lords, who stand impeached of high crimes and misdemeanours until the impeachments depending against them in this House shall be tried.'[1]

Matters hung fire for some little time after the presentation of the two addresses, to neither of which any direct reply was forthcoming.[2] The King contented himself with the vague assurance to the Commons that they might depend upon his employing only such councillors as he could trust. In the meanwhile the names of the impeached lords remained on the Council Book. The Commons ordered a committee to draw up articles of impeachment, but this, by Burnet's account, was only for form's sake.[3] He explains that they considered that they had already done sufficient injury to their enemies, and trusted that the King would not again employ them. As this was their sole object, the Commons were content that the matter should now be allowed to drop. Be this a true account of the situation or not the matter was *not* permitted to drop. The appearance of the Kentish Petition, with its forcibly expressed dissatisfaction with the nation's representatives, stung them to further action. At the same time, the impeached lords moving earnestly for a speedy trial, the Upper House sent a message to the other Chamber suggesting that the articles of accusation should be prepared as soon as possible both in justice to the persons concerned and in order to conform to

---

[1] *L. J.*, vol. xvi, p. 654. See L'Hermitage, W.W., p. 253, April 18/29, 1701. A protest was made against this resolution on the ground that it was unparliamentary procedure 'to take notice in this House of what is represented only by some lords to have passed in the other'. It was signed by Scarsdale, Normanby, Townshend, Abingdon, Bp. of Exeter, Lexington, Bp. of London, Sandwich, Cholmondeley, Caernarvon, Thanet, Weymouth, Ashburnham, Hereford, Granville, Willoughby of Parham, Ormonde, Kent, Rochester, Howard, Poulett, Weston, Jeffreys, and Dartmouth. A debate arose subsequently as to this protest. It was resolved that the reasons should be expunged; a resolution which provoked a second protest against such treatment of a privilege of the House.

[2] For a detailed account of the proceedings of the House of Lords in connexion with the impeachments see *Lords' MSS. 1699-1701*, No. 1615.

[3] Burnet, vol. ii, p. 268.

the methods of Parliament.[1] Thus conjured to proceed, the
Commons submitted the articles against Orford, and also
demanded that sufficient security should be given by the Earl
to abide the judgment of his peers.   The Lords investigated
this demand, and as they could find no precedent, they
informed the Commons of the fact.   The Upper House now
did its utmost to hasten the procedure of the Commons.
As a result of their remonstrances the articles of impeachment against Somers at last appeared on May 19, but none
were forthcoming against Portland and Halifax.   The Lords
reminded the other House of this fact in two messages, in
which they spoke of the hardships under which the aforementioned peers laboured by reason of the delay.   Not until
the 31st did a reply come from the Commons.   In this they
stated that they intended to proceed first with the trial of
Lord Somers.   Secondly, they asserted that for their lordships
to declare that the delay to exhibit articles against Portland
and Halifax was a hardship for those noblemen and not con-
sonant with parliamentary methods, tended ' to the breach of
that good correspondence betwixt the two Houses, which ought
to be mutually preserved '.   The same day the Lords informed
the Commons that they had appointed Monday, June 9,[2] for
the trial of the Earl of Orford, and at the same time they
reiterated their complaint of the hardship under which Halifax
and Portland laboured.   A committee of impeachments met to
furnish material for a reply to the Commons' message.   It
could find no precedent for so long a delay in the past.   So the
Lords were satisfied that they had been amply justified in their
use of the word ' hardship'.   They expressed the hope that
the Commons on their part would be as careful to preserve
amity between the Chambers as the Lords always would be
on theirs.

By this time the Houses had become well embarked upon
their quarrel.   It was clear, especially from their treatment
of the Kentish Petitioners, that the Commons were in a
particularly angry mood.   It was equally clear that the Lords

---

[1] Torbeck's *Parl. Debates*, vol. iii, pp. 175–8.
[2] The date of trial was subsequently postponed.

were determined not to yield to what they regarded as high-handed procedure on the part of the Commons. There was no question of taxation involved here, and the Peers had a much freer hand than in the previous dispute concerning the Irish Forfeitures. If the Commons had then shown themselves resolved to defend their peculiar privileges in money matters, the Lords now showed themselves equally disposed to stand firmly by precedent as regards their judicial privileges.

The Commons sent an aggrieved answer to the Lords' communication of the 31st. They said that in their opinion it was their undoubted right, when several persons stood impeached together, to bring to trial first whichever they thought fit. They considered that their lordships' proceedings were consistent neither with justice nor reason. They wished for Somers to be tried first, and, therefore, they were unable to agree to the day appointed for the trial of Orford. On the 6th of June a free conference took place at which Harcourt, the chief manager for the Lower House, explained that they had desired to confer with their lordships in order to preserve the good relations between the Chambers which they considered the Peers had endangered. In order to prevent differences in the future conduct of the impeachments, the Commons proposed the appointment of a joint committee of both Houses. The Lords certainly at this juncture showed themselves in a most unconciliatory mood. They refused to consent to the Commons' scheme.[1] They expressed astonishment at the expressions used by the other Chamber, which were such as they conceived had never before been used by one House to the other, and which, if repeated, could only have the result of destroying all good correspondence between the Houses. They concluded by the pious declaration that they thought that they had given convincing proof of their moderation and of their sincere desire to preserve the amity between the two Houses.

Meanwhile the Commons were considering the last communications from the other House. They made answer to it

---

[1] *L. J.*, vol. xvi, p. 730. Twenty-one lords protested, averring that a similar joint committee had met in 1679 in connexion with the trials of Popish lords. There was therefore a precedent. Ibid., p. 731.

in an injured tone. They thought they might justly have expected their lordships' compliance in their request. For their part they claimed that they had shown great moderation and a sincere desire for concord; witness their proposal for a joint committee, upon which they still insisted. There were one or two important questions which they considered ought to be settled, viz. whether the impeached peers should come to the bar of the Lords as criminals; whether they were to sit as judges at each other's trials or be permitted to vote in their own cases. If the request for a joint committee were not conceded, they asserted that it would mean the end of the rights of the Commons of England as shown by unquestionable precedents and the usage of Parliament. Another result would be that all impeachments would be rendered impracticable for the future; and impeachments were the greatest bulwark of the laws and liberties of the land. The Peers were quite willing to answer the specific questions of the Commons, but they were still resolved to dispense with the latter's co-operation. Thus they decided 'that no lord of parliament, impeached of high crimes and misdemeanours, shall upon his trial be without the bar'; and, secondly, that no peer could be precluded from voting on any occasion save at his own trial.[1] Another message came from the Lower House, principally directed against the date of the trial. The appointment of so near a date was such a hardship to them and such an indulgence to the accused—so they declared—as could not be paralleled in any parliamentary proceedings. In short, it would be preposterous for them to enter upon the trial of the impeached lords until the Upper House revealed some inclination to make it practicable. They insisted that a later date should be fixed for the trial. But the Lords would not agree. The session was far advanced already, and there was urgent need for haste, if the impeachments were to take place at all before Parliament adjourned.

---

[1] _L. J._, vol. xvi, p. 737, June 12. Against the first resolution there protested : Nottingham, Weymouth, Rochester, Abingdon, Bp. of London, Guilford, Bp. of Exeter, Bp. of Rochester and Torrington. Their reason was that they conceived it very improper to determine the question before the House had heard what the Commons had to say about it.

As for the Commons, they discovered ambiguities in the last message of their antagonists and concluded that there was greater need than ever for the joint committee. It was visible, in Burnet's opinion, that the Commons had no serious charges to bring against the Whig peers and that they were only intent upon finding excuses for delay.[1] A final pretext was found in a speech made by Lord Haversham at a free conference held on June 13.

This conference was opened by Halifax.[2] The case for the Commons was put by Sir Bartholomew Shower, and the reply to it by the Lord Steward, to whose speech the Commons could make no objection. Then, however, Lord Haversham rose to speak. He was a young man, a strong Whig, one never at any time conspicuous for moderation. Originally a member of the Lower House, he had not long been in enjoyment of his peerage. On this occasion he expressed himself in very outspoken fashion, with a flimsy pretence of restraint, charging the Commons with deliberately attacking men whom they knew to be innocent. There was instant outcry at the insinuations contained in the speech. The managers for the Commons looked upon it as containing so great an aspersion on their House that they were obliged to retire. The deeply injured Chamber proceeded to pass a resolution against scandalous reproaches which tended to make a breach between the Houses and to delay the impeachments. They also resolved that the Lords should be requested to inflict a punishment upon their member for his heinous offence. As for the Lords, they sent a message stating that they had been informed of the misunderstanding at the conference and suggesting that as they were anxious not to interrupt public business the best thing to do was to resume the conference. The suggestion was repeated next day, but the Commons preserved the haughtiness of outraged dignity. They were, they said, exceedingly desirous of maintaining friendly relations, but at the same time it would not be consistent with their honour to renew the conference before

---

[1] Burnet, vol. ii, p. 278.
[2] L. J., vol. xvi, p. 742.

reparation was done them. The same day the articles against Halifax were at last produced.

Notwithstanding the determination of the Commons to play no part in it the trial of Lord Somers actually took place on the appointed day, Tuesday, June 17. The Commons might do as they pleased; that was no concern of the Peers who had fixed a date and were going to abide by it. By 57 to 36 [1] they resolved to go into the court of Westminster Hall for the trial of Lord Somers. A message was sent to the other House to say that the Lords intended to proceed immediately to the trial. The Bishop of Hereford and the Earl of Anglesey were excused from attendance, together with Orford and Halifax, who requested to be absent from the trial of their comrade. It was ordered that Westminster Hall should be cleared for the Peers, and thither they took their way, and the solemn farce began. When all were seated, proclamation was made for silence. A second proclamation declared that Lord Somers, who had been charged with high crimes and misdemeanours by the House of Commons, was now upon his trial, and that all persons concerned were to take note of the fact and now come forward to make good the charge. Next were read the articles of impeachment, and the answers made to them by the accused, after which the previous proclamation was made once more. The Lord Keeper [2] stated that the House was ready to receive evidence and desired that their lordships should give attention to it. Then there was silence again. The Upper House sat in solitary state in Westminster Hall. None came to disturb their serene repose; there were no accusers, there was no evidence. After a while Somers moved that his own counsel should be heard; and the case for the defence was thus presented. There was no other case. The space within the Hall where the faithful Commons should

---

[1] The Non-Contents included Somerset, Northumberland, Bp. of London, Scarsdale, Jermyn, Normanby, Nottingham, Derby, Rochester, Caernarvon, Feversham, Marlborough, Plymouth, Abingdon, Thanet, Oxford, Peterborough, Lawarr, Warrington, Denbigh, Lexington, Bp. of Rochester, Hunsdon, Dartmouth, Howard, Weston, Weymouth, Cholmondeley, Jeffreys, Godolphin, Bp. of Exeter, and Guilford. These signed a protest, afterwards erased by order of the House.
[2] Sir Nathan Wright.

have stood remained empty. So the Lords adjourned to their own House.

The House being resumed, it was moved to acquit Lord Somers of the charges preferred against him. A long debate ensued. The opinion of the judges was asked as to what naturally happens when any one accused of felony, treason, and misdemeanour pleads not guilty and no evidence is forthcoming. Finally, the question was put that Lord Somers is acquitted of the charge against him and the impeachment is dismissed. It was resolved in the affirmative by a majority of 55 to 33. Of the latter 30 protested, their reasons for dissent being subsequently expunged from the *Journals*. Once again the Peers proceeded in dignified order to Westminster Hall. When they were assembled in their proper places the Lord Keeper asked each one severally whether he was content that Lord Somers be acquitted or not content; and each, as his name was called, stood up and gave his verdict. The contents numbered 55, the non-contents 32.[1] When all had answered the Lord Keeper declared that Lord Somers had been acquitted, whereupon the Peers returned to their Chamber, where it was ordered that the impeachment should be dismissed, and also that an account of the proceedings of the House throughout the entire matter of the impeachments should be printed.

The House of Commons were not slow to express their wrath at the last outrage on the part of the Peers. They

[1] The Contents were: Barons Haversham, Herbert, Ossulstune, Osborne, Cornwallis, Granville, Berkeley, Rockingham, Lucas, Culpepper, Byron, Mohun, Lovelace, North and Grey, Wharton, Eure, Fitzwalter, Abergavenny; Bishops of Chichester, Lincoln, St. Asaph, Bristol, Gloucester, Peterborough, Norwich, Coventry, Ely, Bangor, Sarum; Viscount Saye and Sele; Earls of Rochford, Romney, Scarborough, Montague, Portland, Berkeley, Radnor, Macclesfield, Shaftesbury, Burlington, Bath, Essex, Kingston, Stamford, Rivers, Dorset, Huntingdon, Carlisle; Dukes of Newcastle, Schomberg, Bolton, St. Albans, Devonshire; the Earl of Tankerville, and the Archbishop of Canterbury.

The Non-Contents were: Barons Jeffreys, Godolphin, Guilford, Dartmouth, Lexington, Jermyn, Howard of Escrick, Hunsdon, Lawarr; Bishops of Exeter, Rochester, and London; Viscount Weymouth; Earls of Warrington, Marlborough, Plymouth, Abingdon, Rochester, Nottingham, Feversham, Scarsdale, Thanet, Caernarvon, Peterborough, Denbigh, Derby, Oxford, Jersey, Lindsey; Marquis of Normanby; Dukes of Northumberland and Somerset. *L. J.*, vol. xvi, p. 756.

passed a resolution affirming that the Lords had refused them justice, had by their pretended trial endeavoured to subvert the rights of impeachment, and had invaded the liberties of the subject by laying a foundation of impunity for the greatest offenders. All the disastrous consequences which must follow upon the delay in granting supplies must, they stated, be laid to the charge of those who had done their best to make a breach between the Chambers. When the Lords sent a message giving official notice of Somers' acquittal and stating that the next Monday, June 23, had been fixed for the trial of Lord Orford, the Commons ordered that no member should presume to appear at the pretended trial upon pain of incurring the utmost displeasure of the House. They then adjourned until Tuesday, June 24.

Meanwhile the Lords resolved that unless the Commons' charge against Lord Haversham were presented by them before the end of the session they would declare him innocent. They also emphatically condemned the resolutions of the Commons, which they hinted had been contrived merely with a view to covering the Commons' own delays.[1] These resolutions they regarded as tending to the destruction of the Lords' judicature and the rendering trials and impeachments impracticable in future. On Monday, June 23, the whole elaborate ceremonial, which had been gone through on the occasion of the Somers' trial was punctiliously repeated, with precisely the same result. The Tory lords had stayed away in sympathy with the action of the Commons, so that all who were present in Westminster Hall voted for Orford's acquittal. The impeachment was accordingly dismissed. The House afterwards took notice that several lords in town had absented themselves, though summoned to attend that day, and that others who had actually been at St. Stephen's had absented themselves from the trial. It was, therefore, resolved that all such peers, if they proved unable to make a just excuse, were to be held guilty of a great and wilful neglect of their duty. On June 24, the last day of the session, Haversham was solemnly absolved from the charge against him, and the

[1] *L. J.*, vol. xvi, pp. 763, 765-7.

impeachments against Halifax and Portland, together with one, long outstanding, against the Duke of Leeds were all dismissed. The famous episode of the impeachments was now ended. But the bitterness it had aroused had been extreme. Bolton had even moved that the King be desired to put an end to a Chamber which in abusing its own legitimate authority was a menace to the affairs of Europe and a seed of discord in the state.[1] The rupture had produced difficulties outside the immediate area of dispute. A Commons' bill for appointing commissioners of accounts had been amended in the revising chamber to the indignation of a Lower House already indignant enough. The King put an end to the troublous parliament as speedily as he could; and thus ended the long series of quarrels between the two Houses. The fifth parliament of the reign, which came to an untimely end owing to William's death, was peaceful.

The rights and wrongs of the dispute over the impeachments of the Junto have often been argued and might be argued indefinitely. The case for the Commons may be found in a pamphlet, entitled *A Vindication of the Rights of the Commons of England*.[2] It is an interesting piece of work if only for the objections which the writer raises against the Cabinet, whose existence had been found such a difficulty in the attempt to bring home their crime to the ministers responsible for the Partition Treaties. But the main argument of Sir Humphrey Mackworth is concerned with the Commons' right of impeachment. The Lower House, he says, made no claim to concur in the sentence; they in no way encroached upon the Lords' judicature.[3] But to the latter's judicial rights the appointment of a time for an impeachment to be held did not appertain. The appointment of a day was a collateral power, which might or might not belong to the judge. If the judge possessed it in the case of impeachments, then the right of the Commons would be rendered impracticable. And if the

---

[1] L'Hermitage, W. W., p. 304: June 24/July 5, 1701.
[2] *A Vindication of the Rights of the Commons of England*, by Sir H. Mackworth (1701), p. 16. Also printed in *Somers' Tracts*, vol. xi, p. 276 *et seq.*
[3] Ibid. (ed. 1701), p. 20.

right of impeachment were defeated, might not that of the control of the purse be defeated also? For what did the latter signify if it was not accompanied by the power to impeach evil ministers, who acted to the ruin of the nation or misapplied money to corrupt purposes? In short, a blow aimed at the Commons' right of impeachment was a blow at the balance of the constitution, and that again was a blow at the common safety of King and people. For 'the power of impeachments . . . in the Commons seems to be an original inherent right in the people of England, reserved to them in the first institution of government by the law of nature, and self-preservation for the common safety of their just rights or liberties.[1] With regard to the Lords' refusal to agree to the scheme for a joint committee, Mackworth avers that according to parliamentary practice, when precedents are doubtful, recourse should be had to the fountain of all precedents, i. e. sound reason, in accordance with which joint committees had been held in the past. The author closes with the declaration that when the question is one of the methods of procedure in cases of impeachment he declines to argue; he considers it necessary only to assert.

Mackworth's pamphlet was answered by a truly remarkable production, *A Vindication of the Rights and Prerogatives of the House of Lords.*[2] The argument of this paper is conceived on too lofty a plane to permit of its author's descending much to details. But he twits Sir Humphrey with claiming to be of no party but that of Reason and Law, and yet defending the proceedings of an assembly which sought to have its enemies condemned unheard; and he claims that it was undeniably the Commons, and not the Lords, that were the aggressors in the quarrel. The Peers deferred the trial from day to day for the convenience of the other House until further delay was out of the question. The same side is taken in the manifesto

---

[1] Mackworth's *Vindication*, p. 32. Cf. another pamphlet in favour of the Commons, *A History of the Last Session of Parliament* (1702).
[2] *Somers' Tracts*, vol. xi, p. 315. The pamphlet was originally published in 1701.

directed against the Commons under the name of Legion.[1]
In this the Commons are accused of having abused their
power, first by their imprisonment of the Kentish Petitioners;
secondly, by delaying public affairs until the enemy was at
the door; thirdly, by impeaching members of the House of
Lords, and then shuffling out of an untenable position by
miserable shifts, 'the end being to blast their reputations, not
prove the fact, that they might be put out of place, and your-
selves put in; finally, by quarrelling with the House of Lords
at a time when peace at home was most necessary.'

There is a poem, possibly by Defoe, on the imprisonment
of the Kentish Petitioners, which puts the case of an injured public against a House of Commons which no longer
represents it.[2]

> And now your wrath is smoking fast
>   Against the Kent petition,
> No man alive can tell for what,
> But telling truths that please you not,
>   And taxing your discretion.

The author concludes that there is only one thing to be done.
An assembly which is not representative must be got rid of.

> For since in vain our hopes and fears,
>   Petitions too are vain,
> No remedy but this appears,
> To pull the house about your ears,
>   And send you home again.

> These are the nation's discontents,
>   The causes are too true,
> The ploughman now his choice repents,
> For though he values parliaments,
>   He's not in love with you.

---

[1] 'Legion's New Paper; Being a Second Memorial to the Gentlemen
of a late House of Commons.' *Somers' Tracts*, vol. xi, p. 267.
[2] *Somers' Tracts*, vol. xi, pp. 259–64.

CHAPTER X

CONCLUSION

THE ultimate causes of the great quarrel between the two Houses is the most interesting question presented by the parliamentary history of the reign of William III. Our own knowledge and experience of the thoroughly organized party system make us too prone to read all parliamentary history from the standpoint of party divisions even in days when the party system, so far from being organized, was really in its infancy. Though the terms Whig and Tory certainly connoted fairly well defined political principles, they are far from being a master-key to the whole meaning of the parliamentary proceedings of the reign. The terms may be positively misleading. Neither party in 1689 had a detailed creed. After the Revolution the position of the Tories was distinctly ambiguous, for by strict rule Tory ought to have meant Jacobite, which it was very far from doing. The party issue becomes confused, if only because it is hard to reconcile Toryism as it was in 1689 with the Revolution Settlement. Moreover, this is not the only cause of confusion. We find politicians acting in a way which on the broad basis of party would be difficult to explain. They are actuated by motives other than party motives. Again and again we find that the parliamentary contest is being fought between the two Houses rather than between the two parties. It is reasonable to inquire whether it would not be a more illuminating way of studying the parliamentary history of the reign to consider the relations between Lords and Commons rather than those between Tories and Whigs. And the discussion of the relations between the two Houses involves the question of the amount of political influence which the House of Lords exercised at the close of the seventeenth century.

Reference has been made in the chapter on the Social Aspect of the Peerage to contemporary lamentations over the personal decadence of the nobility. Similar lamentations were expressed over an alleged decay in their corporate influence also. A favourite argument of the day ascribes the disasters of the Commonwealth and Protectorate to unwise policy on the part of kings themselves. The Tudors' policy, it was affirmed, had been utterly at fault. Their successors had paid the dire penalty attaching to a tactical blunder. The true support and mainstay of the monarchy was the nobility. Yet Henry VII had waged dreadful war upon the nobility. This argument is almost a commonplace in the seventeenth century and beginning of the eighteenth. We must take the theory for what it is worth. We are looking at the situation through the eyes of a supporter of the Stuarts, who is not concerning himself in the least with the nature of the problem with which the Tudors were in their day confronted. The fact was clear to the monarchist of 1700 that whatever might have been the justification of the Tudors' policy for their own generation it had certainly resulted in the sowing of a new crop of dangers for a future generation to reap. Henry VII had been the destroyer of the baronage by a war of proscription. Henry VIII and Elizabeth had been equally culpable, though the method of their warfare had been different. The author of the *Memorial to the Princess Sophia*[1] especially censures Elizabeth's courting of popularity. She neglected the Peers; she smiled upon the House of Commons, so that (to quote Harrington) 'her successors have ever since looked pale before their assemblies. For the House of Peers, which alone had stood in the gap, now sinking down between the King and the Commons, showed that Crassus was dead, and the Isthmus broken. But a monarchy divested of its nobility, hath no refuge under heaven but an army; wherefore the dissolution of this government caused the war, not the war the dissolution of this government.' Says another pamphleteer: 'Had the Lords in Charles I's reign had but the fortieth part of the real

---

[1] *Memorial to the Princess Sophia*, by G. S., p. 38.

power their ancestors enjoyed, there can be no doubt they had kept the balance even, and prevented that unnatural war.'[1]

It is hardly fair to the Tudors to regard them as alone responsible for the decrease in the influence of the nobility. Does strength lie with the many or the few? It is possible to argue either way, as was found in 1719 in the discussions over the Peerage Bill. But whatever be the answer to that question, it is certain that the lavish creations of James I did not enhance the prestige of the House of Lords. It was not so much the number as the character of the new peerages that was at fault. For James made a market of them; sold them right and left. A new nobility, lacking in the *éclat* of family distinction, was raised up side by side with the older baronage, which was not slow to express its resentment. If the House had already been humiliated before the outbreak of the Civil War, infinitely greater was its humiliation afterwards. It failed to effect a reconciliation between the monarchy and the Commons, who thereupon found it to be as useless and dangerous as the monarchy itself and destroyed it altogether.[2] Then followed the days of the nobility's greatest degradation. They were outcast from the social pale of their country. No longer leaders, they became objects of ridicule, targets for jeers and mockery.[3] The restoration of the monarchy in 1660

---

[1] *The Constitution explained in relation to the Independency of the House of Lords.* A pamphlet written on the Stanhope Peerage Bill. It will be found in the British Museum, Political Tracts, 1714-21 (No. 1108).

[2] See Firth's *House of Lords during the Civil War*, p. 74:
'During the first and second sessions of the Long Parliament the House of Lords was the arbiter between the Crown and the Commons. As in 1626 and in 1628 both Crown and Commons appealed to it for support, and once more it endeavoured to mediate between the two. Its inability to effect a compromise led directly to the Civil War, and indirectly to the abolition of the House of Lords itself.'

[3] See Firth's *House of Lords*, pp. 238-9. 'So they jostle him now in the streets, who was wont before, like Mandarins, to make whole streets to give way, and nobody takes notice of him unless some one in seven points at him (perhaps), and says, "There goes a Lord," and this is all the privilege of peerage they have now, besides the having every base fellow without commission to search their house, every tradesman cite them before their Worships at next shire-towns, and every common serjeant drag them away to prison, where they lie in the dungeon or common gaol: and this fine prerogative they have got, who would needs pluck

did not involve the restoration of the nobility to their former power and reputation. For them the restoration was social rather than political. And as the society of the court was so largely frivolous, the social restoration did them but little good, at a time when, as has been said, 'it looks rather as if the spread of the democratic spirit had undermined the moral basis of their claims, so that deference to rank had become a debt grudgingly paid rather than a due willingly rendered.'[1]   Earnest-minded men like Clarendon realized that if the House was to increase its authority it must do so by paying faithful and devoted services to the nation, whereas it was only too prone after 1660 to fritter away its influence by the slackness of its proceedings and the altercations and ill-living of its members, together with the ill-use they were accustomed to make of their privileges.[2]

Charles II regarded the House of Lords as impotent for good or ill, and when William III ascended the English throne, it is plain that he was inclined to share this opinion. He was unwilling to attend the debates of the House, though often urged by Halifax to do so. If only he would come, thought the Marquis, he would realize how necessary the support of the Peers was to him.[3]   He would seem to have lost his temper at Halifax's repeated exhortations. When again asked to attend the debates in January 1689/90 he showed heat, exclaiming that he had no time for it.   The estimation in which in these early days he held the average English peer is revealed by a saying of his in March 1689, quoted by Halifax, that he will raise regiments, but will not give the command of them to peers, as the humour and character of a peer of England did not agree well with the discipline to which a colonel must be subject.[4]   The opinion that the House of Lords now counted for much less than the Commons

away the King, only to be promoted to the King's Bench themselves.' From a sketch of 1652 entitled ' A character of a degenerate nobleman '.
    [1] Ibid., p. 293.
    [2] *Life of Edward Hyde, Earl of Clarendon* (3 vols., 1827), vol. iii, pp. 166–9.   See *Old Parl. Hist.*, vol. xxi, p. 95 (quoted in Firth, p. 294).
    [3] Foxcroft's *Life of Halifax*, vol. ii, pp. 208, 244.
    [4] Ibid., p. 205.

was shared very generally by foreigners. The recent history of England inevitably gave this impression to outside observers, who were in any case likely to be struck by the remarkable vigour of the most vigorous representative chamber in Europe. An interesting instance of this state of feeling is afforded in 1698, when Bolton and Abingdon moved an address in favour of the persecuted Protestants in France, only to be roundly informed that an address from the Upper House could carry but little weight, as their Chamber had not the reputation in foreign countries that the Commons enjoyed.[1]

The pamphlets on the Peerage Bill of 1719, though obviously dealing for the most part with the specific proposals of that measure, yet contain general discussions on the state of the peerage, which are as relevant to the days of William III as to the early days of George I.[2] There are some interesting passages in a reply to one of Walpole's pamphlets against the bill. 'What are the Lords?' the writer exclaims. 'They are few in numbers; they possess merely an imaginary dignity; they represent none but themselves. They can never be popular, but must always remain a mark for envy. Most of them are poor, and few possess a dangerous wealth. They possess no strongholds as they did in ancient days. When considered as a body, they are dissoluble at pleasure. Could there be a description of more harmless creatures?' The constitutional position of the House reminds the author of purgatory. For what is the idea of purgatory? It is a place 'where the great and ultimate decrees of Providence are not altered, but suspended and delayed.'[3] It appears that in strictness the House of Lords is but an imaginary estate, resembling purgatory in this, that affairs pass through its channel, and rest there deposited for a while, but the final decision is always given either by the Crown or the Commons. The Peers can be brought to book by the King, the Commons,

---

[1] F. L. Bonet, B, pp. 119–20: May 13/23, 1698.

[2] For list of these pamphlets see *Retrospective Review*, Series II, vol. ii, 1828, p. 129.

[3] *Remarks on a Pamphlet, entitled 'Thoughts of a Member of the Lower House in relation to the Project for Restoring the Peerage'* (1719), p. 30.

the civil officers, the army, or the mob. 'The Lords in their greatest splendour and authority, with their speaker at their head, what have they to contend with against all these supposed enemies? They have an empty embroidered purse and a black Rod.'[1]

Other writers might be quoted as illustrating what was clearly an opinion held widely both by friend and foe, that the House of Lords, viewed both in its personal and its corporate character, had much declined in authority and prestige. That the opinion should have existed at all is a noteworthy fact apart altogether from the question whether the opinion was justified or not. But, on the other hand, it is necessary not to take these lamentations and diatribes too literally. One must remember that the standpoint of contemporaries was very different from our own. When they spoke of the halcyon days of the House of Lords, from which it had been declining, they were thinking of the period of feudalism, when the third estate had scarcely any practical power, and government was a true oligarchy. Little wonder if the authority of the House in their own day seemed puny and meagre when such was their standard of comparison. But we, with two more centuries behind us, view the condition of parliamentary institutions at the end of the seventeenth century in a very different light. So real were the privileges and exemptions of the noble class that it formed then, in a way quite different from the present, a caste apart. Privilege was not a dead letter; it was perpetually utilized. At no time did the English nobility show the utter aloofness, the indifference to the interests of the rest of the community displayed by the French noblesse. Yet the conception of the dignity of the peer, as of some one on quite a higher plane than his neighbours, was still strong at the end of the seventeenth century.

It was still possible for a supporter of the authority of the Upper House in all seriousness and sincerity to build up a gaudy theory of natural superiority, which seems strange

[1] *Remarks on a Pamphlet*, &c., p. 33.

and somewhat ridiculous to our ears.[1] The foundation of the theory is the undoubted fact that man, as the perfection of the universe, was made paramount on the earth. Hence is adduced the principle that 'superiority and subordination are the ligaments of government'. Then follows a glorification of the great man, and an exhortation to godliness in rulers. After this comes a laudation of the English nobility,

'That know themselves honourably born, of plentiful estates in the country, and that owe their original to virtue, that can never be suspected of ill intentions, against their nation's soil, where the parents, relations, friends, and tenants reside, and must be possessed of their heirs and successors. Altho' they are tender of their rights and privileges, as the supreme court of judicature in England, from which there is no appeal, and are zealous in maintaining them; cannot, I say, without the greatest breach of duty and charity imaginable be supposed to act against the valuable interest of England in general; but on the contrary are the pillars that support the nation, welfare, and grandeur, and their estates in conjunction with others that defend our coasts from the insults and depredations of our enemies.

'These are the English nobles, which being adorned with their own virtues as well as with those of their ancestors, merit esteem, preferment, trust, honour, and fame above all others that would stand in competition with them, in the administration of public affairs, for they are armour of proof against all innovations and whatever might reflect injuries upon our happy constitution of Kings, Lords, and Commons either obliquely or directly.'

Another writer justifies the special judicial prerogatives of the Upper House on somewhat similar grounds.[2] As the peers hold their seats in parliament by hereditary right they are supposed to be above corruption or the influence of a court. As having the greatest share in landed property, they are thought to be most fit to make impartial rules about it, as what they do must affect both themselves and their posterity.

---

[1] *A Vindication of the Rights and Prerogatives of the House of Lords*, in *Somers' Tracts*, vol. xi, p. 315. The pamphlet was first published in 1701.

[2] *The Constitution explained in relation to the Independency of the House of Lords*, p. 11. British Museum Political Tracts 1714-21, No. 1108.

Again, the peers may be expected to be free from chicanery which too often mars the proceedings of inferior courts. In a like strain other writers expatiate upon the calmness, fairness, superior virtues inherent in a House composed of the nobility of the realm.

Such was the sort of theory which justified the peculiar privileges of the peer. It will be noticed that, although most of these had their origin in Parliament, their importance was chiefly personal. A lord who scarcely ever appeared at Westminster, in virtue of his membership of the Upper House, was able to exert the widest authority as a territorial magnate. This territorial power reacted upon the influence of the House of Lords viewed as a corporation. The House was in the main an assembly of great landowners, of men bound together by the ties of common interest, and because of their authority in their respective districts able to wield a great authority in Parliament. Tangible proof of this was given in the extensive nature of aristocratic control over elections and the composition of the House of Commons. The strength of the Upper House itself was enhanced by the fact that it was no assembly of diverse elements: it was in reality an organism. Apart from community of interests, there was the cohesion given by close family connexion, as a glance at the genealogical trees of the peerage will prove. So strong was the sense of common heritage and the corporate character of the peerage that in the world of politics there was always a tendency for a lord to stand more for his House than for his party. Thus the House of Lords was strong in its territorial influence, its distinctive privileges, and its consciousness of essential unity.

When we realize the solidarity of the Upper House, we become possessed of one of the explanations of the parliamentary history of the reign of William III. Whenever the House of Commons came into forceful contact with the corporate sense of the other Chamber it came up against something adamantine. For in the other Chamber there was enshrined not only political aspirations but class consciousness. The Commons failed repeatedly in their attempts to carry their Treason Bills because the Lords saw in those bills a menace to their security. It did not matter whether those bills emanated from the Whig or the Tory party. They were in any case regarded as attacks upon the House of Lords, not as an assembly consisting mainly of one party or the other, but as a united organism. Similarly, the attack upon Somers, Orford, Halifax, and Haversham was felt to be an attack not merely upon them, but also upon the House of which they were members. It was as when the internal disputes of a city are forgotten in the haste to defend the citadel against the escalade of an outside foe.

It was not only as an assembly consisting of a privileged class that the House of Lords enjoyed a superiority which laid it open to attacks from without : it has been generally admitted that, at any rate until the era of Walpole, the Lords were the intellectual superiors of the Commons. ' Until the reign of George III ', says Buckle, 'the House of Lords was decidedly superior to the House of Commons in the liberality and general accomplishments of its members.'[1] The education of many of them may have been defective; they may have been impregnated with narrow prejudices; still they were considerably freer from these failings than the squirearchy from which the Commons were in large measure recruited. It is indisputable that from 1660 to 1714 we must go to the Upper House in order to find the great personalities of the political world. Of these, it is true, several served an apprenticeship in the Lower House; but then the ablest members of the Commons were generally sent ere long to the other Chamber. We may say with confidence that at any given time within the period mentioned, the majority of the most remarkable figures in political life will be found in the Upper and not in the Lower House. The peers were apt to predominate in all the services, either by actually holding places themselves, or by being able to fill them with their nominees. But in particular they were predominant in the great offices of the state. The leading ministers were almost always peers. Because this was so the House of Peers played a foremost part in political affairs, which it subsequently lost.

[1] Buckle's *History of Civilisation* (1869, 3 vols.), vol. i, pp. 451–3.

In those days the connexion between the administration and the Lords was closer and more intimate than the connexion between the administration and the House of Commons. When we realize such facts as these, the privileges of the House, its corporate character, its priority in the executive, its judicial activities, its influence over offices, over elections, over the electorate and its representatives alike, we recognize that from our modern point of view the House of Lords was not the decrepit institution some contemporaries pictured it to be. It was still a strong citadel, a mark for jealousy not contempt.

Even despite its reverses, even after the era of the Commonwealth, the House of Lords still symbolized the traditions of aristocratic government, with which the House of Commons, if it was to progress, could not sympathize. And the aspirations of the Lower House had been fired by the great part it had played against the first Charles, and been encouraged by the continuous duration of Parliament under the second Charles. If the authority of the representative Chamber was to increase, it was inevitable that that of the other House must decrease. The battle to be waged was not against a despotic monarchy only, but against an oligarchical tradition also. It has been pointed out that in William's first parliament a great Whig majority was returned, who conceived that the new settlement was their work, and that they must make the most of the opportunity afforded by the new order. The members of this first parliament were of a distinctly militant type, and on the whole that type was maintained in subsequent assemblies.

There were not wanting those who perceived in the ambitions of the Lower House a danger not only to the Lords but also to the whole nation;[1] who thought they saw the balance of

---

[1] F. L. Bonet, E, p. 13, January 3/14, 1700/1. 'La Chambre des Communes, parce qu'elle est Maitresse des bourses, a forcé les Rois de leur ceder mille privileges qui favorisent à la verité en un tems le Peuple, mais qui rendent les deliberations importantes à l'état de plus en plus dangereuses. Non contente de voir ces anciens privileges establis et la religion affirmie par le secour de S. M. à present regnante, elle ne cesse dans toutes ces sessions d'ébranler la balance du pouvoir qui a rendu cette Nation heureuse et florisante ; de sorte qu'on peut craindre que ce

power which had made the country happy and prosperous threatened by a too violent assembly. The author of the *Memorial to the Princess Sophia* expressed consternation at the growing influence of the Commons. He compared them to wild beasts, who, did they but know their own strength, would destroy mankind. So might the Commons destroy kings and monarchies; no power on earth could govern them. It was fortunate that they could not utilize their full strength. Country gentlemen might manage their own estates excellently well; they could divert themselves with hunting and feasting: citizens could be sharp enough in business—but, God be thanked, all were not cut out for statesmen![1] Such was the pious ejaculation of the man who believed thoroughly in the old order, and considered that the House of Commons should hold only a subordinate position, such as the Lords certainly did their best to maintain for it by means of influence, direct or indirect. We have seen how extensive that influence could still be. On the other hand, it was becoming increasingly difficult for the Lords to secure a considerable following in the Commons. The independent ambitions of the Lower House had been so much encouraged of recent years; its traditions had become so powerful that they exerted a controlling authority over its members. Once brought into fellowship with the body, each new recruit found himself breathing a distinctive atmosphere, which had stronger properties than the forces to which he had been subjected outside the House. The Commons also had its corporate sense. And now to strengthen it there emerged a new class in the Chamber, 'the moneyed class,' of which we begin to hear so much in the reign which saw the foundation of the National Debt and the Bank of England. Over the forces of trade and finance the landed interest had no power whatsoever. Although there was often a good deal of jealousy between them, there was still a distinct affinity between the peerage

desir d'empêcher sur les prerogatives de la Couronne ou que cette jalousie inveterée qui a été de tous tems entre le Roy et le Peuple, après avoir produit pendant un tems la conservation des Privileges et le bonheur de cet etat n'en produise un jour la perte.'

[1] *Memorial to the Princess Sophia*, pp. 31–2.

and the squirearchy. But when the 'moneyed class' began to have a determining voice in the House of Commons, there came into the counsels of the Lower House an interest which had no counterpart in the Lords. There was a new contingent, strong, alert, and proof against a bribe.

There is a most remarkable passage in Burnet's *History*, in which he expresses his opinions on the House of Commons in 1700.[1] The passage might well form a text on the condition of parliamentary government at the opening of the century. He has just been speaking of the death of the little Duke of Gloucester, and his mind is much perturbed, for he writes:

'The nation was falling under a general discontent, and a dislike of the King's personal government, and the King on his part seemed to grow weary of us and our affairs; and partly by the fret from the opposition he had of late met with, partly from ill-health, he was falling into a lethargy of mind: we were, upon the matter, become already more than half a commonwealth, since the government was plainly in the hands of the House of Commons, who must sit once a year, and as long as they thought fit, while the King had only the civil list for life, so that the whole administration of the government was under their inspection: the act for triennial parliaments kept up a standing faction in every county and town of England: but though we were falling insensibly into a democracy, we had not learned the virtues that are necessary for that sort of government: luxury, vanity, and ambition increased daily, and our animosities were come to a great height, and gave us dismal apprehensions. Few among us seemed to have a right notion of the love of their country, and of a zeal for the good of the public: the House of Commons, how much soever its power has advanced, yet was much sunk in credit: very little gravity, order, or common decency appeared among them; the balance lay chiefly in the House of Lords, who had no natural strength to resist the Commons.'

The Bishop was perplexed by the opposition so frequently shown to the King, the country's redeemer. He can find no better word for it than factiousness. That there was always a strong opposition in the House of Commons is obvious.

[1] Burnet, vol. ii, p. 247.

Enemies of the Lower House were content to go no further in search of an explanation of this phenomenon where they were able to ascribe it to self-interest. 'The truth of the matter is', says one already quoted, 'these gentlemen having their wants to lead, and the devil to drive, they can find no other expedient to supply the former and to please the latter as by changing the ministry, and threatening in themselves to accomplish what they aim at; and therefore prosecute the design accordingly with uncommon vigour.'[1]

Vernon, arguing in favour of the calling of a new parliament in 1700, asks, 'In a concluding session do people consider any thing so much as securing their next elections, and does not that naturally run them into an opposition against the Court, and setting up pretences for the good of the country?'[2] Although William at his accession regarded the Commons as decidedly the more important of the two Chambers, he felt no love for them. He complained that they used him like a dog.[3] He resented the very thinly-veiled reprimands which they addressed to him on more than one occasion. It is necessary to remember that opposition to the wishes of the sovereign did not mean that the opposition was necessarily either Whig or Tory. We have to draw a very important distinction between Whig and Tory on the one hand, and Court and Opposition on the other. The ministry was always more or less composite; at no time was it entirely composed of members of the one party. On the other hand, the opposition was also often of a composite character. We read of Jacobites and Republicans joining hands.[4] As to the strength of the republican party in England at this time, we have seen it asserted that Whig and republican were synonymous terms. William's first impression was that 'the Commonwealth party' was the strongest in the country.[5]

---

[1] 'Cursory Remarks on some late Disloyal Proceedings in several Cabals.' *Somers' Tracts*, vol. xi, p. 182.

[2] *Vernon Corr.*, vol. iii, p. 114.

[3] Foxcroft's *Life of Halifax*, vol. ii, p. 207.

[4] F. L. Bonet, D, p. 273, September 6/17, 1700. Cf. 'Cursory Remarks, &c.', *Somers' Tracts*, vol. xi, p. 159.

[5] Foxcroft's *Life of Halifax*, vol. ii, p. 203.

Bonet's statement is undoubtedly an exaggeration, but it is no more inaccurate than Cowper's disclaimer.[1] It is certain that there were many Whigs who were discontented with the Settlement of 1689, and thought it should have gone much further. They had a permanent grievance against the King for his refusal to proscribe the Tories altogether. On the other hand, the Tories who loved monarchy did not love their King. There was, therefore, as much likelihood of opposition against the Court emanating from the one party as from the other. It is the object of the writer of this pamphlet already referred to, *Cursory Remarks*—'a reviling declamatory pamphlet' it has been called—to prove that the House of Commons was only united in its opposition to the sovereign.[2]

It was certainly at times united in one other thing, viz. opposition to the House of Lords. 'There is no more certain maxim in politics', writes Sir Robert Walpole, voicing the current theory, used also by the author of the *Memorial*, 'than that a monarchy must subsist either by an army or a nobility; the first makes it despotic, and the latter a free government. I presume none of those noble personages themselves, who have the honour to make up that illustrious body, do believe they are so distinguished and advanced above their fellow-subjects for their own sakes. They know well they are intended the guardians as well as ornaments of the monarchy, an essential prerogative of which it must be to add to, and augment their number in such proportion as to render them a proper balance against the democratic part of our constitution, without being formidable to the monarchy itself, the support of which is the reason of their institution.'[3] There is reason to believe that William changed his opinion that the

---

[1] Campbell's *Lives of the Lord Chancellors*, vol. iv, p. 421. Bonet, speaking of the question of the Succession on the death of the Duke of Gloucester, declares that Whigs and Republicans are synonymous. D., p. 273.

[2] See *Somers' Tracts*, vol. xi, p. 149.

[3] *Thoughts of a Member of the Lower House in relation to the Project for Restraining and Limiting the Power of the Crown in the future Creation of Peers*, by Sir R. Walpole (1719), p. 9. Published anonymously.

Lords could be of but little use to him, and realized that there was some measure of truth underlying the theory of a natural alliance between crown and nobility.

We have to be careful not to overstate the case. There was at all times an anti-court party in the Lords as there was in the Commons. The House as a body was not enthusiastically friendly to William. Once or twice it read him lectures, though certainly in more deferential terms than the Commons used. The Peers evinced the dislike which they shared in common with the rest of the nation for William's Dutch advisers. For example, they made an address of advice in 1692, prompted by their investigations into the state of the navy and army. At that time the commander-in-chief of the forces was Count Solms; a list of members of the Ordnance revealed the fact that nearly all were Dutchmen. The Lords moved that in future his Majesty's native subjects should be preferred in the army above all others, and that the chief governor of the forces should always be a subject born in His Majesty's dominions.[1] Another reprimand was contained in the Lords' first address in regard to the Partition Treaties. But while there was always an opposition in the House of Lords as well as in the Commons, on the other hand, whereas in the latter House the party of opposition was nearly always predominant, in the Lords it was nearly always subordinate. In the early days of the reign we find the Upper House supporting the King in his projects of indemnity and toleration, when the Commons were bent on proscription and threw out the Comprehension Bill. Later in the reign the Lords support the King in connexion with the Army question and the Irish Forfeited Estates.

The representation of the sovereign's own views in the Lords followed from the intimate connexion between the House and the ministers, who were in those days really the servants of the King. How far ministers continued to be not responsible to the nation was proved by the incident of the Partition Treaties. The Lords, as has been noted, solemnly declared their disapprobation of the methods whereby the

[1] *Lords' MSS. 1692-3*, No. 611, pp. 179–98.

Treaties had been carried through; but they actually rallied to the defence of the ministers themselves, and saved them from punishment for their constitutional misdemeanours. Again, when it is desirable to name a definite number of troops as in the sovereign's opinion the minimum commensurate with safety, the number must be stated in the Upper House, which will take up the cudgels in favour of the wishes of the King. Unfortunately William is too angry to consult with his ministers, and the opportunity is allowed to pass. Again, the second chamber is the one in which the royal will is normally expressed, for the simple reason that it is the revising chamber. By the time a measure has reached the Lords from the Commons, sufficient time has elapsed to allow a definite opinion to be formed upon it. The King has been able to review the situation, to estimate the strength of feeling in the Commons. Premature interference is undesirable, but should the King greatly dislike the measure, he may send a judicious message to the Lords.

William III's conduct conclusively disproves the fallacious notion that the royal power was killed, or even very greatly curtailed, by the Revolution. Not only was he the most important member of his own administration; he did not shrink from making use of his veto upon occasion. 'The power of the Crown', said Burke, 'almost dead and rotten as prerogative, has grown up anew, with much more strength, and far less odium, under the name of Influence.' The process originated long before the reign of George III. William made use of influence, by means of places in the House of Commons, by means of his ministers in the House of Lords. We possess the significant statement in connexion with the debates on the Irish Forfeitures, that it is universally believed that the King 'manages' the House of Lords as seems good to him.[1] But apart altogether from direct influence by the Crown, there was undoubtedly a certain amount of unity of interest between the Upper House and the monarchy. They were both upon the defensive from the attacks of a House, which was militant, innovating. There proved to be an

[1] F. L. Bonet, D, p. 127 : April 9/20, 1700.

affinity between royal prerogative and aristocratic privilege. William, despite his lack of interest in domestic affairs, was bound to have a definite policy. It is summed up in the determination he expressed to Halifax to be the latter's disciple as a trimmer, to go always upon the foundation of a middle party.[1] Latterly he took Sunderland's famous advice to entrust his affairs to ministers mainly from one party; but at no time had William any sympathy with the tenets of either party. The younger Bonet, writing of the ministerial changes in May 1699, notes that the new men, Pembroke and Lonsdale, are like the Secretary of State, Jersey, moderate and far removed from the spirit of faction. He thinks that this proves that His Majesty has a set plan of giving places in the government to men of moderation, irrespective of party.[2] It is certain that William never encouraged the extremists. Something of the spirit of moderation William found in the House of Lords, a chamber open to all the influence of tradition, which because it was hereditary must be conservative in feeling, and essentially interested in the maintenance of equilibrium. William never found a party of trimmers. But surely it is not fanciful to suggest that in the House of Lords he found at times something of the spirit of the middle party?

Discussing the uses of an aristocracy, Lecky[3] says, 'Such men may be guilty of much misgovernment, and they will certainly, if uncontrolled by other classes, display much selfishness, but it is scarcely possible that they should be wholly indifferent to the ultimate consequences of their acts, or should divest themselves of all sense of responsibility or private duty. When other things are equal, the class which has most to lose and least to gain by dishonesty will exhibit the highest level of integrity. When other things are equal the class whose interests are most permanently and seriously bound up with those of the nation is likely to be the most careful guardian of the national welfare. When other things

---

[1] Foxcroft's *Halifax*, vol. ii, pp. 206, 232, 242, 252.
[2] F. L. Bonet, C., p. 110: May 23/June 2, 1699.
[3] W. E. H. Lecky, *History of England in the Eighteenth Century* (7 vols., 1904), vol. ii, p. 221.

are equal, the class which has most leisure and most means of instruction will, as a whole, be the most intelligent. Besides this, the tact, the refinement, the reticent, the conciliatory tone of thought and manner characteristic of gentlemen, are all peculiarly valuable to public men, whose chief task is to reconcile conflicting pretensions and to harmonize jarring interests . . .' The argument is that, theoretically at all events, the composition of the second chamber is such as to make it normally the home of conciliation and moderation. The history of the House in the reign of William III is not such as to call for anything in the nature of high eulogy. Over and over again it gave evidence of its selfishness, its exaggerated sense of its own importance. The case of Oates and its anti-papal measures revealed an intolerant spirit, in the possession of which, however, it was by no means peculiar. Its hostility to the attempts made to purify the Lower House showed its determination to preserve its own predominance, if possible, even at the price of corruption. In its frequent economic legislation it showed no enlightenment, though here again it was in no way behind the thought of the age. Although the Lords acquiesced in the scheme, it was the Commons who first conceived the idea of allowing the licensing of the press to lapse. And in January 1698/9 in a Printing Regulation Bill,[1] which the Commons rejected, the Lords sought to reintroduce the system of superintendence, though it should be added that many of the objectionable features originally in the measure were omitted in the committee stage. On the other hand, we do find the feeling against the licensing principle voiced in the Lords as early as March 1692/3.[2]

[1] See *Lords' MSS. 1697-9*, No. 1339, pp. 271-6. Both Houses were anxious to put down vice, profanity, and atheism. For bill of 1697 see No. 1217, pp. 112-13.

[2] The motion then brought forward is of considerable interest. It was to the effect that 'if the names of printer and author of any book be affixed to, and printed in the same book, that then, and in such case, it shall not be necessary to take out a license for the printing of the said book.' The proviso was lost by twenty-six votes to eighteen, but of the minority eleven, including Halifax, Mulgrave, Marlborough, and Shrewsbury, entered a protest, which assigned among other reasons for dissent from the passing of the expiring Laws Continuing Act the fact that 'it subjects all learning and true information to the arbitrary will and pleasure of a mercenary, and perhaps, ignorant licenser, destroys the

On the whole we may say that though we cannot find in the proceedings of the House of Lords evidence of any outstanding political wisdom and foresight, on the other hand the Peers were well abreast of their age, and the best political thought of the day found expression among them. But together with the intellectual eminence of a Savile, a Talbot, a Stillingfleet, there was all the native caution of an aristocratic chamber. On the one hand there was sympathy for the enfranchisement of literature; on the other, balancing it, the protective instinct to guard against profanity and sedition. The note of compromise and moderation is struck at the very outset. The Lords, in great measure responsible for the Revolution which has indeed been termed aristocratic, were resolved that it should also be a conservative revolution— monarchical, not republican. They were anxious that the inevitable change should not be accentuated, but disguised. This same moderation, shown in the first parliament of the reign, is revealed on all the different occasions in which the Lords came to the rescue of the sovereign ; when they resisted the confiscatory methods of the Commons; when they endeavoured to maintain the standing force which William considered requisite. It is shown again when they protected the rights of private property in their defence of Duncombe. From insular prejudice the Peers were by no means free, but they tried to secure the Dutch Guards for His Majesty. Some of the English jealousy of the Scots appeared in the Upper House in its proceedings in regard to the Darien scheme, but it promoted the King's statesmanlike scheme for a union with Scotland, in a bill for the appointment of commissioners to discuss the project.[1] Partly because the Lords dared specially to recommend the measure, the Commons rejected it. When the Commons showed that the motive of their impeachments of the Junto was largely vindictive, the Lords rallied to the support of the ministers, although they had previously condemned their conduct. They had other reasons

properties of authors in their copies, and sets up many monopolies.'
Thorold Rogers, vol. i, p. 109.
[1] *Lords' MSS. 1699-1702*, No. 1513, pp. 106-7.

for their action in the matter, but certainly dislike of violent methods was one of their reasons. That there was need for a moderating spirit in the England of William III's day, and that the Lords performed a valuable function for their generation in supporting the cause of moderation no one will deny. It was a good thing that there was a strong conservative influence in the country to secure consolidation when there was much temptation to excess. Nevertheless there was good cause for the battle which the House of Commons waged against the alliance of King and peerage, against the obstacle which barred the way to their further advance.

The great struggle between the House closed with a triumph for the Lords. Their lordships, in the words of Legion's Address, 'like the true posterity of those noble ancestors, at the price of whose blood we received our privileges and liberties,' had 'vigorously and gloriously withstood the treacherous and unfaithful proceedings of our degenerated representatives'.[1] They had vindicated the rights of the English people against the usurpation of the House of Commons to the immortal glory of the English nobility. The Commons had imprisoned the Kentish Petitioners; they had been guilty of other arbitrary proceedings. And yet the cause which they had been upholding in their long quarrel with the Upper House, and particularly in their impeachments, was that of the representative principle. We know now that the reign of William III was a critical period in the development of our parliamentary system and in particular of the Cabinet. It is instructive to turn to the writings of the Bishop of Salisbury and to notice how little he comprehended the significance of the situation. He is at a loss to account for the constant, in his eyes ill-conditioned, opposition to the saviour who had succoured the nation in the hour of its extremity. Such factiousness is akin to treason and argues a bad and ungenerous spirit in its authors. So urges Burnet, seeing in the action of the Lower House nothing better than caprice and discontent. To us, on the other hand, the cry of the

---

[1] 'Legion's Humble Address to the Lords', *Somers' Tracts*, vol. xi, p. 275. The address has reference to the Kentish Petition.

Commons appears, so to speak, as the half-articulate voice of the party system, pleading for its fuller development.

It was necessary that the Revolution settlement should have some harmony with the past, in order that its fruits might be lasting. On the other hand, it was desirable that the fruits should be brought to perfection. The principles underlying the Revolution demanded, among other things, the proper organization of the ministerial system. Burnet was horrified at the unprecedented dismissal of a statesman who had done such loyal service as Somers. He did not realize that in order that government may be efficient it is necessary that the ministers shall enjoy the confidence of the House of Commons' majority. It was a semi-conscious desire to assert that principle which prompted the rancorous attacks upon Somers himself and the impeachment of him together with his colleagues. The great stumbling-block in the path of the development of the Cabinet system was the prominence of the sovereign in the party conflict, a sovereign who had to be taught the expediency of employing ministers pleasing to the nation's representatives as well as to himself, a sovereign who took sides in the warfare of Parliament and was a member of his own government. So long as such a condition of things continued there could be no straight issue between Whig and Tory. There would always be a struggle between Court and Opposition. It was necessary that the sovereign should be removed outside the sphere of politics altogether; that he should become the neutral symbol of the essential union which embraces and transcends all political differences. Criticism is an imperative condition of efficient government; an organized party of opposition as indispensable as a ministry. It was for the right to criticize, without being deemed disloyal, that the House of Commons was fighting. The phrase ' His Majesty's Opposition' shows how far we have travelled since Burnet's time. The opposition forces which he condemned were not merely the ill-natured cavillers against a beneficent sovereign; they were performing a legitimate service to the sovereign and to the state. That they were often violent and bad-tempered was the fault not so much of their own dispositions as of the disadvantages of the ambiguous conditions under which they laboured.

The struggle for the principles of representative government and responsibility of ministers involved an attack upon the House of Lords as well as upon the sovereign. Ministers were usually in the Lords, and they were sheltered by the Lords, who keenly defended their own members. Moreover, the Upper House joined with other forces in preventing the House of Commons from being a true representative of the nation. The latter chamber aimed at realizing a complete independence. The endeavour, in which the House was engaged at the opening of the eighteenth century, was not destined to succeed for many a long day. It had no chance of success in the years of Whig oligarchy which followed upon the downfall of the Tory party at the end of the reign of Queen Anne. Complete independence could only come with the appearance of democracy. It was industrialism that forced through the Reform Bill of 1832. In 1688 England was in no sense a democratic country. The Commons had indeed secured a brilliant triumph when they had overthrown monarchy and peerage together, and even after the reaction had set in, they had retained the great prestige of their victory. The principles of government which, though veiled in ambiguity, underlay the Revolution Settlement, presaged a new train of development in the future, which should enhance the authority of the Lower House. On the other hand, the forces of aristocracy were still strong, possibly predominant, despite the moral reverse of the Commonwealth. The Revolution was in its origin essentially an aristocratic and not a democratic movement. The House of Lords, in which the aristocratic tradition was enshrined, still claimed co-ordinate powers with the Commons, together with what they termed 'a natural superiority'. For were they not the King's hereditary councillors—not merely the Upper Chamber in the Legislature, but a special advisory body to the Crown? Privilege and Influence were still powerful weapons in their hands, and although the nobility may have been 'sunk in credit', the personal distinction of its most notable members added the moral weight which only intellectual power and high achievement can bestow.

APPENDIX

THE MANNER OF SITTING IN THE HOUSE OF LORDS

IT is interesting to picture the Chamber as it was constituted in the reign of William III, since it differed very considerably from the present House.[1]

Whenever the King was present in person, he sat at the upper end of the room in a chair of state, over which was spread the cloth of state. Under this and on either hand of the sovereign the royal children might sit. On the right hand of the King was placed a seat, once used for the King of Scotland, and destined for a Prince of Wales. On the right-hand side and set against the wall was a bench upon which sat the two Archbishops. Just below was another bench for the superior Bishops of London, Durham and Winchester. Upon other forms and still on the same side of the House sat the rest of the episcopate.

On the King's left hand were places for the great officers of state—the Lord Chancellor, the Lord Treasurer, the President of the Council, and the Lord Privy Seal. If, as was practically always the case, these were peers, they sat in virtue of their office above all the nobility including dukes, except such as were members of the Royal Family. If it chanced that any of the great officers was not a lord, he sat on the uppermost woolsack. On the same side as the ministers and below them sat the dukes, marquises, and earls in order of their creation; while the viscounts and barons sat on cross benches at the foot of the room.

When the King was present, the Lord Chancellor or Lord Keeper stood behind the cloth of state. Otherwise he presided as Speaker of the House, taking his place on the woolsack athwart the chair of state. Upon other woolsacks sat the judges, privy councillors not being barons, and secretaries of

---

[1] For the following description see any issue during the reign of William III of the *Whittaker* of the day, viz. Chamberlayne's *Present State of England*. In the issue for 1692 the passage to which reference is here made is in Part II, p. 35 *et seq*.

state, king's counsel at law and masters of chancery. Such of these as were not peers had their place in the House as advisers and necessarily possessed no suffrage. On the lowest woolsack were the clerk of the Crown and the clerk of Parliament, the latter having two clerks under him, who knelt behind this woolsack and wrote upon it.

When the King was present, the lords remained uncovered; when he was absent they sat covered, after having at their entrance done reverence to the chair of state. After this, the judges were allowed to take their seats, but they might not be covered until the Lord Chancellor or Keeper signified to them the consent of the peers. The king's counsel and masters of chancery were also allowed to sit, but at no time might they be covered.

The Upper House assembled every day, except on Sundays and great festivals, in the morning, and they might remain until the comparatively early dinner hour of those days. Only very rarely did the House meet after dinner, but sittings were often protracted until late in the afternoon. Though the House itself so infrequently sat after dinner, committees did.

BIBLIOGRAPHY

THE principal authority is the *Journals of the House of Lords* for the period. The space occupied by the reign of William III extends from vol. xiv, p. 101, to vol. xvii, p. 62.

The *Journals* give the outline of the business transacted at each sitting of the House, together with the names of the peers present on each occasion. Their utility is limited, as they provide no information as to the debates or divisions or work done in select committee.

The gaps left by the *Journals* have to a great extent been filled up by the publication of the *Manuscripts of the House of Lords* for the years 1678-1702. The four volumes for the years 1678 to 1693 were published under the authority of the Historical MSS. Commission 1887 to 1895. Four other volumes dealing with the period 1693-1702 have been issued separately, 1900 to 1908, but are uniform with the volumes published by the Historical MSS. Commission.

The papers gathered together in these volumes are of the utmost value, as a great deal of the material is entirely new. They give details which are not recorded in the *Journals*, but are gleaned from the MS. Minutes of the House. Such are proceedings in committees, examination of witnesses before the Lords, questions asked of the judicial advisers of the House, heads of arguments used in debate and at conferences with the Commons, particulars as to the voting in divisions. There are also reports and official papers laid before the House in connexion with its consideration of questions, e. g. of finance, military and naval administration, judicial reform. Thus the MSS. provide the widest information on a variety of subjects outside the sphere of one considering the history of the House only.

The Protests entered by dissentient peers in the Journals are of considerable value. They have been printed in easily available form in J. E. Thorold Rogers's *Complete Collection of the Protests of the Lords* (Oxford, 1875, 3 vols.).

The interest of the Protests is that they provide us with the arguments of minorities, which in many cases might otherwise have remained unknown to us. As it is, owing to the existence of the Protests we know at least as much about the opinions of minorities as those of majorities.

DEBATES.

Information as to Debates is unfortunately very scanty. There is a good deal more information about those of the other chamber. *The Parliamentary History of England, 1066 to 1803,* William Cobbett and John Wright, is the most familiar compilation. Volume x (1809) deals with the reign of William III. Another collection, upon which it is largely based, is to be preferred to it. This is *A Collection of the Parliamentary Debates from 1668 to the Present Time* (14 vols., Dublin, reprinted London, John Torbeck, 1741). This is referred to in the following pages as Torbeck's *Parliamentary Debates.* The type is much larger than that of *The Parliamentary History.* Protests are printed in appendices at the end of the volumes. Another collection of debates is Chandler's *History and Proceedings of the House of Lords from 1660 to 1743* (8 vols., 1742–3 ; Timberland, printer).

The information given in these publications is scrappy and jejune. A good deal of space is occupied by quotations verbatim from the *Journals.* There is little independent material ; and undue notice is sometimes directed to matters of the most ephemeral consequence, while important bills are sometimes passed over with the barest reference. For really interesting accounts of debates the investigator is dependent on two other sources : (1) contemporary letters and memoirs ; (2) the dispatches of representatives of foreign powers to their governments. Such accounts are often fragmentary and haphazard, but they are as a rule more lifelike and arresting than those vouchsafed by the formal collections.

Among correspondence and memoirs giving particulars on parliamentary proceedings may be mentioned, e. g. *Works of John Sheffield, Duke of Buckinghamshire* (2 vols., 1729); *Memoirs of Thomas Bruce, Earl of Ailesbury* (Roxburghe Club, 1890). Ailesbury's memoirs are somewhat confused and not altogether trustworthy, but they are generally entertaining. *The Diary of Henry Hyde, Earl of Clarendon,* in vol. ii of his *Correspondence* (ed. S. W. Singer, 1828), is good for the early days of the reign ; for later years *Letters from 1696 to 1708 to the Duke of Shrewsbury by James Vernon* (ed. G. P. R. James, 1841). *The Hatton Correspondence* (Camden Society, 1878) is more particularly useful for the Revolution period. Some useful newsletters are to be found among the *MSS. of the Earl of Denbigh* (Hist. MSS. Comm., Rep. xii, App., pt. ii, 1873). Narcissus Luttrell's *Historical Relation of State Affairs, 1678–1714* (6 vols., Oxford, 1817) provides occasional details and is invaluable as a guide to chronology.

Some interesting particulars about leading peers are to be gleaned from Queen Mary's own Memoirs, for which see the appendix to *Memorial of Mary, Princess of Orange and Queen Consort to William III,* by Gilbert Burnet, Bishop of Sarum (Edinburgh, 1842).

The fullest sources, curiously enough, are not in English. Extensive use has been made of the following authorities : (1) *Dispatches* of L'Hermitage in *State Correspondence between England and the Netherlands*—MS. transcripts are in the British Museum, Add. MSS. 17677 ; (2) Extracts from the *Reports* of Friedrich Bonet to the court of Brandenburg, printed in appendix to von Ranke's *History of England, mainly in the Seventeenth Century* (trans. Oxford, 1875), vol. vi ; (3) *Dispatches* of Friedrich Louis Bonet (Brit. Mus. Add. MSS. 30000).

For some critical remarks about the work of the brothers Bonet see Ranke, vol. vi, pp. 146–7.

Gilbert Burnet's *History of My Own Time* naturally supplies much material in connexion with proceedings in which its author played a prominent part. The book has to be regarded rather as the memoirs of a political partisan than as the work of an impartial historian. Nevertheless, its value as an authority on the House of Lords in this period is great ; and it is not difficult to guard against its defects. The notes made on the History by Swift, Hardwicke, Dartmouth, and Onslow, which are printed as foot-notes in the 1823 and 1833 editions, contain ample criticisms, so that few questionable statements are permitted to pass unchallenged. Though his ideal of history was high, Burnet's generalizations are rarely satisfactory. His analyses of popular feeling, particularly at elections, are superficial. His pen-pictures of politicians are apt to be biased, and are at times acrid. Party spirit is shown, e. g. in the accounts of the Fenwick case and the Act of Settlement. Indefiniteness is typical of the History ; there is a notable absence of precise dates. Exact numbers in parliamentary divisions are never given. Burnet does not profess to give a full parliamentary history. For obvious reasons the proceedings of the Upper House are much more fully treated than those of the Commons. Privilege questions and private bills are passed over. The Duncombe case, for example, is not mentioned. Inaccuracies of statement are to be found, but they are not very numerous. Sometimes it has been the critics and not Burnet that have been proved inaccurate (particularly James Ralph, who has been shown to be in the wrong more than once by the publication of the *Lords' MSS.*). In short, it may be said that Burnet has all the value which attaches to the Memoirs of a prominent politician, together with some measure of the authority which attaches to historical work, undertaken with ingenuous purpose. References are to the folio edition of Burnet. As the folio pages are marked in the margins of the 1823 and 1833 editions, the folio references are good for all three editions.

No other contemporary or almost contemporary historian is nearly as useful as Burnet. The following, however, may be mentioned : Abel Boyer's *History of William III* (3 vols., 1702–3); Laurence Echard's *History of the Revolution* (1725) ; John Oldmixon's *History of England under the Reigns of the House of Stuart* (1730). Of somewhat later works James Ralph's *History of England during the Reigns of William III, Anne, and George I* (1744) is of interest for its criticisms of Burnet and also for the use made of some original documents. Sir John Dalrymple's *Memoirs of Great Britain and Ireland from the Last Parliament of Charles II to the Battle of La Hogue* (1720, 3 vols.), besides containing a number of valuable original papers, is well worth reading for its own sake. A very readable account of parliamentary affairs is given by Thomas Somerville in his *History of Political Transactions and of Parties from the Restoration to the Death of William III* (1792). But by far the most brilliant narrative is given by Lord Macaulay. It is unfortunate that he often omits to mention his authorities when recounting debates, and on occasion attributes opinions to the House for which, though they may be intrinsically probable, there is no direct evidence, despite the fact that Macaulay gives the impression that he is quoting from actual speeches. The last part of the History, incomplete and unrevised, inevitably provides only a fragmentary account of parliamentary proceedings.

SPEECHES.

There is a woeful dearth of printed speeches. One, by Mulgrave, on the first Place Bill, is printed in his *Works*, vol. ii, p. 95 et seq. Another speech by this eloquent peer, one on a purely personal matter in which he was discreditably involved, is printed in Chandler's and Torbeck's *Parliamentary Debates*; but one would willingly have dispensed with it for one on a more important subject. There is a speech of Warrington's against bishops being allowed to vote in cases of blood (*Works of Henry, Lord Delamere and Earl of Warrington*, 1694, p. 111). But there is no evidence that it was ever delivered or intended to be delivered. Pamphlets in the form of speeches, but quite unauthentic, are common, e.g. *Speech of a Noble Lord against Deposing Kings for Male-administration* (Bartholomew Pamphlets, Bodleian, 1689). One is glad to have such materials as the heads of speeches, e.g. those of Savile, Marquis of Halifax, in Miss Foxcroft's *Life*, vol. ii, pp. 253–7.

MISCELLANEOUS PROCEEDINGS OF THE HOUSE.

For matter concerning privileges of the House and its procedure an annual publication, J. Chamberlayne's *Angliae Notitia, or the Present State of England*, is very useful. Modern authorities consulted on these subjects have been Sir W. Anson's *Law and Custom of the Constitution*; L. O. Pike's *Constitutional History of the House of Lords* (London, 1894); T. Erskine May's *Parliamentary Practice* (10th ed., 1893). For the conduct of peers in connexion with elections see E. Porritt's *The Unreformed House of Commons* (Cambridge, 1903). Contemporary evidence on the subject is provided in several publications of the Historical MSS. Commission, e.g. in the *Harley Correspondence* in the *MSS. of the Duke of Portland*, vol. ii (1891); the *Coke Papers* in *MSS. of Earl Cowper in Melbourne House*, vol. ii (1888); *Rutland MSS. at Belvoir*, vol. iii (1894). The principal judicial proceedings of the House are narrated in the *Complete Collection of State Trials* (ed. T. B. Howell and T. J. Howell, 34 vols., 1828). The space occupied by the reign of William III is vol. xii, p. 598, to vol. xiv, p. 516.

PEERAGES.

The Peerages used have been : J. E. Doyle's *Official Baronage of England* (3 vols., London, 1886); Arthur Collins's *Peerage of England* (ed. Sir F. Brydges, 9 vols., 1812); *Complete Baronage of England, &c.*, by G. E. C[okayne] (8 vols., 1887–98); *The Peerage of England, or an Historical and Genealogical Account of the Present Nobility* (2 vols., printed by E. J. for Abel Roper and Arthur Collins, 1714); *The Jacobite Peerage, Baronetage, Knightage, &c.*, by the Marquis of Ruvigny and Raineval (1904). Lists of peers are given each year by Chamberlayne in *Angliae Notitia*.

It is a pity that Doyle's *Baronage* is not complete, as it is the most valuable of all on account of its admirable arrangement. It is finished from Dukes to Viscounts inclusive, but there are no Barons, i. e. Barons at the time of the publication of the work.

PERSONAL HISTORY.

Individual references to the numerous authorities for the social life of the peerage are quoted in the chapter on that subject. It is unfortunate that there are few modern standard biographies of the leading peers. At present, for example, there are none of Leeds, Nottingham, Shrewsbury, Somers, and Tillotson. The best modern biography is the *Life and Letters of George Savile, Marquis of Halifax*, by Miss H. C. Foxcroft (2 vols., 1898). Miss Foxcroft is also responsible, in collaboration with T. E. S. Clarke, for the *Life of Gilbert Burnet, Bishop of Salisbury* (Cambridge, 1907). From such books, e.g. as the *History of Burley-on-the-Hill*, by Pearl Finch (2 vols., 1901), useful on Nottingham ; *The Whartons of Wharton Hall*, by E. R. Wharton (Oxford, 1898) ; John, Lord Campbell's *Lives of the Chancellors* (7 vols., 1848), on Somers, vol. iv, pp. 62–240, some interesting facts may be gleaned. But generally speaking, in order to learn anything of the prominent personalities in the House of Lords in this period, it is necessary to have recourse to contemporary memoirs, correspondence, &c.

PAMPHLETS.

Many pamphlets are of interest either as criticizing proceedings in the House or, more particularly, as discussing the claims or the influence of the House as a whole. Three main sources have been used: (1) *The Bartholomew Pamphlets* in the Bodleian, which are of value for the Revolution period; (2) Pamphlets included in the collection of *Lord Somers' Tracts* (2nd ed., 1809–15); (3) *Pamphlets on the Peerage Bill of 1719*. For list see *Retrospective Review*, Series II, vol. ii, 1828, p. 129. An especially interesting pamphlet is the *Memorial offered to the Princess Sophia* (1712, reprinted 1815). [See Clarke and Foxcroft's *Life of Burnet*, p. 556, for authorship.] The impression made by the House on contemporaries is admirably mirrored in writings of this description.

INDEX

Abdication, theory of James II's, 140.

Abergavenny, George Neville V., eleventh Baron, 205 f, 220 f.

Abingdon, James Bertie, first Earl of, 4, 122, 128, 142 f, 174, 229.

Abingdon, Montague Venables Bertie, second Earl of, 214 f, 217 f, 219 f, 220 f.

Admiralty, question of its jurisdiction over peers, 67–9.

Ailesbury, Thomas Bruce, second Earl of, his opinion of the nobility, 45 ; on Lords Dover and Sunderland, 120 ; gives James II good advice, 130 ; his attitude to Place Bill of 1692, 182 ; otherwise mentioned, 92, 132 f, 141, 142 f. Quoted, 59.

Ailesbury, earldom of, 4.

Albemarle, Arnold Joost van Keppel, Earl of, 8, 202, 209.

Albemarle, Christopher Monk, second Duke of, 3, 54.

Albemarle, dukedom of, conferred on Henry FitzJames by James II, 6.

Anglesey, James Annesley, Earl of, 115–6, 205, 208 f, 219.

Annesley, Francis, 202.

Army Disbandment, 194, 243.

Arrest, freedom from, 63–4.

Arundell of Trerice, John, second Baron, 142 f.

Arundell of Wardour, Henry, third Baron, 121.

Ashburnham, John, first Baron, 8, 214 f.

Attainder, Bills of, 99–106.

Attendance, enforced . . . in House, 90–3.

Attorney-General, 84–5.

Audley, barony of, 5.

Audley End, 54.

Audley, James Tuchet, fifteenth Baron, 205 f.

Banbury, earldom of. See Knowles.

Bangor, Bishop of. See Lloyd, Humphrey ; Humphreys ; Evans.

Bank of England, opposition to in House of Lords, 192, 235.

Barillon, 120.

Barnard, Christopher Vane, first Baron, 8.

Bath, John Granville, first Earl of, 4, 74–5, 220 f.

Bath and Wells. See Ken ; Kidder.

Beaufort, Henry Somerset, first Duke of, 3, 91–2, 142.

Beauw, William, Bishop of Llandaff, 142 f.

Bedford, William Russell, fifth Earl and afterwards first Duke of, 9, 176 f.

Belasyse, John, first Baron, 121.

Bellamy, Lord, in Shadwell's *Bury Fair*, 36.

Berkeley, Charles, second Earl of, 220 f.

Berkeley, George, first Earl of, 4, 132 f., 142, 192.

Berkeley of Stratton, John, third Baron, 60, 74.

Berkeley of Stratton, William, fourth Baron, 220 f.

Berkshire, Thomas Howard, third Earl of, 91.

Berwick, James, Duke of, 5, 15.

Bishops. See Chapter II. Asked to repudiate William of Orange, 127 ; their anomalous position in interregnum, 136 ; their attitude on question of Irish forfeitures, 209. See also Seven Bishops.

Blair, Sir Adam, case of, 98.

Bolingbroke, Henry St. John, Viscount, 50.

Bolton, Charles Paulet, Marquis of Winchester, afterwards first Duke of, 4, 11, 91, 102, 229.

Bolton, Charles Paulet, second Duke of, 73, 205 f.

Bonet, F. L., his account of Act of Settlement, 167–8 ; on Lords' attitude towards House of Commons' Officers' Bill, 187 ; on dangerous nature of House of Commons, 234–5 f.

Borlase, Humphrey, said to have been created Baron Borlase of Mitchell by James II, 7.

Bradford, Francis, Viscount Newport, afterwards created Earl of, 11, 43.

Brewster, Sir Francis, 202.

Bridgwater, John Egerton, third Earl of, 73, 122, 209.

Holt, Sergeant, 139, 145, 159.
Hough, John, Bishop of Bangor, afterwards of Hereford, 23, 220 f.
Howard of Escrick, Charles, fourth Baron, 214 f., 219 f., 220 f.
Humphreys, Humphrey, Bishop of Bangor and afterwards of Hereford, 19, 23.
Hungerford, meeting between William and James's representatives at, 131.
Hunsdon, Robert, seventh Baron, 219 f., 220 f.
Huntingdon, George Hastings, eighth Earl of, 220 f.
Huntingdon, Theophilus Hastings, seventh Earl of, 15 ; case of his imprisonment, 70-2, 169.

Impeachments, 98-9.
— of the Whig Junto, 212-24, 233, 243-4.
Irish Night, the, 134.
Ironside, Gilbert, Bishop of Bristol, afterwards of Hereford, 19, 22, 219.

Jacobite peerages, 5-7.
James I, his peerage creations, 2, 227.
James II, his peerage creations, 5-7; and Anglican Church, 16-17; his fatuity, 119, 127 ; retreat from Salisbury, 128-9 ; flight from London and capture, 130-4; leaves England, 135 ; his crimes recited in Convention, 140; held to have abdicated, 140-2 ; his letter to Convention, 143 ; his unpopularity with peerage, 147.
Jeffreys of Wem, George, first Baron, 5, 134.
Jeffreys of Wem, John, second Baron, 169, 214 f., 219 f., 220 f.
Jermyn, Thomas, second Baron, 132 f., 142 f., 219 f., 220 f.
Jersey, Edward Villiers, first Earl of, 8, 11, 14, 60, 209, 220 f., 241.
Johnson, Samuel, referred to, 50, 53.
Jones, Edward, Bishop of St. Asaph, 23, 220 f.
Judges, their attendance required in House of Lords, 94-5.
— See also King's Bench.

Ken, Thomas, Bishop of Bath and Wells, 17, 142 f.
Kent, Anthony Grey, tenth Earl of, 4, 127, 142 f., 214 f.
Kentish Petition, the, 214, 215, 224, 244.
Kidd, Captain, affair of, 209.
Kidder, Richard, Bishop of Bath and Wells, 22.

Kingston, Evelyn Pierrepont, fifth Earl of, 220 f.
Kings' Bench Judges, in Devonshire case, 65-7; in case of the Three Earls, 70-2 ; in case of Titus Oates, 159-60.
Kiveton. See Osborne of Kiveton.
Knowles, Charles, 84-5.

Lake, John, Bishop of Chichester, 17, 142 f.
Lamphugh, Thomas, Bishop of Exeter, afterwards Archbishop of York, 19, 22, 24, 132 f., 142 f.
Land Bank, 192 f.
Land Tax Bill of 1692/3, attitude of Lords towards, 189-90.
Langford, Henry, 202.
Latitudinarians, 18, 25.
Law Reform Bill, 117.
Lecky, W. E. H., on the uses of an aristocracy, 241-2.
Lee, Sir Thomas, 108.
Leeds, Thomas Osborne, Earl of Danby, then Marquis of Caermarthen and then Duke of, part played by in Revolution, 125-6, 128, 136 ; in Convention, 138, 141, 142, 144 ; attitude towards Place Bill, 182; attitude towards affair of Dutch Guards, 199 ; opposes Resumption Bill, 206, 209. Otherwise mentioned, 4, 8, 10, 100, 102, 147, 158, 197, 222.
Legion's New Paper, quoted, 224, 244.
Leigh, Thomas, second Baron, 142 f.
Lempster, William Fermor, first Baron, 8.
Levinz, Sir Richard, 202-4.
Lexington, Robert Sutton, second Baron, 214 f., 219 f., 220 f.
Licensing of the Press. See Press.
Lichfield and Coventry, Bishop of. See Wood ; Lloyd, William ; Hough.
Lichfield, Edward Henry Lee, first Earl of, 142 f.
Limerick, capitulation of, 201, 203.
Lincoln, Bishop of. See Barlow ; Tenison.
Lincoln, Edward Clinton, fifth Earl of, 56, 57, 79, 146.
Lindsey, Robert Bertie, Baron Willoughby d'Eresby, afterwards fourth Earl of, 7, 220 f.
Litigation, use made by peers of their privileges in cases of, 72-6.
Llandaff, Bishop of. See Beauw.
Lloyd, William, Bishop successively of St. Asaph, Lichfield and Coventry, and Worcester, 17, 23, 24, 132 f.
Lloyd, William, Bishop of Norwich, 17, 142 f.